# PROBABILITY
## Grades 3–4

# MATH
## By All Means®

## PROBABILITY
### Grades 3–4

## by Marilyn Burns
### A MARILYN BURNS REPLACEMENT UNIT

MATH SOLUTIONS PUBLICATIONS

**Editorial direction: Lorri Ungaretti**
**Art direction and design: Aileen Friedman**
**Typesetting: Rad H. M. Proctor**
**Illustrations: David Healy, First Image**
**Cover background and border designs: Barbara Gelfand**

Marilyn Burns Education Associates is dedicated to improving mathematics education. For information about Math Solutions courses, resource materials, and other services, write or call:

Marilyn Burns Education Associates
150 Gate 5 Road, Suite 101
Sausalito, CA 94965
Telephone (415) 332-4181
Fax (415) 331-1931

ISBN 0-941355-12-8

This book is printed on recycled paper.

**Distributed by Cuisenaire Company of America, Inc.**
**P.O. Box 5026**
**White Plains, NY 10602-5026**
**(800) 237-3142**

# PREFACE

Although the topic of probability is included in the NCTM Standards, it doesn't get very much attention in the elementary grades. I think this is due in part to teachers' limited experience with probability ideas and in part to the lack of instructional materials for teachers to use. The omission of probability from the elementary mathematics curriculum is unfortunate. It's a topic that relates to our lives in many ways. Children bring to the classroom many informal experiences and some basic notions about chance. Also, probability activities give students experiences that relate numerical thinking to a variety of situations.

This unit evolved over several years. I put together and taught the first version of it to third graders during the 1987–88 school year and again in the 1989–90 and 1990–91 school years. The following two years I taught a related probability unit to second graders. Then, in the 1993–94 school year, I again taught the third-grade unit.

Each time I taught the probability unit, I did so differently, both because students in different years responded differently and because I had new ideas I wanted to try out. This book presents many of the activities I used in my most recent experience. I chose those activities that I felt the children responded well to, that teachers would have the most success teaching, and that addressed the probability ideas important for children to learn.

This unit is structured the same way as the other *Math By All Means* units. However, it contains one section that is new to the series—Student Portfolios. In this section, I explain my preparation for having students assemble portfolios, how the children responded, and how parents reacted to reading their children's work.

As has happened in the past, I learned a great deal as I pored over two months of children's work and my daily logs. Also, writing the unit raised a slew of questions for me. While students found the games and activities to be engaging and fun, their responses to the mathematics varied. Some children delved into the probability ideas with interest, thoughtfulness, and insights that astounded me. Others weren't particularly interested (or ready?) to think about the mathematical ideas, but merely enjoyed the games.

Even though I've been teaching probability for years, it continues to intrigue me. I'm interested in learning more about what's appropriate to teach students of different ages and what I can expect them to understand. I'm moving up to fifth grade to try a related unit there, and I welcome your ideas or accounts of your experiences helping students learn about probability.

All of the "From the Classroom" vignettes describe what happened when the unit was taught in a third-grade class. However, the grade level span assigned to the unit indicates that it is suitable for grades three and four. We've made this grade-level designation for two reasons. We know that in any class, there is typically a span in students' interests and abilities, and the activities in the unit have been designed to respond to such a span. Also, teachers who have taught the unit have found it successful with children in several grade levels and have reported that the activities are accessible and appropriate to a range of students.

Marilyn Burns
October 1994

## Acknowledgment

I've been teaching math to Dee Uyeda's third graders at Park School in Mill Valley, California, on and off for years. The children I taught when I first developed some of these units are now nearing the end of high school! I'm deeply grateful to Dee for opening her class and sharing in the excitement about students' progress. I feel enormously enriched from watching how Dee establishes a classroom environment that makes school rich and joyful for children. And I'm grateful for all I've learned from her about how to help children see writing as a natural extension of their learning process.

# CONTENTS

**Homework**                    **221**

**Blackline Masters**           **227**

**Index**                       **253**

# INTRODUCTION

Probability is a topic that hasn't typically been part of the elementary mathematics curriculum. This has been due, in part, to the emphasis of traditional programs on number skills, often leaving limited instructional time for other topics. Also, many elementary school teachers have not studied probability in depth, if at all, and are not comfortable with the idea of teaching a topic they don't understand well. This unit presents a professional development opportunity for teachers to expand their own understanding of probability and learn along with their students.

One of the advantages of teaching probability is that children intuitively have some understanding of the topic from their real-life experiences. For example, they're used to hearing weather reports ("There's an 80 percent chance of rain"), and many children have developed an understanding that the closer the percentage is to 100, the more likely the prediction. They know about tossing a coin to make decisions ("Heads, you go first; tails, I go first") and have developed an understanding about the 50-50 likelihood of heads or tails coming up. They've probably had experience using spinners or dice in games, and although they might not have thought formally about probability when using these materials, their experiences provide a base from which their learning can grow.

This unit builds on students' past experiences and engages them with a variety of games, activities, and investigations in which they're encouraged to predict outcomes and then test their predictions through their first-hand experiences.

## Goals for Probability Instruction

Several important ideas about probability emerge from the activities in this unit. They include the following:

1. **Some events are more likely than others, while some events are equally likely.** Students are usually familiar with this idea informally. The activities in the unit build on that informal understanding, connect it to the standard language of probability, and provide additional experiences.

2. **It's possible to measure the likelihood of events.** Children know that they have a 50-50 chance of getting heads when flipping a coin. Mathematicians would say that heads is one of two equally likely outcomes and, therefore, the chance of flipping heads is 50 percent, or 1 out of 2. The unit helps children learn to assign numerical probabilities to outcomes in a variety of situations, with and without equally likely outcomes.

3. **A sample set of data can be useful for making a prediction about an outcome.** Polls are frequently used to determine public opinion on issues. Of course, pollsters do not ask every citizen for his or her opinion; rather, they base their statistics on a representative sample of the population. Similarly, in this unit children take samples and use the information they gather to make predictions.

4. **Larger sample sizes of data give more reliable information than do smaller sample sizes.** If you flip a coin 10 times, it would be unlikely that heads and tails would each come up exactly 5 times. If heads came up 6 times, that would reflect a 60 percent outcome for heads, although the theory predicts a 50 percent outcome. However, with a larger sample, say of 1000 flips, heads would likely come up closer to 50 percent of the time. In several activities in the unit students compare class data to their individual samples. They learn that larger sets of data provide more reliable information for verifying or challenging their predictions and theories.

5. **Sometimes an experiment produces data that do not exactly match a theoretical probability.** The element of chance makes any set of data subject to variation. Data may validate or challenge predictions, but mathematical explanations are needed to justify theories about probabilities. In the unit students typically encounter situations where their results don't "come out right" or match their expectations. These situations are valuable opportunities for discussing the importance of theories and the role of empirical information.

## Other Mathematics in the Unit

No topic in mathematics exists in isolation from other mathematical areas, and it's important for children to see mathematics as a study of related ideas, instead of as a collection of concepts independent of one another. Therefore, the activities in the unit draw on ideas in various areas of the mathematics curriculum.

For many of the activities, students collect, represent, and interpret data and are thus involved with statistics, an area of mathematics that is closely related to probability. In relation to the number strand, the activities help reinforce learning basic addition facts and adding two-digit numbers and also engage children in thinking about percentages, fractions, ratio, and proportion. From working with spinner faces, students think about dividing up the circumference of circles and measuring the areas of regions within circles, drawing on the areas of geometry and measurement.

## What's in the Unit?

In this six-week unit, third- and fourth-grade children explore probability through a collection of games, activities, and investigations. The activities are structured so that they are accessible to children with limited math experience and ability and have the potential to stimulate and challenge more capable and experienced children.

Children work with four different materials: dice, spinners, Color Tiles, and Two-Color Counters. The variety of materials helps hold children's interest and helps them think about the concepts in different ways. Also, it's important that children see relationships and make connections among mathematical concepts. For example, some of the spinner activities engage children in thinking about equally likely outcomes. Similarly, children have other opportunities to think about equally likely outcomes when they roll one die or toss Two-Color Counters (which are like coins except that they have two colors instead of heads and tails).

During the unit, children participate in whole class lessons, work cooperatively in pairs or small groups, and complete individual assignments. They are encouraged to explain their thinking, and writing is an integral part of their learning. Homework assignments continue class experiences as well as provide ongoing communication with parents about their children's learning. At the end of the unit, students reflect on their learning and put together portfolios of their work.

## The Structure of This Book

The directions for implementing the unit are presented in five components: *Whole Class Lessons, Menu Activities, Assessments, Portfolios,* and *Homework.* Blackline masters needed for the activities are included.

### Whole Class Lessons

Four whole class lessons, each requiring one or two class periods, introduce students to the basic probability ideas presented in the unit. Also, each whole class lesson prepares students for later, independent activities.

The instructional directions for each lesson are presented in four sections:
*Overview* gives a brief description of the lesson.
*Before the lesson* outlines the preparation needed before teaching the lesson.
*Teaching directions* provides step-by-step instructions for presenting the lesson.

*From the Classroom* describes what happened when the lesson was taught to one class of third graders. This vignette helps bring alive the instructional guidelines by giving an over-the-shoulder look into a classroom, telling how lessons were organized, how students reacted, and how the teacher responded. The vignettes are not standards of what "should" happen; instead they are a record of what did happen with 27 children.

## Menu Activities

The menu is a collection of activities that children do independently, either in pairs or individually. The tasks on the menu pose problems, set up situations, and raise questions that help students interact with probability ideas. The menu activities do not build on one another and therefore do not need to be done in any particular sequence. Also, the tasks are designed so that students can do them several times, thus continuing to explore ideas by returning to activities that interest them.

The unit contains eight menu activities: three require the students to work in pairs, four are designed to be done individually, and one can be completed with a partner or individually.

The instructional directions for each menu activity are presented in four sections:

*Overview* gives a brief description of the activity.

*Before the lesson* outlines the preparation needed before presenting the activity.

*Getting started* provides instructions for introducing the activity.

*From the Classroom* describes what happened when the activity was introduced to one class of third graders. As with the whole class lessons, the vignette gives a view into an actual classroom, describing how the teacher gave directions, what the students did, and the results of a follow-up class discussion.

## Assessments

The unit contains seven assessments. They are listed in the Table of Contents and placed near the activities from which they evolve. Also, they are identified in the book by gray bars in the margins.

For specific information about assessing understanding, see the introduction to the Assessments section on page 15.

## Homework

Homework assignments have two purposes: They extend the work students do in class, and they inform parents about the instruction their child is receiving. The Homework section presents suggestions for homework assignments and ways to communicate with parents.

## Portfolios

Putting together a portfolio gives students a chance to reflect on their learning as they review their work, make choices about papers to include, and write about why they chose each paper. Portfolios give teachers a view into what was important to students and how each student perceived his or her learning experience. Also, portfolios provide a vehicle for communicating with parents about what their children have experienced and learned.

This book's Student Portfolios section describes my first experience implementing portfolios with a class of students. As stated in the Preface, this section represents work-in-progress more than a firm suggestion for implementation. I begin by presenting a detailed chronicle of what I did with a class and what resulted. "Reflections on Implementing Portfolios" follows the vignette, summarizing my experience and thinking in four sections:

**Preparing for Portfolios** describes the thinking I did before introducing portfolios to the students.

**Introducing Portfolios to the Class** presents how I explained portfolios to the students and had them review and choose work to include.

**Communicating with Parents** offers a suggestion for presenting portfolios to parents and getting feedback from them.

**Looking Back** describes my reactions to the experience and what I would do differently next time.

## Blackline Masters

Blackline masters are provided for all menu activities, recording sheets, and portfolio reflections.

# Notes About Classroom Organization

### Setting the Stage for Cooperation

Throughout much of the unit, children are asked to work cooperatively, sometimes with a partner, and sometimes in small groups. Interaction is an important ingredient for children's intellectual development. They learn from interaction with one another as well as with adults.

Teachers who have taught the unit have reported different systems for organizing children to work cooperatively. Some put pairs of numbers in a bag and have children draw to choose partners. Some assign partners. Some have seatmates work together. Others let children pick their own partners. Some teachers have students work with the same partner for the entire unit. Others let children choose partners for each activity, allowing them either to change frequently or stay with the same person. Some don't have children work with specific partners but instead with others who have chosen the same activity.

The system for organizing children matters less than the underlying classroom attitude. What's important is that children are encouraged to work together, listen to one another's ideas, and be willing to help classmates. Students should see their classroom as a place where cooperation and collaboration are valued and expected. This does not mean, of course, that children are never expected to work individually. However, it does respect the principle that interaction fosters learning and, therefore, that cooperation is basic to the culture of the classroom.

## A System for the Menu Activities

Teachers report different ways to organize the menu activities. Some teachers use a copy machine to enlarge the blackline masters of the menu tasks onto 11-by-17-inch paper, mount them on construction paper or tagboard, and post them. Although the teacher introduces each activity to the entire class, individual students can refer to the posted directions for clarification. (Note: A set of posters with the menu activities is available for purchase from Cuisenaire Company of America.)

Rather than enlarge and post the tasks, other teachers duplicate about a half dozen of each and make them available for children to take to their seats. Mounting them on tagboard makes the copies more durable. Some teachers put the tasks in booklets, making one for either each child or each pair of students. For any of the above alternatives, children take materials from the general supply and return them when they finish their work or at the end of class.

Some teachers prefer to assign different locations in the classroom for different tasks. For each activity, they place a copy of the task and the worksheets and materials needed in a cardboard carton or rubber tub. At the beginning of menu time, they ask monitors to distribute the tubs to the locations. The number of chairs at each location determines the number of children who can work there.

Each of these systems encourages children to be independent and responsible for their learning. They are allowed to spend the amount of time needed on any one task and to make choices about the sequence in which they work on tasks. Also, the tasks are designed for children to do over and over again, avoiding the situation where a child is "finished" and has nothing to do.

## How Children Record

Teachers also use different procedures to organize the way children record their learning. Some prepare a folder for each child, either by folding 12-by-18-inch construction paper in half or by using regular file folders, and require children to record individually even when working cooperatively. Some teachers prepare folders for partners and have the partners collaborate on their written work. Other teachers don't use folders but have students place their finished work in an "In" basket.

Some teachers have children copy the list of menu activities and keep track of their work by putting a check by an activity each time they do it. Other teachers give children a list of the menu activities by duplicating the blackline master on page 228. It's important that the recording system is clear to the class and helps the teacher keep track of children's progress.

## About Writing in Math Class

For both learning activities and assessments, students write about their thinking. Student writing helps teachers gain valuable insights into what children understand. Helping children learn to describe their reasoning processes, and become comfortable doing so, is extremely important and requires planning and attention. Experience and encouragement are two major ingredients.

I often remind students that their writing is important because it helps me learn about how they are thinking, which helps me become a better teacher. I reinforce, over and over again, that I am the audience for their writing and that they need to provide sufficient details to help me understand their thinking and reasoning processes.

When children are writing solutions to problems, I circulate, offer encouragement, and often push for more. Often when children think their papers are complete, I think they still need revision. "That's a good beginning," I say if they've explained their thinking incompletely. "Use words," I say if they've used only numbers and pictures. "Include numbers," I say, if they used only words and pictures. "Write some more," I say if their explanation is skimpy and lacks detail.

As often as possible in the bustle of classroom work, I have individual children read their papers aloud to me, and I suggest revisions. At times, I point out that they need periods, or capital letters at the beginning of sentences, and I correct their spelling; at other times, I let grammatical errors pass. These sorts of decisions fall in the realm of the art and craft of teaching, and I tailor my decisions to the individual children and to the assignment. I find that, over time, children come to accept revising and editing of their math writing as part of their learning process.

Teachers report different ways they use writing in math class. Some have children write daily about what they did and their reactions to the activities; others have children write on an occasional basis. Some have students keep math journals or logs; others prefer to have children write on paper and collect the class set each time. Some teachers give students free rein about what they write; others structure the writing by raising questions or providing prompts; some use a combination of ways to initiate writing assignments.

In this unit, I had students write daily. I didn't use journals or logs, however, as I preferred to take home stacks of papers rather than stacks of books. I used a variety of approaches to initiate students' writing. At times, I had them write freely about what they did that day and instructed them to describe any discoveries they made or ideas they were still wondering about or unsure of. At other times, usually to help me assess the students' understanding and responses to an activity or idea, I structured an assignment for the entire class by writing on the board directions, questions, or a prompt.

I often used comments, discoveries, or questions from the students' papers to initiate a discussion the following day. In this way, the children came to see that I valued their ideas and that their ideas could contribute to our classroom learning. At other times, I had private conversations with children about what they had written, probing to learn more about what they understood or to challenge an incorrect notion.

Whenever I have students write, my message is consistent: Write only what makes sense to you, and persist until it does. Getting students to express their ideas in writing isn't easy, although it gets easier as the year progresses if they write regularly. In general, I push and push (as in nag and nag), respecting, of course, individual students' differences. I'm convinced the benefits of having students write are substantial, both for their learning and for teachers' assessments.

### Managing Materials and Supplies

Teachers who have taught this unit gave children time to explore the concrete materials they needed to use. Most teachers devoted several weeks at the beginning of the school year to free exploration of materials. Also, all teachers gave students guidelines for the care and storage of materials. The following materials and supplies are needed for the Probability unit:

### Materials

- Dice or number cubes, about one pair per child
- Color Tiles (1-inch square tiles in four colors), one set of 400
- Two-Color Counters (1-inch circular counters red on one side and yellow on the other), one set of 400
- Lunch bags, about 15

### General Classroom Supplies

- Post-it Notes, at least one pad of $1^1/_2$-by-2-inch notes per group of four children
- Paper clips, about two per child
- 5-by-8-inch index cards, about two per child, or tagboard
- Scissors, at least one for each pair of children
- Tape

In addition, recording sheets for individual activities are included in the Blackline Masters section. Most teachers choose to have supplies of each sheet available for children to take when needed.

### A Comment about Calculators

It's assumed that during this unit, and in the classroom throughout the year, calculators are as available to the children as pencils, paper, rulers, and other general classroom supplies. You may occasionally ask students not to use calculators if you want to know about their ability to work with numbers on their own. However, such times should be the exception rather than the rule. Children should regard calculators as tools that are generally available for their use when doing mathematics.

As with other materials, children need time to become familiar with calculators. Some children will find them fascinating and useful; others will not be interested in or comfortable with them.

## A Suggested Daily Schedule

It's helpful to think through the entire unit and make an overall teaching plan. However, it isn't possible to predict how a class will respond as the unit progresses, and adjustments and changes will most likely have to be made. The following day-to-day schedule is a suggested six-week guide. It offers a plan that varies the pace of daily instruction, interweaving days for whole class lessons with days for independent work on menu activities. The schedule also suggests times for discussing menu activities and giving homework assignments.

Class discussions of menu activities are included throughout the day-to-day plan. These are typically scheduled several days or more after the menu activity is introduced, giving children time to experience the activity before participating in a class discussion. Since students will be working on menu activities at their own pace and completing them at different times, it's important to check with children about their progress. At times, you might mention to children that they will discuss a particular activity the next day and should be sure to work on the task so they can contribute to the discussion. Although times for class discussions are suggested in the plan, use your judgment about when it's best to have them. For general information about the importance of class discussions, see the Menu Activities introduction on page 89. For suggestions about how to conduct specific discussions, check the "From the Classroom" section in each menu activity.

**Day 1    Assessment: What Is Probability?**
**Whole Class Lesson: The 1-2-3 Spinner Experiment, Part 1**

Discuss probability with the children. Introduce *The 1-2-3 Spinner Experiment, Part 1* lesson. The children make spinners, do the experiment, and post their results. Then introduce the assessment and have the students write what they know about probability or write about the spinner experiment. Give homework assignment: *Spinners.*

**Day 2    Whole Class Lesson: The 1-2-3 Spinner Experiment, Part 1 (continued)**

Have students post data from the *Spinners* homework assignment. Then continue with the whole class lesson, with children analyzing the data.

**Day 3    Whole Class Lesson: The Game of Pig**

Introduce Part 1 of the lesson. Teach the children how to play Pig and let them play it.

**Day 4    Whole Class Lesson: The Game of Pig (continued)**

The children continue playing Pig. Introduce Part 2 of the lesson and have children collect data for the "How Many Rolls to Get a 1?" chart. Give homework assignment: *The Game of Pig.*

**Day 5    Whole Class Lesson: The Game of Pig (continued)**

Invite students to report their experiences playing Pig at home. Discuss probabilities and strategies for Pig with the class.

**Day 6    Whole Class Lesson: Tiles in the Bag**

Introduce the lesson. As a class, take samples, then record and analyze the data for the two bags of tiles. Empty the first bag to reveal its contents. End class by asking the children to write about their predictions of the contents of the second bag.

**Day 7**   **Whole Class Lesson: Tiles in the Bag (continued)**

Discuss the children's writing about *Tiles in the Bag*. Students play Pig for the remainder of the class.

**Day 8**   **Introduce Menu Activities: Roll Two Dice, Tiles in Three Bags**

Present the directions for the menu activities *Roll Two Dice* and *Tiles in Three Bags*. Students choose menu activities to work on for the remainder of the class.

**Day 9**   **Introduce Menu Activity: Shake and Spill**

Present the directions for the menu activity *Shake and Spill*. Students choose menu activities to work on for the remainder of the class.

**Day 10**   **Menu**

Students work on menu activities. Direct students who haven't done the menu activity *Shake and Spill* to complete it so they can participate in tomorrow's discussion.

**Day 11**   **Assessment: Results from Shake and Spill**

Begin class by discussing the *Shake and Spill* data. Then present the *Results from Shake and Spill* assessment. When children complete the assessment, they choose menu activities to work on for the remainder of the class.

**Day 12**   **Whole Class Lesson: The 1-2-3 Spinner Experiment, Part 2**

Introduce *The 1-2-3 Spinner Experiment, Part 2* lesson. The children make equally likely spinners, do the experiment, and post their results. Give homework assignment: *Spinners*. (Note: This is the same assignment as given in day 1, but with a different spinner.)

**Day 13**   **Whole Class Lesson: The 1-2-3 Spinner Experiment, Part 2 (continued)**

Begin class with students posting their data from the *Spinners* homework. Then continue with the whole class lesson, having children analyze the data and write about the results.

**Day 14**   **Whole Class Lesson: The 1-2-3 Spinner Experiment, Part 2 (continued)**

Discuss the results of the experiment. Then students choose menu activities to work on for the remainder of the class.

**Day 15**   **Assessment: Equally Likely**

Present the *Equally Likely* assessment. When children complete the assessment, they choose menu activities to work on for the remainder of the class. Direct children who haven't yet done the menu activity *Roll Two Dice* to complete it so they can participate in tomorrow's discussion.

**Day 16**     **Introduce Menu Activity: Spinner Puzzles**

Begin class by discussing the class data for *Roll Two Dice*. Then present the directions for the menu activity *Spinner Puzzles*. Students choose menu activities to work on for the remainder of the class.

**Day 17**     **Introduce Menu Activities: Testing Pig Strategies, High or Low**

Present the directions for the menu activities *Testing Pig Strategies* and *High or Low*. Then let students choose and work on activities from the menu.

**Day 18**     **Menu**

Students work on menu activities. Tell children to be sure to finish their spinner puzzles and turn them in to you today. (Look them over before class the next day so that you can talk with children who need to make corrections.)

**Day 19**     **Menu**

Students work on menu activities. Give homework assignment: *Spinner Puzzles*.

**Day 20**     **Assessment: Spinner Statements**

Begin class by having children report their experiences at home with their spinner puzzles. Then present the *Spinner Statements* assessment and have students work on it in groups of four. Groups that finish early choose and work on activities from the menu. Near the end of the period, initiate a class discussion about the spinner statements. Give homework assignment: *Spinner Statements*.

**Day 21**     **Menu**

Begin class by encouraging students to solve the spinner puzzles that other students made at home. Then have students work on menu activities. Ask students to be sure to complete the menu activity *Testing Pig Strategies* so they can participate in a class discussion tomorrow.

**Day 22**     **Menu**

Invite children to discuss their findings from *Testing Pig Strategies*. Then children choose and work on menu activities. Direct children who have not worked on the menu activity *High or Low* to do so before tomorrow's discussion. Give homework assignment: *Pig Strategies*.

**Day 23**     **Assessment: Which Number Wins?**

Begin class with children reporting what happened when they tested Pig strategies with their families. Then children discuss their findings from *High or Low*. Present the *Which Number Wins?* assessment. When children complete the assessment, they choose menu activities to work on for the remainder of the class.

**Day 24**  **Introduce Menu Activities: Spinner Sums, Match or No Match**

Present directions for menu activities *Spinner Sums* and *Match or No Match*. Then students choose menu activities to work on.

**Day 25**  **Menu**

Students work on menu activities. Let students know that they will be discussing *Match or No Match* tomorrow. Give homework assignment: *Probability Vocabulary*. (See the assessment on page 196.)

**Day 26**  **Menu**

Students work on menu activities. Interrupt them about 20 minutes before the end of class to discuss their data and ideas about *Match or No Match*.

**Day 27**  **Menu**

Begin class with continuation of the discussion of *Match or No Match*. Then children write about whether the games were fair. When students finish, they choose menu activities to work on for the remainder of the class. Direct children who have not done the menu activity *Spinner Sums* to do so before tomorrow's discussion.

**Day 28**  **Assessment: Favorite Activity/What I Learned**

Begin class with a discussion of the children's results from *Spinner Sums*. Then present the *Favorite Activity/What I Learned* assessment.

**Day 29**  **Portfolios**

Present Student Portfolios: Identify categories for work, give students their papers to reread, and direct them to choose papers and read their partners' papers. Have students write about their reactions to reading their work.

**Day 30**  **Portfolios**

Students review the work they selected, write reflections, and assemble their portfolios.

## A Letter to Parents

Although parents learn about their child's experiences from homework assignments and papers sent home, it's helpful to give them general information about the unit at the outset. The following is a sample letter that informs parents about the goals of the unit and introduces them to some of the activities their child will be doing.

Dear Parent,

We are about to begin work on a math unit that focuses on probability. In the activities in this unit, children make predictions, collect and interpret data, recognize the usefulness and limits of sampling, learn that some outcomes are more likely than others and some are equally likely, and investigate beginning ways to measure chance. The games, activities, and experiments in the unit engage children with estimating and computing with whole numbers, introduce them to fractions and percents, and provide experience with statistics, geometry, and measurement.

Throughout the unit, children are introduced to the vocabulary of probability: *likely, unlikely, chance, equally likely, certain, uncertain, probable, improbable, possible, impossible, sample,* and more. They are encouraged to use this vocabulary in discussions and writing assignments.

Two lessons engage children with spinners as shown:

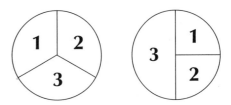

The children predict what will happen with each spinner, spin and collect data, and compare the class statistics from the two experiments.

In another lesson, the students are shown a paper bag in which there are 12 Color Tiles, some red, some blue, and some yellow. Students draw 1 tile at a time, note its color, and replace it. Then, looking at the results from multiple draws, they try to predict how many tiles of each color are in the bag. This investigation reinforces the idea that large samples provide more reliable information than do small samples, while also presenting beginning notions of ratio and proportion.

Another lesson introduces the game of Pig—always a favorite game among children. The game engages children in thinking about the odds when rolling dice, while also providing valuable practice adding two-digit numbers.

In the unit, independent activities extend children's experiences in whole class instruction, and regular assessments provide a way to track children's learning. Also, for homework, they'll be asked to introduce some of the games and activities they're learning to family members and bring results to the class for discussion and further investigation.

Sincerely,

## A Final Comment

The decisions teachers make every day in the classroom are the heart of teaching. Although this book attempts to provide clear and detailed information about lessons and activities, it isn't a recipe that can be followed step-by-step. Rather, the book offers options that require teachers to make decisions in several areas: sequencing activities, organizing the classroom, grouping children, communicating with parents, and dealing with the needs of individual children. Keep in mind that there is no "best" or "right" way to teach the unit. The aim is to engage children in mathematical investigations, inspire them to think and reason, and encourage them to enjoy their learning.

# CONTENTS

# ASSESSMENTS

Assessing children's understanding is an ongoing process. In the classroom, teachers learn about what children know from listening to what they say during class discussions, observing and listening as they work on independent activities, having conversations with individual children, and reading their written work. From a collection of observations and interactions, teachers gain insights into children's thinking and reasoning processes and learn about children's mathematical interests and abilities.

Teachers can assess students' understanding of probability during informal classroom observations and interactions. The following questions can help guide these informal assessments:

Can a child distinguish between events that are likely or unlikely, possible or impossible, probable or improbable, certain or uncertain?

Can a child use the terminology of probability appropriately when describing his or her thinking about activities in the unit?

Can a child interpret measures of chance in real-world contexts, such as understanding the implication of a weather report that indicates an 80 percent chance of rain or knowing that 50-50 means the chance of winning is the same for both teams?

Can a child assign numerical probabilities to outcomes—for example, that the probability of getting heads when a penny is tossed is 1 out of 2 (1/2) or 50 percent, or that the chance of drawing a yellow tile from a bag of four tiles, one yellow, one blue, one green, and one red, is 1 out of 4 (1/4) or 25 percent?

Can a child interpret and use statistical data to make conjectures about probability activities?

Can a child formulate theories about the probabilities of situations, such as "This is more likely because . . ." or "They're equally likely because . . ."?

To supplement the insights teachers gain from informal observations and interactions, the unit offers seven assessments. *What Is Probability?* given at the beginning of the unit, has students discuss what they think probability is and then write down their thoughts. The assessment *Equally Likely* is given after a class discussion of that concept; students write what they think "equally likely" means and provide examples from their lives. In *Results from Shake and Spill,* students examine and analyze the statistical results from a menu activity. *Spinner Statements* focuses children on interpreting probability vocabulary as they work in small groups to evaluate 17 probability statements in relation to a spinner. In *Which Number Wins?* students write about the probabilities of getting high or low sums when rolling dice. *Probability Vocabulary,* given near the end of the unit, asks students to write sentences that explain the meaning of the probability terms they have learned. Finally, for *Favorite Activity/What I Learned,* students write about their experiences in the unit, giving the teacher valuable information both about individual children and about the unit itself.

# ASSESSMENT  What Is Probability?

Probability has not traditionally been part of the elementary mathematics curriculum; therefore, students may not be familiar with this area of mathematics. However, even though students may not have heard the word *probability* before or studied probability formally, more than likely they have had some informal experiences with the topic and have some intuitive understanding of it.

Begin a discussion by telling the students that over the next several weeks they'll be learning about probability, and you're interested in finding out what they already know about it. Ask if they have any ideas about what probability is. If no one volunteers, introduce the idea with some examples that the children can relate to their own lives. You might say, "When you study probability, you make predictions about things that you're not sure about, things that probably will or probably won't happen." Give some examples:

> When you listen to the weather report, you often hear that it's likely to rain or that there's an 80 percent chance of rain. Then you have to decide whether to take an umbrella.

> When you ask your parents for permission, they sometimes say "maybe," which could be yes or could be no. You have to wait to find out if you may do what you asked about.

> When you flip a penny, it's possible for either heads or tails to come up. Both possibilities are equally likely. Because it's a 50-50 chance, you have to pick one and hope for the best.

> If the telephone rings, it's very likely that someone will be on the other end of the line when you answer. It's possible that the person will hang up without talking to you, but it's almost certain that he or she will talk to you.

Title a sheet of chart paper "Probability Words" and list the probability terminology as you use it—*likely, chance, 50-50, possible, certain.* Then ask the children to think about other things that they're not sure will happen, about events that may be likely or unlikely.

If you feel the children have some familiarity with probability, you may want to have them write about their ideas. However, remember that the purpose of this introductory assessment is to give you a feel for the overall experience of the class. It isn't essential to have children write at this time, unless you would like to have specific information about each student.

After this discussion, start the unit with the first whole class lesson, *The 1-2-3 Spinner Experiment, Part 1.* (See page 24.)

## FROM THE CLASSROOM

I wrote *Probability* on the board and asked the students to raise their hands if they thought they could read it. About half of the students raised their hands, and I asked the class to read the word. I repeated it and had all the students say it in unison.

"In this math unit," I said, "we'll learn about probability. Who has any idea what probability is?" Nine students had been in my second-grade class the previous year, but only two had comments to offer.

"It has something to do with percents," Andrew said.

"Can you give an example?" I asked.

"Well, if something is 50 percent, then it has a chance of happening," he answered. I posted a sheet of chart paper, titled it "Probability Words," and wrote the word *chance.*

Charlie had a different idea. "It's like what the weatherman says," he said.

Seth chimed in. "Sometimes there's a 20 percent chance of rain," he said.

"What does that mean?" I probed.

"It isn't very sure," Seth answered, "but the weatherman isn't always right."

"It means there isn't a very good chance it will rain," Lori added.

"I don't know about probability," Emelia said, "but I'm getting the idea that it's about things that can happen."

Tomo had an idea. "If there's a 20 percent chance it will rain, then there's an 80 percent chance it won't." Tomo enjoys thinking about numbers and is quick to quantify situations.

"It means it's not certain," Abby added.

As the children spoke, I continued listing the probability terminology they used, supplementing their ideas with other words I wanted to introduce. I listed: *likely, unlikely, chance, 50-50, equally likely, certain, uncertain.*

Finally, I said to the children, "In this unit, we're going to learn about probability through different kinds of activities. We'll be using spinners, dice, Two-Color Counters, and Color Tiles. We'll play games and do experiments. And we'll talk and write a lot about probability."

From this conversation, I learned that most of the children hadn't had much experience with probability. Of the seven children who shared their ideas, five of them had been in my class last year. They weren't able to recall much about what we had studied, but they seemed to be familiar with some of the language of probability.

I took only 10 minutes for this introduction and then immediately began the first whole class lesson, *The 1-2-3 Spinner Experiment, Part 1.* (See page 24.) At the end of class, I asked the children to write about what we had done so far with the spinner experiment, about probability in general, or about both if they wished. Because I think success with writing assignments depends on children having something to write about, I did not want to impose a written assessment on students who may have no idea of what to write about.

Most of the students referred to weather reporting, since it had played an important part in our brief discussion. Erin, for example, wrote: *Some times you yous* [use] *probability and you don't even nodice. like if it's cloudy outside you say shoud I bring a unbrella?*

Lori wrote: *Probability is like 50-50 which means its like 50% it will rain and 50% it will not rain. There are words that discribe probability, too! Like certain, uncertain and likely. You might need probability in your job as a weather reporter when you say it is 40% rain and 60% not rain.*

Tomo wrote: *Today I learned about "Probability". This is an example of Probability. It is 60% chance that it's going to rain. 0% is the lowest and 100% is the highest. If there is 50% chance of raining and 50% chance thats it's not going to rain no one will know. I think Probability is important because if your T.V. brakes you could look at the <u>whether</u> and think if it's unlikely or likely going to rain.*

Tomo's paper showed his interest in quantifying situations.

> Probability
> Today I learned about "Probability". This is an example of Probability. It is 60% chance that it's going to rain. 0% is the lowest and 100% is the highest. If there is 50% dance of raining and 50% chance thats it's not going to rain no one will know. I think Probability is important because if your T.V. brakes you could look at the <u>whether</u> and think if it's unlikely or likely going to rain.

Amanda had quite a bit to say: *Probability is mostly guessing. It is equal chance. Like when they say on the news it will be a 50 persent chance of rain. That means it will proboply or proboply not rain. The higher percentage is more likely to rain. If was a lower percentage it would be unlikely to rain. That is how they tell the wether. No one really knows what the wether is going to be. Sum times the news raporters are really wrong.*

*The inportance of probability in your life is to know what to wear in srtin days, or when you go camping in the summer you are not going to bring pants and swet shrts. You are going to bring tank tops and shorts.*

Amanda had a good deal to say about probability in relation to predicting the weather.

> ## Probability
> Probability is mostly guessing. It is equal chance. Like when they say on the news it will be a 50 persent chance of rain. That means it will proboply or proboply not rain. The higher percentage is more likely to rain. If was a lower percentage it would be unlikely to rain. That is how they tell the wether. No one really knows what the wether is going to be. sum times the news raporters are really wrong!
>
> The importance of probability in your life is to know what to wear in srtin days, or when you go camping in the summer you are not going to bring pants and swet shrts. You are going to bring tank tops and shorts.

About half of the children wrote about probability in general. Tom gave a general description. He wrote: *Probadiliy is like you do game of chance and you win or lose. I think the chance of winning could be 20% or another thing could be 50%.*

Tom wrote a general description of probability.

> ## Probadiliy
> Probadiliy is like you do game of chance and you win or lose. I think the chance of winning could be 20% or another thing could be 50%!

Some children talked about how probability might serve them in their lives. David, for example, added a sentence at the end of his description of the spinner experiment. He wrote: *I would use probability if I turned out to be a baseball anouncer.*

Alan wrote: *Probability is like likely and unlikely. Probability is like fifty-fifty equally likely. 80-20 is not equally likely. When I am a base ball player I will yose probability like this. I will pradict if we are going to win.*

And Lee Ann wrote: *If you really want to be a math teacher and teach kids about probability you Need to Know!*

# CONTENTS

# WHOLE CLASS LESSONS

The unit includes four whole class lessons. Each lesson introduces students to a different way of investigating probability and prepares them for independent menu activities.

In the first lesson, *The 1-2-3 Spinner Experiment, Part 1,* children make spinners and use them to collect and analyze data. After discussing their findings, they write about what they did and what they learned.

In *The Game of Pig,* partners take turns rolling dice and mentally adding sums. The game engages children in thinking about the odds when rolling dice, while also providing valuable practice adding two-digit numbers.

*Tiles in the Bag* introduces students to using sampling with replacement to make predictions. Using a paper bag with 12 Color Tiles inside, they draw 1 tile, record its color, and return it to the bag. They repeat this action for three sets of 12 draws, each time predicting how many tiles of each color might be in the bag.

The last whole class lesson, *The 1-2-3 Spinner Experiment, Part 2,* has students use spinners to investigate the concept of equally likely. Using the same procedures as in the first whole class lesson, students collect data, make predictions, and write about their findings. They also write about and draw other spinner faces that might match the data.

When teaching the unit, it's helpful to intersperse whole class lessons with menu activities. Introducing some of the menu activities early in the unit provides students with options during later whole class instruction, when students typically finish work at different times. (See "A Suggested Daily Schedule" on pages 9–12 for one possible day-by-day plan.)

## WHOLE CLASS LESSON   The 1-2-3 Spinner Experiment, Part I

**Overview**

The whole class lesson, *The 1-2-3 Spinner Experiment, Part 1*, introduces children to probability through an experiment in which one outcome is more likely than others. The experiment provides experience with collecting and analyzing data. The probability of spinning each number provides a context for talking about fractions and percents and engages students in comparing the areas of the regions of a circle. Also, making their own spinners gives children practice in following directions and helps develop their fine motor skills.

The menu activity *Spinner Puzzles* (see page 122) extends this lesson by having children design spinner faces to match statements about what should happen in spinner experiments. Also, in the menu activity *Spinner Sums* (see page 165), students collect data using spinners from both this whole class lesson and *The 1-2-3 Spinner Experiment, Part 2*. (See page 67.)

**Before the lesson**

Gather these materials:
- Spinner Faces #1, one per student (See Blackline Masters section, page 232.)
- 5-by-8-inch index cards, one for each pair of students
- Spinner recording sheet, one to two per student (See Blackline Masters section, page 231.)
- Directions for Making a Spinner, copies for students and one copy enlarged and posted (See Blackline Masters section, pages 229–230.)
- Paper clips
- Plastic straws, one $1/4$-inch length per student
- Scissors
- Tape
- "Probability Words" chart from *What Is Probability?* assessment (If you haven't started this, post a sheet of chart paper and title it "Probability Words.")
- Sample spinner made as explained in the "Teaching Directions" section
- Three labels—1, 2, and 3—posted on the bulletin board to designate areas for children to post their spinner recording sheets (Number 3 will need a larger space.)

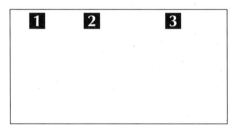

**Teaching directions**

- Show children the spinner you made. Ask what they notice about its face. Spin the spinner and point out how the indicator line tells what number the spinner lands on.

■ Demonstrate for the children how to make a spinner. Post an enlarged copy of the directions to refer to as you make the spinner.

1. Cut out the spinner face.

2. Cut the 5-by-8-inch index card in half. Mark a dot near the center of one of the halves. Draw a line from the dot to one corner of the card.

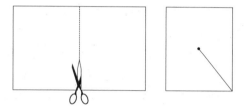

3. Bend up the outside part of a paper clip. This part should point straight up when the paper clip is lying flat on your desk.

4. Use the paper clip to poke a hole in the center of the spinner face and through the dot near the center of the index card.

5. Push the bent end of the paper clip through the hole in the index card and use tape to secure the rest of the paper clip to the bottom of the card. Make sure the side of the card with the line is facing up.

6. Put the $\frac{1}{4}$-inch length of plastic straw and then the spinner face on the paper clip.

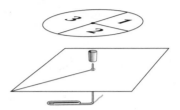

7. Cover the tip of the paper clip with a piece of tape.

■ Demonstrate for the children how to do the spinner experiment:

1. Write the numerals 1, 2, and 3 at the bottom of the first three columns on the spinner recording sheet.

2. Spin the spinner and record the number it lands on in the lowest square of its column. Point out to the students that they should start writing at the bottom of the columns. Do five or six spins, recording the number each time.

**Spinner Recording Sheet**

|   |   |   |   |   |   |   |   |   |
|---|---|---|---|---|---|---|---|---|
|   |   |   |   |   |   |   |   |   |
|   |   |   |   |   |   |   |   |   |
|   |   |   |   |   |   |   |   |   |
|   |   |   |   |   |   |   |   |   |
|   |   |   |   |   |   |   |   |   |
|   |   |   |   |   |   |   |   |   |
|   |   |   |   |   |   |   |   |   |
|   | 3 |   |   |   |   |   |   |   |
|   | 3 |   |   |   |   |   |   |   |
| 1 | 2 | 3 |   |   |   |   |   |   |

1 2 3

3. Tell the children that they will continue spinning and recording until one number reaches the top of its column. You may want to complete the experiment to be sure the children understand.

4. Cut out the three-column strip and post it under the 1, 2, or 3 on the bulletin board, depending on which number reached the top.

| | | 3 |
|---|---|---|
| | | 3 |
| | | 3 |
| | | 3 |
| | | 3 |
| 1 | | 3 |
| 1 | 2 | 3 |
| 1 | 2 | 3 |
| 1 | 2 | 3 |
| 1 | 2 | 3 |
| 1 | 2 | 3 |
| 1 | 2 | 3 |

5. Write the numerals 1, 2, and 3 at the bottom of the next three columns on the spinner recording sheet to prepare to repeat the experiment. Most likely it won't be necessary for you to model another experiment; the students should understand what they are to do from your first demonstration.

■ Ask the students to predict which number has the best "chance" of reaching the top of the record sheet. Point out that although it's "possible" for 1, 2, or 3 to reach the top, mathematicians would say that it's more "probable" that 3 will reach the top—it's not "certain," but it's more "likely." Use the language of probability as often as possible when you introduce and discuss the activity. As you introduce new probability words—*chance, possible, probable, certain, likely*—write them on the Probability Words chart. When you write words such as *possible* and *likely,* it's a good time also to write *impossible* and *unlikely* to introduce children to these opposites.

■ Have the students make their spinners. Distribute copies of the directions for students to refer to. (See Blackline Masters section, pages 229–230.)

■ After each child completes and posts the results from two or three experiments, discuss the distribution of the posted recording sheets. Most likely, more recording sheets will be posted under 3 than either 1 or 2. Have children explain why this happened. Also, point out that it's important to collect a great deal of data because larger samples are more reliable than smaller samples for making predictions. (Add the words *data* and *sample* to the Probability Words chart.)

■ Analyze the data. To count how many times each number came up in all the experiments, remove the recording sheets from the bulletin board and have the students cut each of them so that the 1s, 2s, and 3s are in separate strips. They should discard empty squares. Demonstrate how to tape strips together, making long strips of 1s, 2s, and 3s.

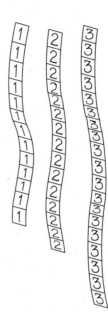

If you have room, compare the lengths of the 1s, 2s, and 3s strips by laying them out on the floor. If you don't have room, have the students cut the strips into 10s, clip together 10s to make strips of 100, and count the 100s. Students can put the extra squares in a central location for others to use to complete 10s. Ask students to report the number of squares they've counted and record their counts on the board. Have the class figure the total number of times the spinner landed on each number.

■ Discuss the results. Ask questions such as:

How do the class results compare with your prediction?
How did your individual experiments compare with the class results?
Why do you think mathematicians say that a large sample of data is better for analyzing information than a small sample of data?

■ If you'd like, have the children write about what they did, what they had predicted, and what the results were.

## FROM THE CLASSROOM

"Today we're going to learn to make a spinner and use it for a probability experiment," I said to the class. I showed the children an example of the spinner we would use.

"What do you notice about the face of the spinner?" I asked.

"It has three numbers on it," Alan said.

"And it has lines," Doug added.

"The number 3 has more space," Abby said.

"The number 3 takes up half," Andrew said.

"It looks like 1 and 2 are the same size," Emelia said.

I spun the spinner and the children were impressed that it spun so smoothly. "Watch as I show you how to make a spinner like this," I said. I posted an enlarged copy of the directions (see pages 229–230) and referred to it as I made a spinner. The children were interested and watched attentively as I demonstrated.

"Do we each get to make one?" Seth asked.

"Yes," I said, "but before you each make your own spinner, I'm going to explain the experiment you'll do." I showed them a Spinner Recording Sheet. It had 9 rows and 12 columns. I wrote *1*, *2*, and *3* underneath the first three columns.

"The experiment is to spin the spinner and each time record the number in its column," I explained. I did five spins, recording the number each time, pointing out to the students that they should start recording each number at the bottom of its column.

Spinner Recording Sheet

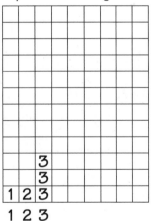

"Do this until one number reaches the top of its column," I said. "Then cut off the three-column strip and post it under 1, 2, or 3, depending on which number reached the top." I referred the children to the bulletin board on which I had posted the three numerals.

"I think 3 will win," Lee Ann said. "It's the biggest."

"It kind of has to because it takes up more space," Abby said, repeating what she had noticed earlier.

"I think 1 and 2 should come up even," Charlie said. "They're the same."

"So you think it's most likely that the number 3 will fill its column first and that 1 and 2 are equally likely," I said, using the probability terminology I had introduced earlier. I referred to the Probability Words chart I had begun. The children nodded.

"But neither of them is as likely to finish first as the number 3." The children nodded again.

"Do you think it's possible for 1 or 2 to finish first?" I asked.

"Kind of," Alan said, "but not too much."

"I hope 1 wins on mine," Elliot said.

"I'm rooting for 2," Doug said.

"Well, remember that this isn't a game where winning or losing is important," I said. "It's a mathematical experiment about probability. After you each do the experiment, we'll have a lot of information to examine." After pointing out that the squared paper was good for three experiments, I distributed the materials and directions for making spinners.

### Observing the Children

All the children were eager to make a spinner, and the task kept them busily engaged. Some children deftly constructed the spinner, recalling what to do from my demonstration. Others referred to the directions. Some got help from children at their table. A few came to me for help— some before even trying, and others to be sure they were right after they'd done something.

As students finished, I directed them to get a spinner recording sheet for the experiment. After about 25 minutes, all of the children had made a spinner and completed the experiment at least once. About a third of the class had completed it two or more times. The bulletin board was filling up with evidence that 3 had reached the top more often than 1 or 2.

Five minutes before the end of class, I called the children to attention. They were enjoying the experience of spinning and recording, and I had difficulty getting them to stop work.

"It's almost time for recess," I said. "Let's take a look at the data you've been posting." I hadn't as yet introduced the word *data*, so I added it to the Probability Words chart.

"Look," Andrew said, "that one came out exactly right."

"Which one?" I asked. He came up and pointed to one recording sheet that had the column of 3s filled in and five squares each in the 1s and 2s columns.

"Why do you think that's exactly right?" I asked.

"Because the 1s and 2s came up even," he said, "and they're about half."

"I see one that's in the wrong place," Abby said, and she came up to move a recording sheet that was erroneously posted under the 1, even though 3 had reached the top first.

The recess bell rang. "We'll look at the information again tomorrow," I said. "In the meantime, if you do any more experiments, please post your data. Also, I'd like you to write about what you learned today. You can do that right after recess."

The children focused on different things in their writing. Elliot, for example, wrote about why 3 had a better chance. He wrote: *It's more likeley that three is going to come up becuase it has a bigger space then the two and one.*

Eric gave a more precise explanation of his prediction. He drew a picture of the spinner face and wrote: *On this spinner there are the numbers*

one two and three. *My prediction of what number would come up most was three because three has a holl hafe* [whole half] *to itself and one and two only have a fourth to there selfs.*

Alan gave complete instructions for making a spinner and then wrote about the probabilities, revealing his partial understanding: *Three has a 50-50 chance. 2 has 30-70 chance. 1 has a 40-60 chance. I predicted 3. I was right. I thought it was unlikely to get a one. But I was wrong.*

Lisa mused about her own experience doing the experiment and then commented about the chance of the numbers. She wrote: *I thought it was interesting the way 2's would be loosing and 3's would be winning and then suddenly the 2's would catch up and win. I also learned that on this spinner the 3's have a bigger chance because they have a bigger space.*

Lisa commented on her experience doing the experiment and having the number 2 win.

Probability facts

I thought it was interesting the way 2's would be loosing and 3's would be winning and then suddenly the 2's would catch up and win.

I also learned that on this spinner the 3's have a bigger chance because they have a bigger space.

Rather than writing about the probabilities, Lee Ann focused on describing the experiment. She wrote: *Our class made spinners and then did a experiment. The experiment was to take a piece of a paper with squars. Twelve squars to be exact. We would spin our spiners. Whatever number the line hit is what number you would write in one of the squars. It goes on and on until one number wins!*

Probability

Ms. Burns today. I learned that 3 is most likley to turn up. But if you put 1 and 2 together then it is a 50% 50%.

3 takes up ½ of the spinner, the 1 and 2 only take up ¼ of the spinner. Therefore 3 is the most likely is the most likely to win.

I think probability is important in life. I use it everyday. For example, my mother asks me how much food I want for dinner. And then I have to predict how much food I will eat.

Probability
Today we learnd that one and tow have 25%, but 3 haves a better chanes but on the spiner 3 has a bigger space to land on. But what I don't get is why did she make the three have a bigger space.

*(left)* Andrew explained why the spinner was more likely to land on 3 than on 1 or 2.

*(right)* Ajani wondered why the 3 had a bigger space on the spinner.

**A Class Discussion**

Many of the children did the spinner experiment several more times. By the next day, the bulletin board was crammed with recording sheets. I began class by asking for volunteers to explain the activity to Timmy, who had been absent the day before.

Alan showed Timmy a spinner and explained how to do the experiment. Lori pointed out that each recording sheet was posted under the 1, 2, or 3. "You put it under the number that got to the top," she explained. Seth told Timmy about the odds. "There's a 50 percent chance that 3 will come up because it takes up half the spinner," he said, "and the 1 and the 2 each have a 25 percent chance."

"Does the 3 have a bigger chance because it's a bigger number?" Timmy asked.

"No," Lisa answered. "It's because Ms. Burns divided the spinner in half and gave half to 3, so it has the most chance."

"How can you tell which number comes up?" Timmy then asked. Alan pointed out the line on his spinner.

"Let's examine the data you collected," I then said. I took one of the posted recording sheets, cut it into three separate columns of numbers, and snipped off the blank squares. I did the same for another recording sheet and then taped the two columns of 3s together, the two columns of 2s together, and the two columns of 1s together. I continued with another sheet, cutting it and taping each column onto the corresponding strip. Then I held up the three strips I had made.

"What do you notice?" I asked.

"I see 3's the longest," Lee Ann said.

"And 1's the shortest," Eric said.

"What if we continued and did this for all of the record sheets?" I asked. "Do you think 3 would still be the longest?" Most heads nodded yes.

"What about the 1s and the 2s?" I asked.

"I think there will be more 2s," Amanda said.

"How come?" I probed.

"Because there are more 2s already," she said, referring to the three strips I had constructed.

"I think she's right," Erin said.

I looked at the recording sheets on the board and chose one where the number 1 had reached the top and there were few 2s. I cut out the three columns and taped them onto the strips. The 1s strip was now almost as long as the 2s strip. Several children giggled.

"I still think there will be more 2s," Amanda said.

"I think there will be more 1s," Andrew countered.

"Why do you think that?" I asked.

"Because I think that the 1 really has a little more space on the spinner than the 2," he said. "I don't think you drew the line exactly."

"I think the best way to find out is to do it," I said. "Mathematicians always say that the more data you have, the better you're able to understand or make a prediction about what's going on." I added *prediction* to the Probability Words chart and continued. "So I'll give each group some of the recording sheets, and you'll cut and tape your strips as I did. Then we'll tape together all of the 1, 2, and 3 strips and see how they compare. Decide how to organize the work at your table so you can get the job done."

"What if the strips are longer than the room?" Tomo asked.

"We can compare them in the hallway if we have to," I said. "In the meantime, as you finish your strips, lay them on the rug."

The children got busy. After about 15 minutes, three lines of strips were on the rug, and I realized that I had underestimated the length of the strips. The children had been prolific in producing data, so I changed my plan.

"What we need to know," I said, "is how many 1s, 2s, and 3s there are. I have an idea. We'll count the number of squares in each column. The easiest way I know is to count by 10s." Several children started counting aloud by 10s, and others joined in. I let them go to 120 and then called for their attention.

"To count the squares by 10s," I said, "we can cut the strips into lengths with 10 squares in each." I took a strip of 2s, counted 10 squares, and cut them off. I used my strip of 10 to measure another strip of 10, and another, continuing until I had 12 strips.

"Let's count by 10s and see how many squares I have," I said. When the children reached 100, I stopped and put a paper clip on the 10 strips.

**NOTE** While it's important to have a clear teaching plan for a lesson, it's just as important to change the plan as needed. The goal of the lesson—not the plan for implementing it—should be the driving impetus.

"You do the same," I said. "Take strips, cut off 10s, and use a paper clip to make a group of 100. If you have extra individual squares or strips of 10, put them on the front table. If you need some individual squares or another 10, use the ones on the front table or ask someone at another table who is working on the same number."

"Do we do this alone or with partners?" Lisa asked.

"Either way," I answered. "If you work alone, take one of the shorter strips with 1s or 2s on it. If you'd rather work with a partner, then take a 3s strip."

The children took strips and scattered about the room, spreading out to cut and tape. There was a good deal of trading as children made 10s and then clipped strips into 100s. After about five minutes, the strips were organized for a class count. I did the 1s first, recording the 100s as the children reported them:

*200*

*100*

*100*

*100*

*100*

*200*

"That's 800," Charlie said.

"How did you add them?" I asked.

"I just counted, like 200, 300, 400, 500, 600, and 200 more makes 800."

"But there are some extras on the front table," Timmy said.

I counted those. There were 32 more 1s.

"So that's 832 altogether," Lisa said.

"Let's do the 2s," I said, and I recorded as children reported:

*200*

*100*

*100*

*100*

*300*

"That's 800 again," Seth blurted out. "That's amazing."

"Nope," Timmy said, "there are extras."

I counted 68 more 2s.

"I think 868 and 832 are pretty close to being the same," Charlie said.

"So how many 3s do you think there will be?" I asked.

Tomo called out. "You just go 800 plus 800, and it's 1600."

"Why did you add 800 and 800?" I asked.

"Because 3 has half the spinner," he said.

"I think it will be 1700," Emelia said.

"Why?" I asked.

"Because I added 32 and 68 and that makes another 100," she replied, "so I added 100 onto 1600 and got 1700."

Timmy again reminded us of the extras.

"Oh, yes," I said, "let me count them." There were 75 extra 3s on the front table.

"I think there will be 1275," Andrew said. "I just don't think there will be so many 3s."

"Let's find out," I said.

As the children reported, I wrote on the board:

300
100
100
100
100
200
200
100
100

The children added the numbers. "There's 1300," Lori reported.

"That means there are 1375," Seth corrected her.

"So Andrew was closest," Tomo said, a bit disappointed.

"All of your predictions were sensible," I said. "It was unlikely that there would be exactly twice the number of 3s as 1s or 2s, and all of your answers were reasonable and possible."

Lee Ann then made a comment that indicated she was still thinking about the number of spins for 1 and 2. "I don't think 832 and 868 are close," she said. "The small numbers are two times different."

"What do you mean?" I asked.

"The 68 is about two times 32," Lee Ann explained, "so they can't be close."

I thought for a moment and then said, "Suppose I brought in two baskets and filled each with the same kind of candies, one with 832 candies and the other with 868. I don't think you'd be able to pick out which basket has more."

"Well, maybe," Lee Ann said, not willing to abandon her idea.

"If you had 832 in one and 1375 in the other," Alan said, "it would be easy to tell them apart."

"I agree, Alan," I said. "Or if I had just 68 candies in one and 32 candies in the other, it would also be easy. As Lee Ann said, 68 is just about twice 32. But a difference of about 30 doesn't matter when the numbers are large, like 832 and 868."

"If you add them together," Tomo said, "you get 1700." It took me a moment to realize that he had added 832 and 868.

"What does the number 1700 tell you?" I asked. I always try to give a context for numbers and, for Tomo, I try to keep the focus on the purpose of adding and the information the answer provides.

"It was Emelia's guess," Tomo said.

"I know another thing," Charlie said. "It means that we spun the 1s and 2s 1700 times altogether."

"But we didn't get that many 3s," Tomo said.

"Some of you seem mathematically disappointed with the results of our experiment," I said. "Part of learning about probability is to think about what should happen and then compare it with the results and see what we can learn. We'll be trying other experiments, and we'll have the chance to talk more about what we'll find out. For now, I'd like you to write about what we did today and what you learned."

Doug described how the class taped the strips, but he did not comment on the results.

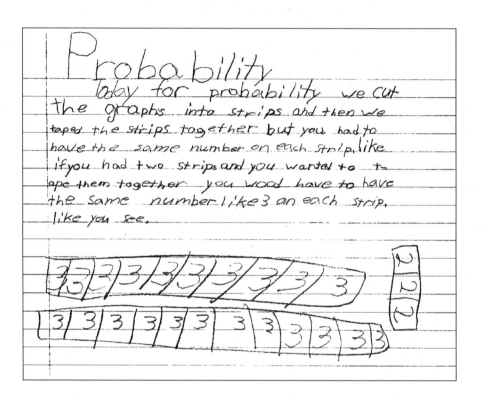

> **Probability**
>
> Today for probability we cut the graphs into strips and then we taped the strips together but you had to have the same number on each strip, like if you had two strips and you wanted to tape them together you wood have to have the same number like 3 on each strip, like you see.

The children's writing revealed their different opinions about the data. Erin, for example, wrote: *Today when we added up all of the data for the spinner proget for 1, 2, and 3 I was surprised that both one and two almost got the same amont 832 for ones's and 868 for the two's.*

Charlie had a different opinion. He wrote: *I was not surprised that the third section had the most squares because of it's 50% out of a 100% circle and 1 and 2 are 25% but I was suprised that section 2 came in second. 1 and 2 had equal chances and it was interesting 2 won.*

Abby ended her paper by writing about her surprise: *So it did not turn out just how I thot but it came out pretty close.*

Lisa was also surprised—not about the probability but about the amount of data we collected. She wrote: *Today when we were all done taping the strips together, I noticed how much longer they were to what I thought. I thought they would only go down to Mr. Thomase's room. If we had put it out in the hallway it would probably go around the whole school. If we had added all the 2's and 1's and 3's together in one long strip it would probaly go down the ramp and through the annex building hallway.*

Probability

Is lost 2s were in second plase threes won. Because on the spiner the three has a bigger plase the the one and the 2. Ushiley three comes up.

(left) Elliot explained why the 3s "won."

(right) Abby recapped the experiment and then described the results of analyzing the data.

| What happend before | cut chart Probability fchart |
|---|---|
| yesterday we made spinners and played a game the spinners looked like this ③. As you can see the three has more of a space than the 1 and 2 so you would prob- ably land on three more and the more threes means the threes should win. | Today we took all the charts down from the bourd and cut them to see wich number came out the most. As I prediced it was three becouse three had a bigger space than two and one. the three had 1300 little squares!! But two and one only had 800 each but if you put 800 and 800 together it makes 1600 So it did not turn out just how I thot but it came out pretty close. |

When helping children learn about probability, it's important that teachers don't lead students to think that results from an experiment are "better" if they more closely match a prediction. Children need to be encouraged to think from a theoretical base and then have the chance to discuss the implications of actual experiments.

# WHOLE CLASS LESSON    The Game of Pig

## Overview

In *The Game of Pig,* children use dice to think about probability and practice adding mentally and on paper. To play the game, children roll the dice and keep a running total of the numbers that come up. Rolling a 1, however, gives the player a score of zero for that turn; rolling two 1s causes the entire score the player has accumulated so far to return to zero. The game gives students the opportunity to think about the likelihood of rolling a 1 or a pair of 1s and also to notice what sums come up more often than others.

The menu activity *Testing Pig Strategies* (see page 145) extends *The Game of Pig* lesson by having the children test strategies against one another. Also, the assessment *Which Number Wins?* (see page 162) provides additional experience with investigating the probabilities of sums generated by rolling two dice.

## Before the lesson

Gather these materials:
- Dice, two per pair of students
- Rules for Playing Pig, enlarged and posted (See Blackline Masters section, page 233.)
- One sheet of chart paper, entitled "How Many Rolls to Get a 1?"
- One sheet of chart paper, entitled "Strategies for Pig"

## Teaching directions

### Part 1: Playing Pig

■ Show the children a pair of dice and have them report what they know about dice. Make sure that children who aren't familiar with dice have a chance to examine them.

■ Teach the rules for playing Pig. Select a child to play a game with you. Present the rules:

1. The goal of the game is to be the first to get a score of 100 or more.

2. Draw two columns on a sheet of paper. Label one with your name and one with your partner's name.

3. Players take turns. When it is your turn, roll the dice as many times as you like, keeping a running total of what you roll. Don't write down the sums, but add them mentally and say them aloud so your partner can check.

4. When you decide to stop rolling, record the total for that round in your column. Then add it to your total sum from the previous rounds.

5. If a 1 comes up on one of the dice, your turn ends and you score zero for that turn. If both dice show 1s, your turn ends and your total score so far goes to zero.

■ As you model the game, use a large sheet of paper or write on the board to show the children how to keep score. Make two columns, one for you and one for the student who plays with you. Start by rolling several times and, assuming you don't get a 1, after each roll have students add the numbers to help you keep your running total. When you decide to stop rolling, record your score.

■ Then have the student take a turn. Continue taking turns until either one of you reaches 100 or you think the children understand how to play and keep score. Distribute enough dice so that all the students can play in pairs. (Note: If you don't have enough dice for children to play in pairs, they can play in groups of three or four.)

## Part 2: How Many Rolls to Get a 1?

■ After the students have had the chance to play at least three games, engage the class in an investigation of the frequency of rolling 1s. Ask: "What do you think the chances are of rolling a 1 with one die?" Also ask students how often they thought a 1 came up when they were playing Pig.

■ Demonstrate for the children how to collect data about how many rolls it took to roll a 1. Roll a die and have the children count the rolls until a 1 comes up. Record on the board the number of rolls it took. Repeat for five trials. Then post the "How Many Rolls to Get a 1?" chart and list numbers, starting with 1 and continuing until you reach the bottom of the chart. Use a tally mark to indicate the number of rolls it took to get a 1 on each trial.

### How Many Rolls to Get a 1?

| | |
|---|---|
| 1 | I |
| 2 | I |
| 3 | |
| 4 | II |
| 5 | |
| 6 | |
| 7 | I |
| 8 | |
| 9 | |
| 10 | |
| 11 | |
| 12 | |
| 13 | |
| 14 | |
| 15 | |
| 16 | |
| 17 | |
| 18 | |
| 19 | |
| 20 | |
| 21 | |
| 22 | |
| 23 | |
| 24 | |
| 25 | |
| 26 | |

■ Explain to students that each of them is to do at least five trials and record the data on the class chart.

■ Discuss the data on the "How Many Rolls to Get a 1?" chart. (You may want to wait a few days after posting the chart so that children can continue to add tally marks. A larger sample gives more reliable information.) Ask: "What do you notice about the data on the chart?" "Considering the data on the chart, what strategies would you now recommend for playing Pig?"

Post the "Strategies for Pig" chart paper and record the strategies the students suggest.

■ Have the children write about the strategies they used to play the game. Explain that soon they'll have the chance to test the strategies on the chart in a menu activity.

■ Optional: Collect data about rolling two 1s. Post a piece of chart paper and title it "How Many Rolls to Get Double 1s?" List numbers as you did on the other chart, making two columns so that you can fit more numbers. The children collect data by rolling dice and counting the rolls until two 1s come up at the same time. They record their data with tally marks. In a class discussion, the students compare the results on the two charts and offer explanations about why they are different.

# FROM THE CLASSROOM

## Part 1: Playing Pig

To introduce *The Game of Pig*, I held up a pair of dice and asked the children what they knew about them.

"There are dots," Doug said, "one, two, three, four, five, and six dots."

"They have six sides," Emelia said.

"They're squares," Elliot offered.

"No, they're cubes," Abby said.

"Each die is called a cube," I confirmed, "and its faces are squares."

"They have eight corners," Seth said.

"Yes," I agreed, "a cube has eight corners and six faces. How many edges do you think it has?" I ran my finger along several edges to show what I meant.

Some of the children called out answers. "Eight." "Four." "Sixteen."

"Let's count," I said. We verified that there were 12 edges.

"You use them to play games," Erin said.

"You can't control what you get when you roll it," Tom said. "Anything can come up."

"I'm going to teach you how to play the game of Pig," I then told the class. "To play, you need a partner and two dice."

"Why is it called *Pig?*" Elliot wanted to know.

"Because if you're too piggy when you play," I answered, "you can lose the game. Watch and you'll see how."

I invited Charlie to play with me to introduce the game. I posted a sheet of paper, drew a line down the middle, and labeled one column "Ms. Burns" and the other column "Charlie."

"Do you want to go first or second?" I asked Charlie.

"You go first," he said, "I don't even know how to play."

"We take turns," I explained. "When it's your turn, you roll the dice and figure the sum." I rolled the dice and got a 4 and a 2.

"So I have 6," I said. "That's my score so far. I can roll again and add on to my score or stick with the 6. I think I'll roll again." I rolled, and this time a 6 and a 4 came up.

"That's 10 more," I said. "I had 6, so what's my score now?" Several children called out 16.

"Again, I can roll again or stick," I continued. "But there could be a problem if I keep rolling. If a 1 comes up on either one of the dice, then I lose all I've added in my head, and I get a score of zero for the round. So I have to decide if I'll be piggy and keep rolling, or if I'll stick."

Several children had opinions and called them out. "Roll." "Stick." "No, keep going."

I quieted the class and said, "I'll roll again. I have 16. Whatever I roll next, I have to add on to 16 in my head. I keep adding in my head until I stick." I rolled the dice, and a 5 and a 3 came up.

"That's 8 more," I said. "Raise your hand when you've figured out how much 16 plus 8 is." I waited a few moments and called on Alan.

"It's 24," he said.

"Now I'm going to stick," I announced, and recorded 24 in my column. I then passed the dice to Charlie. He rolled and got a 2 and a 1.

"Uh-oh," I said. "Remember the rule. If a 1 comes up on either die, you score zero for that round." I recorded a zero in Charlie's column. Some of the children groaned, others laughed, some expressed sympathy to Charlie, some cheered. I admonished the few who cheered, reminding them that we were studying probability and trying to learn more about the mathematics of chance. When all of the children were quiet, I began a second round.

I rolled two 4s. "That's 8," I said. "I'll roll again." I did so and rolled a 3 and a 2.

"I had 8 and now I have 5 more," I said.

"That's 13," Tomo blurted out. I gave him a stern look and reminded him about raising his hand.

"I think I'll stick," I said.

Some children thought I was being too timid. "No, keep rolling." "Do it again." "Take a chance."

"No," I insisted, "I'll stick. Watch me record, so you can learn how to do it. Whenever you stick, you write the sum on your paper and add it to the score you already had." I wrote the 13 under the 24 and had the children help me add to get my new score of 37.

| Ms. Burns | Charlie |
|-----------|---------|
| 24<br>+13<br>—<br>37 | 0 |

I gave Charlie the dice. He rolled and got a 6 and a 5. "That's 11," he said.

"I agree," I said. "It's important that you check your partner by adding the numbers yourself. Are you going to roll again or stick?"

"I'll go again," Charlie said. This time he rolled a 4 and a 2. "That's 6 more. What do I do?"

"Add the 6 to the 11 in your head," I said.

Charlie thought for a moment. I caught Tomo's eye before he blurted out again. But I didn't stop Andrew or Lee Ann in time. I reminded them about raising their hands.

"Yes, it's 17," Charlie said.

"Are you going to roll more or stick?" I asked.

Other students gave Charlie advice: "Roll." "Stick." "Go again." "No, take it." As children called out advice, I felt as if we were on a television quiz show. I calmed them down.

"I'm going to roll," Charlie said. Some children cheered; others groaned. He rolled and got two 2s.

"That's 4 more," he said, and counted on his fingers. "So I have 21." He looked at my score of 37. "I'll roll again," he said, with some confidence. But his confidence was short-lived. He rolled a 5 and a 1, and clapped his hand to his forehead.

"Oh, no," he said, grinning. "It's a wipeout." I recorded another zero in his column. The children were getting very excited and anxious to play.

"There's one more rule," I said, calling for their attention. "If you get 1s on *both* dice, then you not only lose what you were adding in your head for that round, but your entire score goes back to zero."

This latest information added to the children's glee. Their energy was high, and they began talking among themselves. "He should've stuck." "No, he was just unlucky." "I'd stick after my first roll." "I wouldn't. I'd take a chance."

"Can we play now?" Timmy asked.

"In just a minute," I answered, and quieted the class. "The game is over when one person gets 100."

"Do you have to get exactly 100?" Lisa asked.

"No," I answered, "it's okay to go over 100."

There were no further questions, so I distributed two dice to each pair of children and let them play the game.

## Observing the Children

As I circulated, I spent most of my time answering children's questions and helping them to record correctly. I've come to expect confusion when I first introduce an activity. With *The Game of Pig*, children are usually confused about what part they do in their heads and what part they record.

Lori and Amanda were writing down every number they rolled. Then when Lori rolled a 1, she couldn't remember which numbers were from this round and which were from the previous round. Amanda was frustrated, and the two girls came to me for help. I explained again how they were to add in their heads until they decided to stick, and then to record.

"Should we start again?" Amanda asked.

This game between Lori and Amanda was over in four rounds.

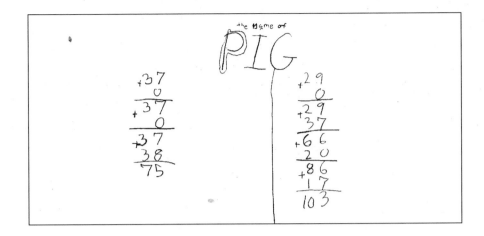

"You'll have to decide that," I said. "Don't worry about the mix-up. With a little practice, you'll both catch on."

Ajani came to ask me if he could use a calculator. Calculators were available for the children, and I was curious why he asked me. "Because you said we had to add in our heads," he said.

"Can you add the numbers in your head?" I asked.

"Yes," he nodded, "but there are a lot on the paper." He showed me how he had recorded each number as it came up and had a column of 10 or 11 numbers. "I never got any zeros," he said.

"But I did," his partner, Antonio, said, joining us. He had three zeros in his column. I wasn't sure how the boys were playing the game, but decided to deal with the adding issue first.

"Let's see if you can add the numbers you wrote," I said to Ajani. "You watch, Antonio, to be sure you agree." Though it was a slow process, Ajani worked his way down the column to reach the correct total of 37. Then I explained again to the boys how they were supposed to add in their heads until they decided to stick and then record and add the number to their previous score. They decided to start again. Ajani didn't ask me about the calculator again. If he had, I would have told him that he could use the calculator to check but that he should do the adding in his head as well.

Emelia rushed up to me. "I have a strategy," she said. "Don't roll too much because 1s come up a lot!" She raced back to her partner.

Charlie was playing with Tom. He was shouting, "Oh, no, I don't believe it! I don't believe it!" He was waving his fists in the air triumphantly. I went over to ask him what was so exciting.

"Look," he said, "I had all these zeros." He pointed to a column of eight zeros. "Then I got 96 in one turn. I never rolled a 1."

"If I didn't see it, I wouldn't believe it," Tom said.

"How come you stuck at 96 and didn't keep going?" I asked.

"I didn't want to be *too* piggy," he said wryly.

I watched Carrie and Maura play. Maura is unsure of herself numerically, but Carrie was helping. However, I noticed she didn't add the numbers in her head, but each time counted on from her previous roll, using her finger to touch each of the dots on the dice. Although Carrie can add in her head when asked to, she seems to feel safer when counting one by one. "It's better this way," she said to me.

About six of the children in the class also used this strategy of counting dots. Although I'd like the children to become comfortable with adding numbers in their heads, I've learned it's something I can encourage but not force. Two of the six children were in my second-grade class last year. They've made progress in some areas, but their insecurity with numbers persists. I continue to talk with the whole class and individual children about strategies for adding and to provide many opportunities for them to combine numbers. What's important to me is that I continue to encourage the children and not make them feel deficient.

Even though Lee Ann got off to a bad start, she wound up winning the game. (See right-hand column.)

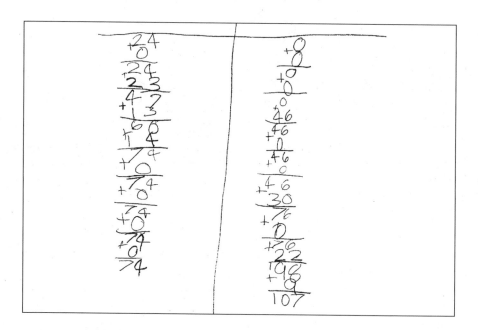

## Part 2: How Many Rolls to Get a 1?

The next day, I had the children play Pig for the first half of the class. Then I called them to attention to introduce Part 2 of the lesson.

I began a class discussion. "Raise your hand if you think you know the chance of rolling a 1 with one die," I said. I waited, scanning the class. As I waited, more and more children raised their hands. When it seemed that about two-thirds of the students had their hands raised, I called on Erin.

"It's 1 out of 6," she said.

"Explain why you think that makes sense," I responded, writing *1 out of 6* on the board.

"Because there are six numbers—1, 2, 3, 4, 5, and 6—," she explained, "and 1 is just one of the six numbers."

"Erin is right," I said. "Does anyone have another way to explain why 1 out of 6 makes sense?" I called on Seth.

"There are six chances," he said, "and only one of the chances is a 1."

I nodded and asked, "Does anyone have another way to explain?" No one did.

**NOTE** Allowing time before calling on a child gives all of the children a chance to think about the question. Wait time also gives children the message that the teacher would like them to think and isn't necessarily interested in a quick response.

I then asked, "When you were playing Pig, what did you notice about how often the number 1 came up?"

The children's viewpoints varied. Some thought that 1 came up often. "Every other roll, practically," Amanda said. Some thought that it depended on whether you were lucky.

"I rolled once and got to 86 before a 1 came up," Elliot said. Other students said you couldn't tell; it was always different.

"Sometimes it comes up on your first roll," Lee Ann said, "and sometimes it takes forever."

"We're going to do an experiment, so we can learn about how often 1 comes up when we roll a die," I said. "I'm going to roll a die and see how many rolls it takes for a 1 to come up." I asked the children to count my rolls as I watched for a 1. When a 1 came up on the third roll, I wrote the number *3* on the board to remember it. I repeated the experiment four more times, each time recording the roll on which the number came up: 7, 3, 9, 5.

"You'll each do this experiment five times as I did," I said. "Watch as I show you how to record your data on a class chart." I posted the "How Many Rolls to Get a 1?" chart and listed the numbers from 1 to 10 on it. I put two tally marks by the number 3 and one tally mark each by 5, 7, and 9 to indicate the number of rolls it took me to get a 1 on my five trials.

"But it's possible to take more than 10 rolls," I said, "so I'll add more numbers." I continued numbering on the chart until I reached the bottom of the paper; I had numbered from 1 to 26.

| How Many Rolls to Get a 1? |
| --- |
| 1 |
| 2 |
| 3    II |
| 4 |
| 5    I |
| 6 |
| 7    I |
| 8 |
| 9    I |
| 10 |
| 11 |
| 12 |
| 13 |
| 14 |
| 15 |
| 16 |
| 17 |
| 18 |
| 19 |
| 20 |
| 21 |
| 22 |
| 23 |
| 24 |
| 25 |
| 26 |

"It's also possible that you'll roll more than 26 times before a 1 comes up," I said. "If that happens, we'll add another sheet of paper and continue numbering."

"How many times do we do it?" Timmy wanted to know.

"At least five times," I said. "You can do more if you'd like. I'll leave the chart up and we'll talk about it tomorrow. The more data we have, the more reliable the information on the chart will be. Any other questions?" There were none, and I told the children they could continue playing Pig after they recorded their data. Then they got to work.

### A Class Discussion

To begin class the next day, I told the children that I would give 10 minutes for those who needed to add data to the "How Many Rolls to Get a 1?" chart. "The rest of you can play Pig until I call for your attention," I said.

After 10 minutes, I initiated a discussion about the data on the "How Many Rolls to Get a 1?" chart.

## How Many Rolls to Get a 1?

```
1  |||| ||||| |||| ||| |||| ||
2  |||| ||| ||| ||| ||| ||| |||| |
3  ||| |||| ||| |||| |||| ||| ||| |||
4  ||||| |||
5  ||||| ||| ||
6  ||| |
7  |||
8  ||
9  ||| |||
10 ||||
11 ||
12 ||||
13 |
14 ||
15 |
16 |||
17 |
18 | |
19
20 ||
21 |
22
23
24 |
25
26 |
27
28
29
30 |
31 |
32 |
33
```

"What do you notice from examining the data?" I asked. I called on Charlie.

"A 1 seems to come up on the first roll a lot," he said. I recorded Charlie's statement on the board. I find that recording children's statements gives importance to the children's thinking and provides a record of the children's ideas for us to revisit as the discussion progresses. Also, recording children's ideas in writing helps give them models for how to do their own writing.

"Does this describe what you noticed?" I asked Charlie. Charlie read what I wrote and nodded. I ask this question to give children the message that by rereading their writing they can check that they've communicated their ideas correctly.

I called on Elliot. "The numbers with just one number have the most." I recorded his statement.

"I'm not sure what you mean," I said. "I'm confused by 'numbers with just one number.'"

"I know," Lee Ann said, "he means one-digit numbers have the most tallies." I looked at Elliot. He nodded, so I wrote Lee Ann's interpretation under Elliot's statement.

"Do Elliot's and Lee Ann's sentences both say the same thing?" I asked.

"Kind of," Lisa said, "but I'm not sure."

"He means 'numbers with just one digit,'" Lee Ann said. Elliot nodded his agreement.

Lisa still looked unsure. So did several other students. I explained the meaning of the term. "The one-digit numbers are the numbers from 1 to 9," I said, pointing out the one-digit numbers on the chart. This seemed to clear up the children's confusion.

Amanda spoke next. "The farther down on the chart to the big numbers, there are less tally marks," she said. I recorded her statement.

"Why do you think that's so?" I asked.

"It's harder to roll that many times and not get a 1," she said.

"But when I was playing Andrew, I almost got 100 on one turn without a 1," Timmy said.

"Me, too," Tom chimed in.

"Did you do that once, a few times, or a lot of times?" I asked.

"Just once," Timmy answered.

"I did it twice," Tom said, excitedly, "and Charlie did it one time." Students burst into individual conversations about their experiences having 1s come up. I quieted them and reminded them to raise their hands to offer their ideas. Then I called on Emelia.

"It's not likely to roll that much and not get a 1," Emelia said.

"But I did it," Timmy insisted. Timmy was more interested in his own experience than in a more general theory. This is typical for some children at this age.

"Does anyone notice anything else from the data?" I asked, to refocus the discussion on the chart.

Eric raised his hand. "The tallies drop down in a slant from 1 down," he said. I recorded Eric's statement.

"Oooh, that's what I was going to say," Abby lamented.

"Keep looking," I suggested, "and see if you notice something else." I called on Seth.

"On the higher numbers, all got mostly only one tally," Seth said. I recorded his idea.

No other children volunteered, so I asked, "How can these observations help you think about strategies for playing Pig?"

"I think you should roll just one time and then stick," Charlie said. His idea related to the observation he had made earlier. I posted a sheet of chart paper, titled it "Strategies for Pig," and recorded Charlie's idea:

1. Roll once and stop.

Doug raised his hand. "I don't get it," he said, "because on the chart you only roll with one die, so it's not like Pig."

"I disagree," Lori said. "I think it's like Pig because with two dice there's even a better chance of getting a 1."

"Well, maybe," Doug said, "but it's not exactly the same." Doug often pushes for precision in descriptions. "I think the best strategy is to go for it," he added. Underneath Charlie's idea, I wrote:

2. Go for it.

"Explain that strategy," I said.

"You just keep rolling until you get a big number," he said. "I've been winning Elliot a lot that way."

"What do you consider to be a big number?" I asked.

"Like 65 or 70," he answered.

"I've been doing it, too," Erin confirmed.

"It doesn't work for me," Ajani said, "I keep getting zeros."

"What other ideas do you have for strategies?" I asked.

Lisa raised her hand. "I think you should roll just three or four times and then stop." I recorded this.

"How do you decide whether to roll three times or four times?" I asked. Lisa thought for a moment and then shrugged.

I called on Eric. "I roll high enough so my friend is behind me," he said. "Then I stick." I added Eric's strategy to the list.

Andrew offered next. "I use a combination," he said. "I look at my partner's score, and if I'm behind I take chances and roll more, but if I'm ahead I stick, so I don't get double 1s. So, it all depends." I recorded Andrew's strategy. His idea was sophisticated for a third grader, and I could see that many children weren't sure about his thinking. One wonderful aspect of a game like Pig is that it allows children to participate at different levels of sophistication and still enjoy the activity, get practice with mental addition, and think about probability.

Kristin had a different strategy. "When I roll," she said, "if I get 15 or 20, I stick. But if I only have a little number, I keep rolling." I recorded Kristin's strategy.

I reviewed the list aloud for the class:

1. Roll one time and stop.
2. Go for it.
3. Roll three or four times and stop.

4. Roll high enough so your friend is behind.
5. Use a combination and pay attention to your partner's score.
6. When you get to 15 or 20, stick.

"Any other strategies?" I asked. There were no more suggestions.

"You'll have the chance to try these strategies and test them on a menu activity," I said. "Right now, I'd like you to write about the strategies you've been using these last few days."

**The Children's Writing**

The students' writing revealed their different thoughts about strategies for playing Pig.

Emelia wrote: *My strategy was take one turn, and if it was a high number stick, if it was a low number, take one more turn and stick. Once I got a dubble one with 15 but I still won.* (When I asked Emelia what she considered to be a high number, she thought for a moment and answered, "8 or more.")

Pig

My strategy was take one turn, and if it was a high number stick, if it was a low number, take one more turn and stick.

Once I got a dubble one with 15 but I still won.

PIG

My ~~strategi~~ is to roll the dice until I get higher then my partner. And if I'm already higher then my partner I only roll the dice once.

*(left)* Emelia commented that rolling double 1s didn't have to be a disaster.

*(right)* Tomo explained his strategy.

Tomo used a different strategy. He wrote: *My strategi is to roll the dice until I get higher then my partner. And if I'm already higher then my partner I only roll the dice once.*

When Charlie wrote about his strategy, he included his ideas about the probability of the dice: *I have noticed in pig that rolling one time and sticking with that roll will get you farther then 3 rolls or 4 because you don't give the 1 enuff chance to come up. 1 seems to have a 20% chance of coming up, double 1 comes up about 10% and all the others come up about 85%.*

Lisa had a similar strategy. She wrote: *I think you should roll three or four times (if your a high player like me). Because after three or four times ones begin to apear. I hate when ones apear. I think you should drop one dice then the other (That gives you a much better chance of not geting a one.) But! Remember to roll the one in hand again!*

Lisa had a strategy and a suggestion for controlling the dice.

> $\mathsf{S}$trategy for pig
>
> I think you should roll three or four times (if your a high player like me). Because after three or four times ones begin to apear. I hate when ones apear. I think you should drop one dice then the other (That gives you a much better chanc of not geting a one) But!. Remember to roll the one in hand again8.

Andrew also described his thinking about the mathematical probabilities. He wrote: *I noticed that it's risky to roll when you've scored a lot of points in that round. I think the chances of 1 coming up is about 1 in 6. I think the chance of 2 ones coming up 2 out of 12. The reason I think this is because there are six numbers on the dice. the number 1 is only one of them.*

Timmy wrote: *I have a stratagy that you don't roll orver 4 times becuase it is likely that you would get a 1 and your turn would be over or you would stat at 0 agen. This is what happened when I had 91. I rolled and got 1 1s.*

Doug described his charge-ahead strategy. He wrote: *I learned that you should roll a lot because whats the wirst that can hapen to you, you lose your turn. So I figured you mite as well just keep on rolling.*

Carrie tried several different strategies. She wrote: *At first, I alway rolled to try to get more, but, I always got a one. So, I started taking <u>whatever</u> I got on the first roll. That didn't seem to work, so I started being a pig again, and always rolled over and over, to get more. <u>Surprisingly,</u> It worked! Anyway, I just wanted to tell you that I usually stop rolling <u>somewhere</u> around "30" or "40."*

Strategy for Pig

At first I alway rolled to try to get more, but, I always got a one. So, I started taking whatever I got on the first roll. That didn't seem to work, so I started being a pig again, and always rolled over and over, to get more. Surprisingly, It worked! Anyway, I just wanted to tell you that I usually stop rolling somewhere around "30" or "40."

strategys for pig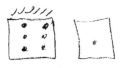

If you get a 4 don't stick. Don't stick if the number is below 4 or 5 O.K? If your numer is above 4 or 5 stick O.K? If my partner was winning and I got a little roll I would roll agan. If I got a high roll I would stick. A high roll is eneaything higher than 5 6 or 7.

*(top left)* Carrie described her struggle to find a successful strategy.

**(top right)** Tom described how he used a combination of strategies.

*(right)* Elliot didn't have much luck with his strategy.

PIG

Pig is a very fun game. I discover never roll more three times. I lost a lot of games of pig. It's a chance game because you don't know what the dice is going to be. Doug won all the time. I never won.

**How Many Rolls to Get Double 1s?**

I was interested in having the children think about the likelihood of rolling two 1s, so I structured a similar experience with two dice. After the students were involved with menu activities, I began class one day by posting a sheet of chart paper entitled "How Many Rolls to Get Double 1s?"

"For this chart," I said, "you'll roll two dice and count the rolls until double 1s come up. Do it five times, just as you did for the other chart, and post your data. We'll talk about the data at a later time."

I numbered the chart to 60. "I wonder if this is far enough," I mused aloud. None of the children commented, and I decided to let them try the experiment without further information.

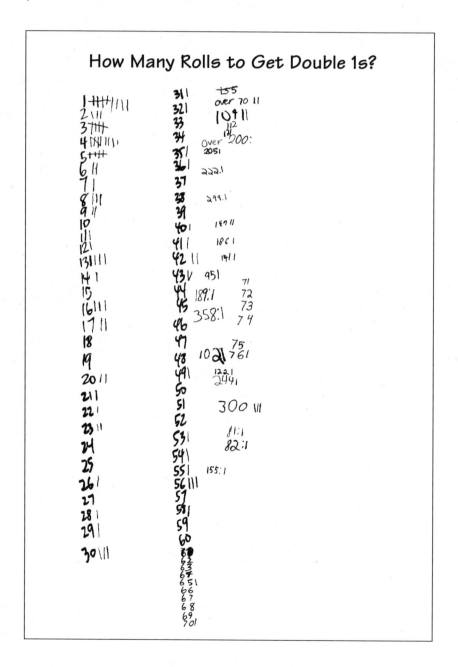

Over the next several days, children made tally marks on the chart. They were surprised that it often took so long before they rolled two 1s. It took some children more than 60 rolls and, when this happened, they wrote the number of rolls it took and made a tally mark next to it. The children didn't seem to care that the extra numbers they wrote were not in sequence.

A few days later, after all of the children had had time to record their data, I asked the class to compare the two charts. "What do you notice about the shape of the data on the two charts?" I asked.

"They're more bunched up near the top on the first one," Erin said.

"Why do you think that happened?" I asked.

"I don't know," Erin shrugged.

"I do," Andrew said. "It's not so hard for a 1 to come up on one of them. But it's harder for 1s to come up on two of them."

"But I got two 1s easier than I got one 1," Timmy said.

"Not me," Lori said. "It took me much longer."

"Do you notice anything else about the charts?" I asked.

"They're like opposite," Amanda said. "There are more at the top of the first chart and more on the big numbers on the other." She then changed her mind. "Well, they're not really opposite, but different."

"They're kind of spread out more on the chart of double 1s," Seth said.

"Yeah, the tally marks just drip down the chart," Doug observed.

There weren't any other comments, so I asked another question. "What does the information on the charts say about which is easier," I asked, "to roll a 1 on one die or to roll double 1s on two dice?" The children looked at the chart and several raised their hands. Many didn't seem to understand my question. I called on Charlie.

"It's easier to roll with one die," he said. "The marks are more on the higher numbers on the other chart."

"Why do you think that happened?" I asked.

"Because it takes more rolls to get two 1s," he said. "I agree with Andrew."

"Any other ideas?" I asked.

No other children raised their hands, and I decided not to push further. I didn't feel the need to bring the discussion to a formal mathematical conclusion. Not all of the children would understand if I discussed the mathematics in more detail, so I decided to leave the charts posted and let the students continue to think about them on their own.

## WHOLE CLASS LESSON ■ Tiles in the Bag

**Overview**

*Tiles in the Bag* introduces students to sampling with replacement as a way to predict how many of each color are in a bag of Color Tiles. The activity not only involves children with taking samples and analyzing data, but also presents them with the opportunity to think proportionally.

The menu activity *Tiles in Three Bags* (see page 105) extends the *Tiles in the Bag* lesson by challenging children to use sampling with replacement to match bags of tiles with descriptions of their contents.

**Before the lesson**

Gather these materials:
■ One lunch bag with 8 red and 4 yellow Color Tiles
■ One lunch bag with 8 blue, 2 red, and 2 yellow Color Tiles

**Teaching directions**

■ Hold up the lunch bag with 8 red tiles and 4 yellow tiles in it. Don't reveal the exact contents, but tell the students that you put 12 Color Tiles in the bag and that some are red and some are yellow.

■ Ask children what might possibly be in the bag. Record on the board the combinations they suggest. If a student suggests a combination that you've already recorded, point to it and ask for one that isn't already on the list.

■ After you've listed about eight combinations, ask the students if they can think of a way to be sure they've thought of all the combinations possible. If no student suggests reordering them, you may choose to do so to help the children see what combinations are missing. Altogether, 11 combinations are possible:

| | |
|---|---|
| 1r | 11y |
| 2r | 10y |
| 3r | 9y |
| 4r | 8y |
| 5r | 7y |
| 6r | 6y |
| 7r | 5y |
| 8r | 4y |
| 9r | 3y |
| 10r | 2y |
| 11r | 1y |

Note: Some students may suggest zero reds and 12 yellows or 12 reds and zero yellows. These are numerically correct, but they aren't possible because they don't meet the condition that two colors are in the bag.

■ Tell the students that they'll now collect information to help them predict what is in the bag. Explain that they'll take turns drawing out one Color Tile from the bag (without peeking inside), recording its color, and returning the tile to the bag. Tell the students that this procedure is called "sampling with replacement," meaning that you take out a sample and record it, then return (or "replace") it to the bag. (You may already have written the word *sample* on the Probability Words chart, but it's useful to add *sampling* or *sampling with replacement.*)

■ Choose a child to record the data for the class demonstration. Write *Red* and *Yellow* on the board and instruct the student to make a tally mark each time someone draws a tile. Call on volunteers to draw tiles.

■ After 12 samples, ask the children what they think might be in the bag. Have them explain their reasoning for their predictions. Take 12 more samples to see if the students would make the same predictions or different ones. Discuss. Then repeat for a third set of 12 samples. Finally, empty the bag and reveal its contents.

■ Do the same experiment with the second lunch bag with eight blue, two red, and two yellow tiles. Hold up the bag and tell the children that the bag also has 12 tiles in it, but it has red, yellow, and blue tiles.

■ As with the first bag, ask students for possible combinations. However, do not try to list them all. (There are 1000 possible combinations!) Don't tell the children that there are too many to list, but let them suggest possible combinations until they realize that there are many more than there were with the first bag.

■ Have the class take three or four sets of 12 samples with replacement. Discuss with the students what they think is in the bag.

■ Do not reveal the contents yet. Instead, have the children write about their predictions. Their writing will give you insights into their thinking. Write the following prompt on the board:

> I predict there are ____ red, ____ yellow, and ____ blue tiles because _____
>
> _____

■ The next day, you may want to ask volunteers to share their ideas by reading their writing aloud to the class. Finally, as with the first bag, reveal the contents.

**NOTE** When giving a writing assignment, a prompt on the board helps children focus on the purpose of the assignment, organize their thoughts, and get started writing. However, prompts should be offered as suggestions, not as mandates. What's important is that children write what makes sense to them and also what clearly communicates their thinking.

## FROM THE CLASSROOM

I showed the class a lunch bag in which I had put 8 red and 4 yellow Color Tiles. I purposely didn't tell how many of each color there were. Instead, I told the children, "I put 12 Color Tiles in this bag. Some are red and some are yellow. What could possibly be in the bag?"

I waited a moment until about a half dozen children had raised their hands. I called on Tom. "Six red and six yellow," he said. I recorded on the board:

6r      6y

"What else could possibly be in the bag?" I asked. I waited to give the children a chance to think. When about 10 students had raised their hands, I called on Emelia.

"It could be 10 red and 2 yellow," Emelia said. I added her prediction to the board:

| | |
|---|---|
| 6r | 6y |
| 10r | 2y |

"And what else could there be?" I asked. Now more than half of the children had raised their hands, as more of them understood the question. After I recorded each suggestion, I asked if anyone had another combination. The list grew longer:

| | |
|---|---|
| 6r | 6y |
| 10r | 2y |
| 7r | 5y |
| 1r | 11y |
| 11r | 1y |
| 4r | 8y |
| 9r | 3y |
| 5r | 7y |

Several times students suggested combinations that I had already recorded. In each instance, I just pointed to it and asked if the student could find a combination that I hadn't yet put on the list.

Charlie suggested 12 red and zero yellow. His suggestion sparked Eric into offering 12 yellow and zero red. I added both combinations to the list, even though they weren't possible because I had said that there were some red and some yellow tiles in the bag. However, no one commented, so I let it go, planning to talk about these two combinations after I had listed all of them. Finally, no one could think of any more:

| | |
|---|---|
| 6r | 6y |
| 10r | 2y |
| 7r | 5y |
| 1r | 11y |
| 11r | 1y |
| 4r | 8y |
| 9r | 3y |
| 5r | 7y |
| 12r | 0y |
| 0r | 12y |
| 3r | 9y |
| 8r | 4y |
| 2r | 10y |

"I think it's hard to tell if we've found all the possible combinations because they're not written in any order," I said. "You can't see any pat-

tern." We had been talking about the importance and value of patterns since the beginning of the school year.

Andrew had a suggestion. "You could do them so the reds go 1, 2, 3, like that," he said. (If no student had made this suggestion, then I would have suggested it.) I reordered the combinations as Andrew suggested, starting with zero red and 12 yellow.

| | |
|---|---|
| 0r | 12y |
| 1r | 11y |
| 2r | 10y |
| 3r | 9y |
| 4r | 8y |
| 5r | 7y |
| 6r | 6y |
| 7r | 5y |
| 8r | 4y |
| 9r | 3y |
| 10r | 2y |
| 11r | 1y |
| 12r | 0y |

"Oooh, look at that," Amanda said, "the yellows go down—12, 11, 10, 9, 8, 7, 6, 5, 4, 3, 2, 1, 0." Several other children joined her as she counted backward.

"That's really neat," Lori said, impressed with the orderliness of the numbers.

"I think there are two combinations on our list that really couldn't be in the bag," I said. "Does anyone have an idea which two I'm thinking of?"

There was silence for a minute. Then Abby's hand shot up. "The ones with zeros," she said. "You can't have zeros because then you'd only have one color."

"Oh, yeah," several children agreed. I crossed out the two combinations with 12 and zero in them.

"So, how many possibilities are there?" I asked. Several children called out responses. "Ten." "Twelve." "Eleven." I counted aloud with them to verify that there were 11 possibilities.

"Who can explain why we don't have a very good chance of guessing exactly what's in the bag?" I asked. Several children had ideas.

"It's hard to guess the right one with so many," Lisa said.

"It's harder than the spinner," Doug said, "because that only had three numbers and this has lots."

"It's only a little chance to guess right," Tomo added, "about maybe 10 percent or 20 percent." Tomo is always interested in quantifying situations.

"A mathematician would say that you have only 1 chance out of 11 possibilities," I said, "and 1 out of 11 isn't very good. We're going to do an experiment to get some information so you'll more likely make a correct prediction."

I explained that we were going to collect information by drawing out one Color Tile at a time, recording its color, returning it to the bag, and then repeating this procedure. "Mathematicians call this *sampling with replacement,*" I explained.

I asked for a volunteer to make tally marks on the board to keep track of what we drew, and I chose Seth. I wrote on the board:

> Red
> Yellow

"Make a tally mark each time someone draws a tile," I instructed Seth.

I asked Ajani to draw first. "Don't look inside," I said. "Just reach in, pull out a tile, and show it to the class." Ajani drew out a red tile, and Seth made a tally.

"We'll take 12 samples," I said, "and then see what the data show." After 12 draws, we had drawn 9 red tiles and 3 yellow tiles. I had Seth write *9* and *3* beside the tally marks.

| | | |
|---|---|---|
| Red | 卌 IIII | 9 |
| Yellow | III | 3 |

"What do you think?" I asked.

Children had different ideas. A few thought there might be 8 red and 4 yellow. Some thought 9 red and 3 yellow. Some thought 7 red and 5 yellow. As children made predictions, I asked them to explain their reasoning.

"I think 8 and 4," Abby said.

"Because?" I prompted.

"Because it's close to 9 and 3," Abby elaborated, "and you can't be sure 9 and 3 is really right."

"I think it could be 7 red and 5 yellow," Lee Ann explained, "because we could have been picking the same red tile over and over again."

"I think 9 and 3 because that's what came up," Timmy said.

"Let's take 12 more draws," I said. "Then you can look at the data and see if you feel more sure about your prediction or want to change your mind." I wasn't sure if it would be best to keep the samples of 12 separate from each other or to have the children look at a larger sample of 24 draws. I decided to look at the data both ways and drew a line to help Seth keep the sample sets separate. This time, 6 red and 6 yellow came up.

| | | | | |
|---|---|---|---|---|
| Red | 卌 IIII | 9 | 卌 I | 6 |
| Yellow | III | 3 | 卌 I | 6 |

**NOTE** Asking children to explain their reasoning reinforces for them that you're interested in their thinking, not just in their answers. After a while, children no longer need to be prompted but learn to explain their reasoning when they respond to a question.

"So, what has come up altogether both times?" I asked. Some children counted the tally marks; others added the numbers. We had 15 reds and 9 yellows. Again, I asked the children to predict. It seemed easier for them to think about the problem by considering the two samples separately, since the numbers related to the number of tiles in the bag.

"Now I think 7 and 5," Alex said, "because 6 and 6 makes it more even."

"Maybe it's 6 and 6," Lisa said.

"I still stick with 8 red and 4 yellow," Abby said. When I probed her reasoning, she just shrugged. "It just could be," she said.

No one thought that 9 red and 3 yellow was likely; a few thought maybe it was 6 and 6. I suggested we take another 12 samples. The children were willing.

As children drew tiles, others began to cheer, some when a red tile was drawn, others when it was yellow, and some each time, just enjoying the cheering. Then a bit of booing started. I stopped the experiment.

"You need to remember that this is a math experiment," I said. "It's not about winning or losing, but about seeing how we can make predictions from information. I know you're excited, but the cheering and booing aren't appropriate. We've got five more draws to make. Let's do them quickly and quietly."

Children continued to draw tiles. Most of the other children watched calmly, but a few continued to cheer, this time much more softly. I didn't stop again but completed the sample of 12. This time seven red and five yellow came up. I thanked Seth for tallying, and he returned to his seat.

| Red | 卌 IIII | 9 | 卌 I | 6 | 卌 II | 7 |
|-----|---------|---|------|---|-------|---|
| Yellow | III | 3 | 卌 I | 6 | 卌 | 5 |

"It has to be 7 and 5," Doug said. "It just has to."

"Are you absolutely certain?" I asked.

"Well, not really," he answered, "but pretty sure."

"Let's see how many times red and yellow came up in our three samples," I said. I wrote the three samples on the board:

$$9r \qquad 3y$$
$$6r \qquad 6y$$
$$7r \qquad 5y$$

I waited a bit and then called on Lori. "It's 22 reds," she said.

"How did you get that answer?" I asked.

"I knew 9 plus 6 was 15 from last time," she said, "and then I counted—16, 17, 18, 19, 20, 21, 22." She used her fingers to keep track.

"I did it another way," Andrew said. "I knew 9 plus 6 was 15, and 5 more makes 20, so I had 2 more left from the 7, so it's 22."

"Let's figure out the number of times yellow tiles were drawn," I said, pointing to the 3, 6, and 5. I waited. More hands were up for this one.

"It's 14," Joseph said, "because 3 and 6 makes 9, and 1 more makes 10, and 4 more makes 14."

After a few more children had explained how they added, I focused their thinking on the contents of the bag. "What do you think you know for sure about what's in the bag?" I asked.

"There's tiles in it," Doug said, always with his wry view of things. Others laughed.

"What else?" I asked.

"I know there are more red tiles," Charlie said. "I'm really sure." Others agreed.

"Is it possible that there are more yellow tiles?" I asked.

"Yes," several answered.

"But there probably are more red," Seth said.

"It's likely," Lori said, using the word proudly.

"Let's see them," Timmy said, getting impatient. I emptied the contents of the bag and showed the class that there were 8 red and 4 yellow. Some students cheered and some seemed disappointed.

"It's important to remember," I said, "that the data from an experiment won't exactly match what you predict *should* happen. Mathematicians say that if we do many, many draws, then the results of the experiment should be close to what the probabilities predict."

## A Second Experiment

I showed the children the other bag of tiles. "In this bag," I said, "I also put 12 Color Tiles, but this time I put in some red, some yellow, and some blue. What could possibly be in this bag?"

I called on several children. "Maybe 4, 4, and 4," Ajani said.

"It could be 1 red, 1 yellow, and 10 blue," Lee Ann said.

"I think 6 red, 6 yellow, and . . ." Abby stopped to think. "Oh, no," she continued, "that can't be. It could be 6, 3, and 3."

As the children gave possibilities, I listed them until they realized that many different arrangements were possible. (There are 1000 possible combinations.) Then I had the children begin to take samples. I asked Elliot to record.

We used the same procedure as before, this time taking four samples of 12 each. We translated Elliot's tally marks to numbers, and children added mentally to find the total number of draws for each color. I recorded on the board:

|       | 1r  | 2y  | 9b  |
|-------|-----|-----|-----|
|       | 0r  | 3y  | 9b  |
|       | 2r  | 2y  | 8b  |
|       | 3r  | 2y  | 7b  |
| Total | 6r  | 9y  | 33b |

"What do you think?" I asked.

"There's definitely more blue," Charlie said. The class agreed.

"There's 1, maybe 2 red tiles," Timmy said, "and 1 or 2 yellow tiles."

"I think there are 9 or 8 blue tiles," Amanda said, "because they came up more."

"And I think 2 yellow for the same reason," Lisa said.

I was interested in each child's thinking. However, I know that not all children are willing to express their ideas in a class discussion, so I asked the children to write about their predictions. I wrote a prompt on the board to help them get started:

> I predict there are ____ red, ____ yellow, and ____ blue tiles because _____
>
> _____

"How much do we write?" Joseph asked.

"As much as you need to explain your thinking as clearly as you can," I answered.

"It's almost time for recess," Eric pointed out.

"Get your papers organized," I said. "Then, when you return from recess, you can do the writing."

Elliot drew the tally chart and explained his prediction.

# Probability with Tiles

I predict there are 4 reds, 2 yellows and 6 blues because on the tally board most pepole picked out mostley blues. less people picked out yellows and reds.(The tally board looks like this.) It's more lickely to get a blue more then the other colors. I think because most kids got it.

**The Children's Writing**

The children's predictions about the contents of the bag varied. Six children predicted that there were 7 blue tiles, 3 yellow tiles, and 2 red tiles. Tomo's explanation was typical: *I predict that there are 2 reds, 3 yellows, and 7 blues. Because not many kids got a red so I thought that there are less reds. I predict that there are 3 yellows because some kids got a yellow but not that many. I am* <u>certan</u> *that there are less yellows in the bag. I predict that there are 7 blues because most kids got a blue. I am* <u>certan</u> *that there are a lot of blues in the bag.*

Tomo based his reasoning on the results from the draws.

> Probability with Tiles
> I predict that there are
> 2 reds, 3 yellows, and 7 blues. Because
> not many kids got a red so
> I thought that there are
> less reds. I predict that
> there are 3 yellows because
> some kids got a yellow but not
> that many. I am ~~certan~~ that
> there are less yellows in the
> bag. I predict that there
> are 7 blues because most
> kids got a blue. I am
> <u>certan</u> that there are a
> lot of blues in the bag.

Charlie made the same prediction. He wrote: *I predict there are 2 red, 3 yellow and 7 blue because I am convinced that blue has more squares for if you look at each round blue dominates over red and yellow. I think yellow will be a little more then red. If you look at the rounds yellow does show up a little bit more then red. Also I took off a few numbers because some were probily chosen twice. I based red on that it wasn't chosen very much and probily less then its total.*

Four children predicted 8 blue, 2 red, and 2 yellow. Abby wrote: *I predict there are 2 red, 2 yellow, and 8 blues because in the first round there was 1 red, two yellows, and 9 blues. But in the second round there were no reds there were three yellows and 9 blues. By than I was sure that there were more blues than reds and yellows but I was not certan that there were more yellows than reds. In the third round it was a tie between red and yellow (they both got 2) and blue got 8. In the 4th round there were three reds and 2 yellows and 7 blues. I gathered up all the data and disided I thot it was 2 red, 2 yellow, and 8 blues.*

Abby explained how her thinking evolved over the four rounds of samples

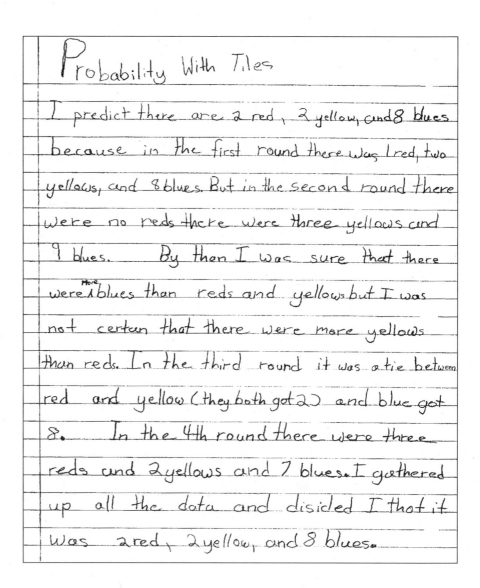

Probability With Tiles

I predict there are 2 red, 2 yellow, and 8 blues because in the first round there was 1 red, two yellows, and 8 blues. But in the second round there were no reds there were three yellows and 9 blues. By then I was sure that there were ^More blues than reds and yellows but I was not certan that there were more yellows than reds. In the third round it was a tie between red and yellow (they both got 2) and blue got 8. In the 4th round there were three reds and 2 yellows and 7 blues. I gathered up all the data and disided I thot it was 2 red, 2 yellow, and 8 blues.

Lisa made the same prediction as Abby. However, her reasoning was based on how she imagined the tiles sat in the bag. She wrote: *I predict there are 2 red, 2 yellow, and 8 blue becuse red only came 2 times and Ms. Bearns shook well, so the red were probably at the bottom of the bag*

*at all the other moves. I think there are 2 yellow because I think they were on the sides of the bag and a lot of people reach in the middle. I think there are 8 blues because since Ms. Bearns shook the bag so well, everybody reaches in the middle, where I think most of the blues go. But I also think the blues go on the sides and bottom too.*

Three children predicted 9 blue, 2 yellow, and 1 red. Andrew, for example, wrote: *I predict there is 1 red, 2 yellow and 9 blues because: 1. I think that there is one red because red only came up 6 times total. And in the one round it didn't come up at all. 2. I think that there are 2 yellows because it came up a little more then red. 3. I think blue has 9 because it is the only number I can use with my other two predictions.*

Janos's prediction showed that he was not thinking about the mathematics of probability but about the popularity of the different colors. He wrote: *I predict there are 4 red 4 yellow 4 blue becase red is just as popular as yellow and plus yellow is the color of the sun and blue is the color of the sky. so what I'm trying to say is I think they are equally popular so that's what I'm trying to say.*

Kristin commented that the samples never came up the same, so her prediction was a guess.

> # Tiles in the Bag
>
> I predict that there is 7 blues, 3 yellows, and 2 reds, because sampling isn't always right. The samples weren't anything twice, and I just made a guess. For blue I put that down because each time the blue had more. I put 3 yellows down because, well it was a guess from the chart. 2 reds because once the red got "0."

After reading the papers that night, I jotted down the various predictions and the number of children who made each of them:

| | | | |
|----|----|----|----|
| 2r | 3y | 7b | 6 |
| 2r | 2y | 8b | 4 |
| 3r | 4y | 5b | 4 |
| 1r | 2y | 9b | 3 |
| 3r | 3y | 6b | 2 |
| 2r | 4y | 6b | 1 |
| 4r | 4y | 4b | 1 |
| 1r | 4y | 7b | 1 |
| 1r | 3y | 9b | 1 |
| 2r | 2y | 7b | 1 |

I noticed that the last two predictions were impossible because neither added up to 12 tiles. I wanted to talk about these two predictions with the students, but I didn't want to embarrass the two children who had made careless errors. So I decided to talk with each of them individually before sharing the predictions with the entire class.

The next morning I approached Joseph first. "When I read your paper last night," I began, "I noticed that your prediction of 9, 3, and 1 adds up to more than 12 tiles."

"Oh, yeah," Joseph said, noticing his error immediately.

"Would you like to change your prediction?" I asked. Joseph nodded and looked at the data still posted on the chalkboard.

"I think maybe there's only 2 yellow," he said, and changed *3 yellow* to *2 yellow*. "That works," he said. I agreed.

Timmy's response was different. When I pointed out that 7 + 2 + 2 added up to less than 12, he became nervous and a little upset. This reaction was typical for Timmy. "What should I do?" he asked anxiously.

"There are 12 tiles in the bag," I said. "For a prediction to be possible, the numbers for the three colors should add up to 12."

"Which one should I change?" Timmy asked.

"You can change whatever you want," I said. "Maybe it would help if you read what you wrote."

Timmy read aloud: *"I thout that there was 7 blue 2 yellow and 2 red. I thout that it was a good pirdicktion because it seemed like blue whould get a lot of taley marks becuse there was a lot more tiles."* I directed Timmy's attention to the data still on the board.

"Maybe I should make it 8 blue," he said. "Wait, let me see." And he counted on his fingers to be sure that 8, 2, and 2 added up to 12. "Is that okay?" he asked me tentatively.

"That would make 12 tiles in your prediction," I responded. "Do you think it's a reasonable prediction?"

He looked at me, as if searching for confirmation. I didn't react. "I'll go with 8, 2, and 2," he said, "because there were a lot of yellows." He changed his paper.

I'm never sure how to deal with Timmy's lack of confidence. He was in my second-grade class the previous year, and I could see improvement. But he often lacks focus and is scattered. He responds when I work with him one-on-one, and I try to do so as much as possible.

**A Class Discussion**

After talking with Joseph and Timmy, I listed all of the children's predictions on the board. However, I didn't indicate the number of children who had made each prediction, as I didn't think that information was useful for the discussion. Nor did I list Joseph's and Timmy's original predictions.

| | | |
|---|---|---|
| 2r | 3y | 7b |
| 2r | 2y | 8b |
| 3r | 4y | 5b |
| 1r | 2y | 9b |
| 3r | 3y | 6b |
| 2r | 4y | 6b |
| 4r | 4y | 4b |
| 1r | 4y | 7b |

"Wow, there were a lot of different ones," Lori said. Other children also seemed surprised at the variety of predictions.

"Are they all possible?" I asked.

"What do you mean?" Amanda asked.

"Well," I responded, "for the first one, I know that 7, 3, and 2 add up to 12, and I know there are 12 tiles in the bag, so that's a possible combination." I put a small check next to the first prediction.

"The next one is possible, too," Doug said.

"How do you know?" I asked.

"Because 8 and 2 makes 10, and 2 more makes 12," he answered. I put a check to indicate that it was possible.

"Three 4s make 12," Lee Ann said, "so I know 4, 4, and 4 works." I checked that prediction.

The children continued adding to verify that all of the predictions were possible. I wondered if it would have been okay to have left Joseph's and Timmy's predictions on the list. It was too late now, and in retrospect, I'm glad I took the time to talk with the boys before the discussion.

"So they're all possible," I said. "Are they all probable?"

"I'm not sure 4, 4, and 4 is," Emelia said.

"How come?" I probed.

"Well, because we had so many blues taken out of the bag," she said, "and that says there is the same of each. It doesn't make sense."

"Is it possible that there could be four of each color in the bag?" I asked.

"Yes," Charlie answered, "but it's not too likely."

"You're saying that it's possible, but not probable," I said, paraphrasing to help the children get used to the language of probability.

"It could be possible," Seth said, "but it's not as good a prediction as some of the others."

"I think it could be good," Abby countered, "because you can't tell what's in the bag and what people pick out."

"Well, let's look at what's in the bag," I said. I took the tiles out, one by one, and piled them up by colors. We counted and found 8 blues, 2 reds, and 2 yellows. There were oohs and ahhs.

# WHOLE CLASS LESSON    The 1-2-3 Spinner Experiment, Part 2

**Overview**

In each of the previous three whole class lessons—*The 1-2-3 Spinner Experiment, Part 1*, *The Game of Pig*, and *Tiles in the Bag*—some outcomes were more likely than others. In the first spinner experiment, the spinners were twice as likely to land on the number 3 as on the number 1 or 2. When dice were rolled to play Pig, some sums came up more often than others. In both of the two sampling experiments for *Tiles in the Bag*, more tiles of one color were in the bag.

In this activity, the children again use spinners, this time to investigate a situation in which it's equally likely for each number to come up. The lesson helps children expand their thinking about measuring the likelihood of events.

The assessment *Equally Likely* (see page 83), given after this lesson's discussion, is helpful for assessing students' understanding. The menu activity *Spinner Puzzles* (see page 122) extends this lesson by having children design spinner faces to match statements about what should happen in spinner experiments. Also, in the menu activity *Spinner Sums* (see page 165), students collect data using spinners from both this whole class lesson and *The 1-2-3 Spinner Experiment, Part 1* (see page 24).

**Before the lesson**

Gather these materials:
■ Spinner Faces #2, one per student (See Blackline Masters section, page 234.)
■ 5-by-8-inch index cards, one per pair of students
■ Spinner recording sheets, duplicated on color paper, one to two sheets per student (See Blackline Masters section, page 231.)
■ Paper clips, one per student
■ Scissors
■ Tape
■ Three labels—1, 2, and 3—posted on the bulletin board to designate areas for children to post their spinner recording sheets

**Teaching directions**

■ Discuss with the class the meaning of *equally likely*. Ask children to explain the meaning and give examples. Add *equally likely* and, if it comes up, *50-50* to the Probability Words chart.

■ Show children the spinner face (#2) for this lesson and the spinner face (#1) from the previous whole class lesson. Ask them to describe how the spinners are the same and different.

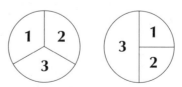

■ Review the procedures the students used for making spinners and doing the first spinner experiment. (See pages 24–28.) Ask them to predict the outcome with the new spinner face.

■ Have the students make the new spinners, do the experiment, and post the results.

■ After each child has completed and posted the results from two or three experiments, initiate a class discussion. Hold up a completed recording sheet and ask students whether they would predict these results came from spinning the old spinner or the new one. Why? Repeat, choosing recording sheets that could reflect probabilities from both spinners. Remind students that predictions are more reliable with larger samples of data.

■ Analyze the data. Have the students use the same procedure as in the first spinner experiment: cutting, taping, making strips of 10s, clipping strips together into groups of 100, and reporting their totals. Record on the board the number of times the spinner landed on each number.

■ Discuss the results with the class. You may want to use the following questions:

How do the class results compare with the results of the first experiment?

How do the results compare with your prediction?

(If appropriate: How can you explain the difference between our class results and what we predicted?)

Did your individual experiments match the class results? Why or why not?

Why do mathematicians say that a large sample of data is better than a small sample of data?

■ Have the children write about the experience. The following prompts on the board might be helpful:

> The results were _____.
> My prediction was _____.
> I learned that _____. (Write about how the results compared with your prediction.)

■ In another class discussion, pose the following question: "If you saw the results of our experiment but hadn't seen the spinner face, how would you predict what the spinner face might look like?" Have the children talk about this question in pairs and then share their ideas with the class.

## FROM THE CLASSROOM

To begin the lesson, I wrote on the chalkboard:

*equally likely*

"Raise your hand if you can read this," I said. Most of the children raised their hands. All but three of the children in the class were adequate or fluent readers.

"Let's say it softly together," I said.

I was interested in finding out what the children thought about the idea of equally likely. I asked, "Who would like to explain what equally likely means, or give an example of how to use it?" I waited a few moments to give children a chance to think and then called on Abby.

"It's like a 50-50 chance," she said. "Like if you had 12 cubes, and there are 6 of one color and 6 of another color, it's equally likely for them to come up." I was impressed by Abby's clarity. Earlier in the year, and all during last year when she was in my second-grade class, Abby tended to daydream. Now she seemed to be paying keen attention to what was going on. I wasn't sure if it was her interest in probability or a shift caused from maturing, but it pleased me to see her come alive in class discussions and in her writing.

"I agree with what Abby said," I responded, adding *equally likely* and *50-50* to the Probability Words chart. "Does anyone have a different way to describe equally likely?" I called on Doug.

"I have an example," he said. "It's equally likely that it will rain." The day was clear and sunny, and I wasn't sure what Doug was thinking.

"Do you think it will rain today?" I asked.

He looked out the window. "Well, no," he said, "but if there were some clouds and it was sunny too, then it could rain."

"How would a weather reporter describe a day that was sunny and cloudy?" I asked.

"I don't know," Doug responded. My questioning seemed to make Doug unsure of himself. Also, I felt uncertain about how to respond to him.

"Would there be an equally likely chance of rain or no rain?" I asked.

"Well, it could be," he answered. "But not today."

I wanted to give Doug some time to reconsider his idea, but I didn't want to reject his idea as wrong or not good enough. "Equally likely usually refers to comparing the probability of two or more things," I said. "Let's listen to some other ideas and hear some other ways to think about equally likely."

I called on Lori next. "On our spinner, it was equally likely for a 1 or 2 to come up," she said, "because 1 is a quarter of the spinner and 2 is a quarter of the spinner." I drew the spinner face on the board as a reminder to the rest of the class.

"And 3 is half of the spinner," Seth added.

"A quarter and a quarter makes a half," Tomo contributed.

"Any other ideas about how to describe equally likely?" I asked. I called on Andrew.

"It's equally likely that a monster will invade the earth as there are people skating on the rings of Saturn," he said. The class laughed, and Andrew grinned triumphantly.

Charlie said, "That means it's a 100 percent chance that neither will happen."

"Or it's a zero percent chance that they will happen," Erin added.

I was surprised at some children's ease with the idea of equally likely and the use of percents to measure probability.

"Any other ideas?" I asked.

Doug raised his hand. "I want to try again," he said.

"Okay," I responded.

"It's equally likely that Al Gore or some other . . . you know, some other . . . person will get elected," Doug said, struggling for a word.

"Do you mean *candidate?*" I asked.

"That's it, that Al Gore or some other candidate will get elected," Doug repeated.

"Yes," I commented, "it can be equally likely if they each have a 50-50 chance. Any other ideas?" The class was quiet.

"How can you talk about equally likely when you toss a coin?" I prompted. Several hands shot up. I called on Lee Ann.

"It's equally likely to get heads or tails," she said. Others nodded.

Tom raised his hand. "I'm not sure that's true with a quarter," he said. "I think one side is heavier than the other."

"That may be true," I said. "I don't know for sure."

I then showed the children the spinner face I had prepared for this lesson.

"How does this spinner face compare with the one we used for the other experiment?" I asked. "How are they the same, and how are they different?" Many children raised their hands. I called on Erin.

"Well, they both have lines and numbers," she said, "but the numbers don't have the same amount of space."

Alan added, "There's not as much space for the 3."

"There's a 50 percent chance for each of them to come up," Joseph said.

"Yeah," Seth said, "they're equally likely." Joseph and others nodded in agreement. I realized that they were erroneously using 50-50 as synonymous with equally likely. This was one of those teaching moments when I realized that I had contributed to misunderstanding by using 50-50 to describe certain situations, and some students were now attaching the language to a different situation. I decided to deal with the confusion by presenting a contradiction to their thinking.

"What's confusing to me," I said, "is that you thought that the 3 on the other spinner had a 50 percent chance. But on this spinner, 3 has even less space and I don't see how it can have a 50 percent chance of coming up."

The class was quiet, considering what I had said. I continued, "On the other spinner, the 3 had a 50 percent chance and the 1 and 2 each had a

25 percent chance, and 50 and 25 and 25 adds up to 100 percent. The 100 percent is for all the possibilities together."

"Oh, I know," Doug blurted out, "it's 35, 35, 35."

"What do you mean?" I said, choosing not to reprimand him for calling out.

"The 1 is 35 percent, the 2 is 35 percent, and the 3 is 35 percent," he said. I wrote three 35s, one underneath the other, on the chalkboard.

Tomo added quickly. "It's 105," he said.

"It's too big," Andrew called out.

I'm often torn between trying to keep discussions orderly and encouraging and allowing students to be spontaneous. This time, however, I decided that I had better remind them to raise their hands before the calling out continued. "Raise your hands if you have an idea," I said.

I waited a moment and called on Amanda. "Try 32," she said. I wrote three 32s in a column. Tomo added again, but this time he raised his hand.

"It's 96," he said. "Now it's too small."

I called on Alan. "Do 33," he said.

It was easy for the children to add the column of three 33s and get 99. "You can't get any closer," Doug commented.

"Yes, I can," I responded. Doug frowned.

"How about 34?" Charlie asked. I wrote the three 34s, and after a minute only three children had answers. I waited until about six more students had raised their hands. I called on Lori.

"It's 102," she said. "It's too big again."

"See?" Doug said. "I told you you can't get any closer." I stood and waited, giving the children time to think.

"I know," Andrew said excitedly, "it's $33\frac{1}{2}$."

"Oh, that's a good idea," Lisa said. I wrote $33\frac{1}{2}$ three times.

"This may be hard to add," I said. Some of the children agreed, but Andrew felt up to the task.

"You have 99," he said, "then $\frac{1}{2}$ and $\frac{1}{2}$ makes 1 more, and that's 100, and then you have $\frac{1}{2}$ more so it's $100\frac{1}{2}$." I wasn't sure that all of the children followed Andrew's reasoning, but I confirmed that he was correct.

"It's still not exact," Tomo commented.

"I have an idea," Emelia said. "I know that if you have something and you break it into three parts, then each part is a third. So I think that $33\frac{1}{3}$ would work."

Emelia is particularly talented in mathematics, and I knew that most of the children had not learned this. I wrote $33\frac{1}{3}$ three times and added them aloud, using the same method Andrew had. I added three 33s to get 99 and then $\frac{1}{3} + \frac{1}{3} + \frac{1}{3}$ to get 1 more. Hearing me add aloud can help children learn about an unfamiliar idea.

"So, what do we know now about the probability of the numbers on the spinner?" I asked. This had been a long and unexpected digression, and I was anxious to get the children involved in the spinner experiment.

Abby raised her hand. "Each number has a $33\frac{1}{3}$ percent chance," she said. "They're all the same."

"But I think that the 1 looks like it takes up a little bit more room," Tom said.

"I think the 2 space looks a little bigger," Eric said.

"When I drew the spinner face, I tried to be exact and give each number the same amount of space," I said. "But they might be a little off. What do you think will happen if we use this spinner for the same kind of experiment we did with the other spinner?"

"In the other one," Emelia said, "we got 832 1s and 868 2s, and they were the same size. So, I don't think they'll come up exactly the same, even if they are the same size, but close."

"But they would come out the same if the spaces were exact," Tomo said.

"I don't think so," I said. "I think each number will come up *about* the same number of times, but it's unlikely that 1, 2, and 3 will come up the exact same number of times. We'll make new spinners now, try the experiment, and post the results. I duplicated the recording sheets on blue paper, so we won't get these mixed up with the ones we used for the first spinner experiment."

Corrine raised her hand. "I don't know how to make a spinner," she said. "I had the chicken pox last week." Antonio and Timmy raised their hands also to indicate they had been absent when I taught the class to make spinners.

"I can show Corrine," Abby said. I asked Alan to help Timmy and Janos to help Antonio. I distributed the materials, and the children got to work.

### Observing the Children

As I circulated, I offered help when needed. Antonio, Corrine, and Timmy seemed to be getting good help from the others at their tables. I helped some of the children poke holes. I helped Mercedes tape her paper clip in place. I reminded Maura to put the straw on her paper clip before putting on the spinner face. When Janos looked confused after spinning the spinner, I pointed out to him that he hadn't drawn the line on the base to determine which number came up. I fixed Joseph's spinner by adjusting the tape he had used to cover the tip of the paper clip; it was so close to the spinner face that it restricted the spinning.

As the children settled into spinning and recording data, I had the chance to listen to their conversations. Although the children were involved with the activity, many of them were chatting about things other than math. Lori, Lee Ann, and Amanda were discussing birthdays.

"Mine is next week," Lori said, "January 18."

"Mine's in two months," Amanda said.

Lee Ann counted on her fingers. "Mine's in 10 months," she said.

As I walked away, I heard Lori say to Amanda, "I'm sorry I can't invite you to my party, but I can only invite eight." I turned around to see Amanda's reaction; she didn't look disturbed.

When I stopped by Tomo's desk, he asked, "When can we do fractions?"

"Didn't we just do some thinking about fractions?" I responded.

"But when can we do more of them?" he asked.

"We'll talk about fractions whenever they come up," I answered.

"Can't we do some sheets of fraction adding?" he persisted.

I answered, "I think it's important to use ideas, like fractions, when they help us solve a problem. I haven't planned for us to do sheets of problems with them." Tomo seemed disappointed. He likes the orderliness of columns of numbers.

Alan and Timmy were talking about their weekend. "I went out in the rain and got all wet," Timmy said.

"Did you get in trouble?" Alan asked.

"No," Timmy said, "my mom made me take a hot shower, though."

"That sounds like punishment to me," Alan replied.

Tom came up to me with his recording sheet. "Look, it's like a shoe," he said. He had trimmed his sheet and was pleased with the shape.

|   |   |   |   |   |   | 3 | 3 | 3 | 3 | 3 |
|---|---|---|---|---|---|---|---|---|---|---|
|   |   | 2 | 2 | 2 | 2 | 2 | 2 | 2 | 2 | 2 |
| 1 | 1 | 1 | 1 | 1 | 1 | 1 | 1 | 1 | 1 | 1 |

He raced off to post it on the bulletin board.

"I hope 3 wins," I overheard Andrew say to Elliot.

"Me, too," Elliot said.

"How come?" I asked.

"Because I like big numbers," Andrew said.

"I don't think 3 is a very big number," I replied.

"Well, it's the biggest on the spinner," he answered, spinning his spinner. "Oh, rats," he commented, "there's another 2."

"Ooooh, it was almost a tie," Corrine said as I walked by. She showed me her recording sheet. The number 2 had come up 12 times, 1 had come up 11 times, and 3 had come up 5 times. Corrine reached for the scissors to cut her paper so she could post it.

At the end of class, I told the children we would analyze the data the next day, then dismissed them for recess.

### A Class Discussion

The next day, I removed some of the children's recording sheets from the bulletin board and gathered the class on the rug for a discussion. I had chosen recording sheets that had different configurations of results. I began by holding up Elliot's recording sheet. Although 3 had reached the top first, 1 and 2 were each just one square behind.

|   |   | 3 |
|---|---|---|
| 1 | 2 | 3 |
| 1 | 2 | 3 |
| 1 | 2 | 3 |
| 1 | 2 | 3 |
| 1 | 2 | 3 |
| 1 | 2 | 3 |
| 1 | 2 | 3 |
| 1 | 2 | 3 |
| 1 | 2 | 3 |
| 1 | 2 | 3 |
| 1 | 2 | 3 |

"If I showed you this recording sheet," I said, holding it up for the children to see, "and asked you to predict whether it was a result of spinning the old spinner or the new one, what would you predict?"

"It's the new one," Lori said.

"How come?" I asked.

"Because it's on blue paper," she explained, "and we did all of the recording sheets for the second spinner on blue paper."

This was true, but not what I had in mind. "Yes, that's an obvious clue," I answered. "Suppose we had used the same color paper for both experiments. What would you predict from looking at the data?"

I called on Seth. "It would have to be the new one," he said, "because even though 3 won, the others got so many."

"It could be the other one," Tomo said. "I got one like that when I did it."

"But it isn't usual," Doug countered.

"Is it possible this could have resulted from either spinner?" I asked. The children nodded or said yes.

"I think that the new spinner is more likely to produce this result," I said, "but it is possible for it to have happened with either."

I showed the children several similar recording sheets and then held up one on which 2 was at the top, 1 was two squares behind, and 3 filled only two squares.

|   | 2 |   |
|---|---|---|
|   | 2 |   |
| 1 | 2 |   |
| 1 | 2 |   |
| 1 | 2 |   |
| 1 | 2 |   |
| 1 | 2 |   |
| 1 | 2 |   |
| 1 | 2 |   |
| 1 | 2 |   |
| 1 | 2 | 3 |
| 1 | 2 | 3 |

"What about this one?" I asked.

"It would be the new one, too," Lisa said. "There are hardly any 3s, and 3 had so much more space on the other."

"And 1 and 2 are so close," Amanda answered.

"But it's funny that there are hardly any 3s," Tom said.

I showed a third recording sheet that more closely resembled the results for the first spinner. (See top of page 75.)

"Even though this looks as if it were from the old spinner," I said, "it was done with this new one. Making decisions from just a little bit of information isn't very reliable. It would be like drawing just one tile from the bag and then trying to predict how many of each color there were."

| | | 3 |
|---|---|---|
| | | 3 |
| | | 3 |
| | | 3 |
| | | 3 |
| | 2 | 3 |
| | 2 | 3 |
| 1 | 2 | 3 |
| 1 | 2 | 3 |
| 1 | 2 | 3 |
| 1 | 2 | 3 |
| 1 | 2 | 3 |

I showed Lee Ann's recording sheet next.

"My experiment worked like the old spinner," Lee Ann said, "but different."

| | 2 | |
|---|---|---|
| | 2 | |
| | 2 | |
| | 2 | |
| | 2 | |
| | 2 | |
| | 2 | |
| 1 | 2 | 3 |
| 1 | 2 | 3 |
| 1 | 2 | 3 |
| 1 | 2 | 3 |
| 1 | 2 | 3 |

"What do you mean?" I asked.

"Well," she said, "it would be like the old spinner if 2 was in the big space and 1 and 3 were in the other spaces."

"That's weird," Doug said.

"How can that happen?" Amanda said.

"It's important to remember that mathematicians say that a large sample is more reliable for making predictions," I explained, "that making a prediction from just a small amount of data isn't a good idea. That's why we'll combine all of our experiments and analyze the data together."

I then reviewed for the children how to count the number of 1s, 2s, and 3s on the recording sheets. As in the first spinner experiment, I demonstrated for them how to cut the strips apart and tape the 1s, 2s, and 3s separately.

I wrote the directions on the board to remind them:

Cut strips.
Tape 1s, 2s, and 3s separately.
Cut strips into 10s.
Clip together strips of 10 to make 100s.
Count the 100s.
Put extra pieces on the front table.

I gave one last direction. "If you finish before we're ready to count," I said, "then play Pig with a partner."

I distributed recording sheets to each table. It took the class about 20 minutes to do all the cutting and taping. Some groups organized themselves for efficiency. At Amanda's table, for example, while Eric cut pieces of tape and placed them on one edge of the table, the other students cut recording sheets, giving the 1s to Kristin, the 2s to Amanda, and the 3s to Elliot. Eric later switched to cutting the longer strips into strips of 10. In other groups, however, children began by working independently, each child cutting apart recording sheets and taping separate strips for 1s, 2s, and 3s; later they combined their strips and cut them into strips of 10.

Finally, all the students were ready for the count. I asked the students at each table how many they had for the number 1, and I recorded their counts on the board:

200
300
300
400
100
100
200

"How many altogether?" I asked. "Raise your hand when you think you know."

I called on Lori. "It's 1600," she said.

"How did you figure it?" I asked.

"I added 300 and 300 and got 600 and 400 more makes 1000," she explained, "and then I added the two 100s together and got 200, and that made three 200s, so I went 200, 400, 600. So I added 600 and 1000 and I got 1600."

"But there are 68 extras," Timmy said. He had counted the extras on the front table.

"So that's 1668," Lori adjusted her answer.

I collected the data for the other two numbers in the same way. I wrote the final results on the board:

| 1 | 2 | 3 |
|---|---|---|
| 1668 | 1908 | 1411 |

"I knew 2 would win," Antonio said.

"We did a lot of spins," Kristin said.

"I can add them all together," Tomo offered.

"Me, too," Andrew said. When the two boys did the arithmetic, they came up with different answers. I asked them to confer with each other until they agreed.

"It's 4987," they reported.

"So, we did about 5000 spins altogether," I said.

"That's more than we did for the old one," Doug said. "We only did around 3000 for them."

"That's a lot of spins," Erin said, rolling her eyes.

"When we look at all of our data together," I said, "we have the benefit of much more information to consider than if each of us looked only at our own experiment."

I wasn't sure how to talk about the results with the children. They enjoyed cutting and taping the strips and counting the 100s. However, they didn't react to the implications of the information, either commenting or questioning why the totals were different. I decided not to discuss the results further at this time but to have the students write about their thoughts. In a way, I was buying time so I could think about how to process the information with them. I thought I could use their papers to begin a discussion the next day.

To help the students, I suggested a structure for their writing. As I typically do, I put several prompts on the board. The children know that these are suggestions for them to use, not requirements. I wrote:

> The results were _____.
> My prediction was _____.
> I learned that _____. (Write about how the results compared with your prediction.)

## The Children's Writing

Children focused on different aspects of the activity in their writing. Janos, for example, wrote: *The results were victory for 2. I learnd equal doesn't mean sucses for all, but 2 must be lucky this time. I thogt that three would win but I was rong, very very very very very! rong. I desovered Equallay dosen't always mean the same!*

Abby described how we counted and reported the class results. At the end of her paper, she wrote about the discrepancy: *I was very suprised. I learned that even if it is equally likely to come up, most of the time it won't be perfectly the same number.*

Ajani reported the class results and what he learned about measuring the probability of three equally likely events, but he didn't offer any interpretation of the data. He wrote: *The resultes were one has 1,668 two has 1,908 and three has 1,411 and all together there was 4,987. Two won. I learned that 50 50 is for twos. But three is 33 1/3% 33 1/3% 33 1/3%. I can't wait until we can make are own spiner.*

Janos commented about the discrepancy between the mathematical definition of equally likely and the results of our experiments.

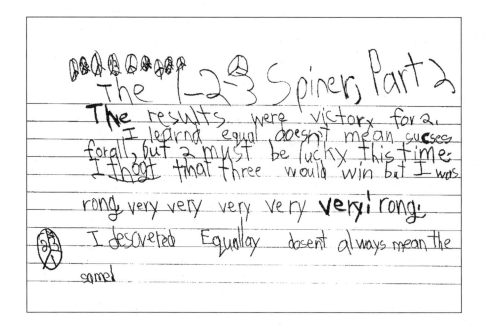

The 1-2-3 Spiner, Part 2

The results were victory for 2. I learnd equal doesn't mean cucses for all, but 2 must be lucky this time. I thogt that three would win but I was rong, very very very very **very** rong.

I descoveted Equallay dosent always mean the samel

---

Abby explained the process we used to count and report the data, then commented on the results.

The 1-2-3 Spinner Part 2

Today we learnd about equally likely. We took down the data from the bord and we each got a an amount of the charts. We cut them up and counted them. We seporated them into tens. I got 143 but I had to give the 43 to the extra pile. Then we told the teucher how many hundreds we had and she put it down on the dry bourd. Then when we were done we added it up. Peaple spun 1 1668 times

Then we did the same thing with 2. It came out with 1908. Then we did the same thing with 3. It came up with 1411 but all together we spun..... 4987! I was very suprised. I learned that even if it is equally likely to come up, most of the time it won't be perfectly the same number.

Doug's humor often seeps into his writing. For this assignment, he wrote: *Andrew and Tomo very much disliked the socres because they were voting very hily for the threes but they had to live with it. The reason they wanted three was because they wanted the hy numbers. Look on the bright side at least the 2s won. I bet there going to say lets do it again. I would probably feel the same if I were them but I am not.*

Having children write on a regular basis helps me understand how they think about mathematical situations. Tomo, for example, calculates numerically whenever he can. For this assignment, he wrote: *The resultes were pretty strange. Because they were all diferent numbers even when the spinner's number's space were all the same. This time #3 lost. #3 had only 1,411. And #2 won. Andrew and I wanted #3 to win because we both like high numbers. #2 had 1,908. #1 was in 2nd place. There were only 1,668 ones. #2 had 497 more then #1. #2 had 240 more then #3. #1 had 257 more then #3. The total of every number is 4,987.*

Tomo's paper shows his interest in computing.

> (①②③) The 1-2-3 Spinner, Part 2
>
> The resultes were pretty strange. Because they were all diferent numbers even when the spinner's number's space were all the same. This time #3 lost. #3 had only 1,411. And #2 won. Andrew and I wanted #3 to win because we both like high numbers. #2 had 1,908. #1 was in 2nd place. There were only 1,668 ones. #2 had 497 more then #1. #2 had 240 more then #3. #1 had 257 more then #3. The total of every number is 4,987.

Lisa's writing often doesn't relate to the mathematics but looks at the activity in some other way. She wrote: *I thought one would come out more. Because whenever I spun it seemed like it would always land on the left side even though it didn't. I think the reason why 2 got the most was because I noticed a lot of people spin toward the right and that is toward the two. But when I saw the spinner I thought they were a equally likely chance because they were all the same size.*

### Another Class Discussion

To decide how to structure another class discussion, I thought about the differences in the children's papers. It's typical to have a spread in children's mathematical sophistication, and I wanted to find a way to engage all of the students in thinking about the mathematics. I decided to pose a new question, using an idea I got from Emelia's paper.

Emelia drew a spinner face that she thought related more closely to the class results.

> ### The 1-2-3 Spinner Part 2
>
> The results were the threes had the least amount 1411 Spins of spins, the twos had the most spins 1908 Spins and the ones were in the middle with 1668 spins. If I hadn't seen the spinner I think it would look like this ⊘ The diffrens between the ones and twos was 240. The diffrens between the twos and threes is 508 The diffrence between the 1s and threes is 257.

**NOTE** From time to time, it's important to reinforce for children that their writing is important and valuable and helps reveal their thinking. Remind them that the teacher is the audience for their work and uses their papers to think about how better to help all students learn.

I began class by commenting to the students about the wide variety in their papers. "Some of you explained how we counted the data," I said, "some of you reported the results, some of you wrote about predictions, and others gave reasons for the results. There were a lot of different ideas, and your writing helped me understand how you were thinking."

Then I presented the new question. "I got an idea from Emelia's paper. If you saw the results of our experiment but hadn't seen the spinner face, how would you predict what the spinner face looked like? Talk about this with your partner first, and then you can share your ideas." This question seemed to engage the children, and there was an immediate buzz in the class. Some students took out paper and pencil and made sketches. After a few minutes, I called the class to attention. Almost half of the students raised their hands to share.

I called on Amanda first. "Can I come up to the board and draw my idea?" she asked. I agreed. She drew two spinner faces.

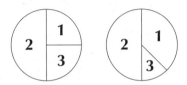

"First I thought that a spinner like the first one, but with the 2 in the big space, would be good," Amanda explained. "But I decided it was a little off. Now I think the spinner would look like this one. I think that's a better guess." Several children responded that they had the same idea.

I called on Elliot next. "Mine's a little different," Elliot said. He came up and drew his idea on the board.

"It's kind of like both of Amanda's," he said. No one else had drawn a spinner face exactly as Elliot had, and the others seemed impressed.

Emelia came up to share what she had drawn on her paper. She carefully drew her spinner idea on the board.

"I tried to give 2 more space, but not so much," she explained. Several others commented that their ideas were similar.

Tom's spinner and explanation elicited discussion from the others.

He explained, "I think that the chance is 70 percent for 2 and 20 per-cent for 1 and 10 percent for 3." After thinking about this for a moment, Charlie's hand shot up. Seth's and Lee Ann's followed. I called on Charlie.

"It can't be 70 percent for 2," he said. "That's more than half and you have about half on your spinner." Tom looked at his spinner, reconsider-ing for a moment, and then changed his sketch.

"Oooh, I know," Lee Ann said. "It's about 50 percent for 2 and 30 per-cent for 1 and 20 percent for 3."

Doug had a different idea. "I think it's 50, 40, and 10," he said.

"It can't be 50 percent for 2," Andrew said. "We didn't get half 2s." None of the other children seemed to understand Andrew's idea, and Andrew wasn't able to explain it. It was an intuitive thought, and a correct one, as Andrew's intuitive thoughts often are, but Andrew didn't have a way to explain it mathematically.

Several other children came up to draw their ideas, but most were repe-titions of Amanda's or Emelia's ideas. However, I felt it was valuable for all who wanted to share to do so. Not only is it good practice for them to represent their thinking visually, but all had different ways to explain their spinners.

After this discussion, I told the children to return to working on the menu.

# ASSESSMENT Equally Likely

One important idea in probability is that some events are more likely than others, while some events are equally likely. In this assessment, each child writes about what *equally likely* means and gives at least one example to explain his or her definition.

During the whole class lessons, children encounter situations that demonstrate how likely events are. In the first spinner lesson, the spinner is designed so that it's more likely for the number 3 to come up than either 1 or 2, but 1 and 2 are equally likely. In the second spinner lesson, the numbers 1, 2, and 3 are equally likely to come up. In both experiments of sampling tiles in the bag, more tiles of one color are in the bag and, therefore, students are more likely to draw that color. The data the students collect for these investigations most likely will verify the predicted probabilities (more or less, of course).

This assessment is appropriate after children have completed the whole class lessons and participated in class discussions about the likelihood of events—more likely, less likely, and equally likely. Discussions help children think mathematically about the experiments and connect their experiences to the language of probability. Also, it's helpful to use the assessment topic for a class discussion a day or two prior to having the students write. Children will usually be more successful with writing assignments after they've had chances to explain their ideas orally.

## FROM THE CLASSROOM

"When we talked a few days ago about the idea of equally likely," I began, "several of you offered different ways to explain it." I reviewed the ideas the children had expressed, reminding them that Abby had talked about Color Tiles, Doug about elections, Lee Ann about coins, Lori about spinners, and Andrew about monsters and Saturn.

"Today I'd like to begin class by having each of you write about equally likely," I said. I reminded the children to write their names and the date in the upper right-hand corner and the title in the center. I wrote a prompt on the board for them to use if they wished:

Equally likely means _____.

"You should explain what equally likely means and then give at least one example," I said.

"Can we use the same idea we did the other day?" Lori asked.

"Yes, that would be fine," I answered.

"But we don't have to, do we?" Abby asked.

"No, you don't have to," I responded.

"What if you can't think of any idea?" Timmy asked. "Can we use one of the examples from before?"

"That would be fine," I said, "as long as you write what makes sense to you."

I gave one last direction. "When you finish writing," I said, "choose a menu activity to do or play Pig."

The children got to work. I circulated, reminding some to put their names and the date on their papers, reminding others about the title. I encouraged them to check the Probability Words chart. "It can help you spell some words," I said, "and also might give you some ideas about what to write."

When children thought they were finished, they brought their papers to me and read them aloud. Some of the children gave clear definitions with examples, and I accepted their papers.

For example, Ajani wrote: *Equally likely means that something has the same chance as the other like for an example it is Equally likely that a rat will gro six feet tall as a man will shrink five feet.*

Several children were inspired by the example Andrew had given the other day about monsters and skating on the rings of Saturn.

Andrew's example was appreciated and imitated by other children.

> ### Equally Likely
>
> Equeally likely means that 2 or more things have the same amount of chance to happen for example it is jcust as likely that gadzilla will jcemp out of someone's TV and invade the earth as their are aliens with snowshoes for feet playing ice hockey on the rings of Scaturn.

Lisa wrote: *Equally likely means that if something is impossible, then if can think of another impossible thing there both equally liekly because there both impossible. For example it is impossible that people will start walking upside down on the rings of Jupiter as it is that the statue of libruty will come alive. It is equally likely that a refrijirator will come alive as it is books will start coming alive.*

Eric wrote: *Equally likely means wen say you were playing a board game. And say each person gets a serten amount of peces. But if both people don't get the same amount of peces it wouldn't be fare. Because equally likely aways is fare. One of my class mates named andrew said it's equally likely that a monster is going to attack the earth. And that there's people scating on the rings of satarn. I thought it was funny. how about you?*

Erin wrote: *Equally likely means that two things have the same chance of haping like it's equally likely that if you flip a coin you can get heads or tails. it's a 50-50 chance. or it's equally likely that dinosors live on the moon as it is that humans live on pluto.*

Erin included a concrete example and a whimsical example.

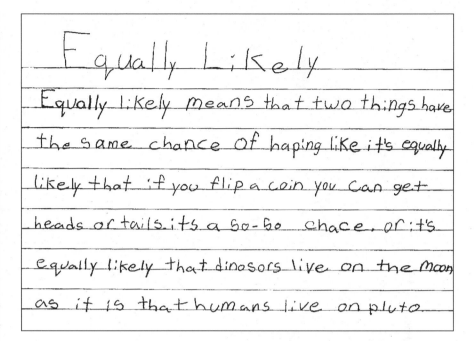

> # Equally Likely
>
> Equally likely means that two things have the same chance of haping like it's equally likely that if you flip a coin you can get heads or tails. its a 50-50 chace. or it's equally likely that dinosors live on the moon as it is that humans live on pluto.

I asked some children to make revisions before I accepted their papers, pushing for more clarity or examples. For example, Elliot finished quickly and brought his paper to me. He had written: *Equally likely menas like it was all cloudy. The weather caster man says it's 50% likely it's going to rain today. One example. There's a 100% impossible a elephant is going to fly.* I told Elliot that equally likely had to do with two or more things that had the same probability of happening.

"What should I do?" he said.

"Your paper tells about a 50 percent chance of raining and a 100 percent chance that an elephant can't fly," I said. "You need to include an example of two things that have the same probability."

"Oh, I get it," Elliot said, and went off to write some more. A little later, he returned. He read his new sentence: *The ground can talk is 100% impossible also.* "Now there are two things the same," he said.

I accepted Elliot's paper. His understanding was fragile, and I decided not to push him to write more. I hoped that Elliot would learn more about equally likely and how to explain it by listening later as other children read their papers.

Corrine's paper showed the same confusion. She had written: *Equally likely means it is zero perseant that Plouto will hit the sun.* When I told her that equally likely had to do with comparing the probability of two things, Corrine added to her paper: *Equally likely menas it is zero perseant that Uranis will hit Neptoon.*

Other children gave only examples in their papers, but I knew from those examples—and from their class participation and conversations with me—that they understood more than they had expressed in writing.

Timmy, for example, wrote: *Equally liekly menas that Bill Clinten had the same chanse of getting elected as George Bush did getting picked to be pressedent.*

Mercedes wrote: *Equally likely means that it is 50-50% chance that it can rain, or that it will be sunny and hot, that's the example.*

When Doug brought his paper to me, he had difficulty reading it. "It's too messy," he said. "Can I copy it over?" I nodded, surprised that he was willing to do so. I thought that Doug was interested in communicating his ideas and upset that his writing was hard to read. He brought his paper back a little later: *Equally likly means well for an example it is Equally likly monkeys can fly as dogs can fly but mayby thats not true if you cunsiter jumping over tree to tree is flying. I will give you another example. Andrew made up it is equally likly marshans will invade earth as marshins are skating on the rings of Saturn.*

In a later class discussion, I had children who were willing read their papers. More than half were eager to do so. Some papers elicited comments from others. Emelia, for example, had written: *Equally likely means there is the same chance of one thing happening as there is for another thing to happen, for example it is equally likely that the story of rupunsel will come true so as to the story of star wars comeing true, a 0% persent chance for both.*

Emelia showed her understanding by assigning a zero percent chance to her examples.

Equally Likely

Equally likely means there is the same chance of one thing happening as there is for another thing to happen. for example it is equally likely that the story of rupunsel will come true so as to the story of star wars comeing true, a 0% persent chance for both.

"That's not so," Doug said. "*Star Wars* could come true."

"But it isn't true," Emelia said.

"But it could be," Doug insisted.

Charlie read next: "*Equally likely means 50-50% chance like if there were two 4th grade teachers it is equally likely you will get either teacher next year. So 50-50% chance is just something has a equal chance of happening as not.*"

"That's not how they put kids in class," Andrew said. "I was changed from one class to another last year. Sometimes they pick."

"I think they put kids together who can work good together," Lori said.

I intervened. "My question is: Do Emelia's and Charlie's papers show that they understand what equally likely means?" Several children nodded. "It's okay to disagree about the examples, but I also want you to think about whether the writer understands what equally likely means."

Abby used examples from the activities we had been doing in class.

> # Equally likely
>
> Equally likely means 50-50 chace and 50-50 chance means if there are two dice it is equally likely for number 6 to come up on each dice. It is equally likely for there to be marshons on mars as ther are plutoshons on pluto. It is equally likely that 1 or 2 will win on the bord (or 3). It is equally likely that josh will spin one two or three on the spinner.

Later, when I read through the papers, I sorted them into three piles. In one pile, I put 14 papers, all of which had an explanation and at least one example. In a second pile, I put 6 papers; these had examples of equally likely events but didn't provide explanations or definitions. The remaining 7 papers showed either limited or fragile understanding about the meaning of equally likely.

After reading the children's papers, I realized that the class had a general misunderstanding about equally likely. Although a 50-50 probability often describes equally likely events, it's possible for equally likely events to be described differently, as in the $33\frac{1}{3}$ chance of the 1, 2, or 3 coming up in Part 2 of the spinner experiment. (See page 67.) Most children ascribed 50-50 to any equally likely events—not just when there were two. I made a note to myself to talk about this with the children.

# CONTENTS

# MENU ACTIVITIES

The activities on the menu were selected to offer children a variety of ways to think about probability. The menu was constructed with the consideration that not all children engage with or experience concepts in the same way; it includes activities that appeal to different interests and aptitudes.

The menu activities offer opportunities for children to extend their experiences with the whole class lessons. *Roll Two Dice* and *Testing Pig Strategies* extend the whole class lesson *The Game of Pig*. *Tiles in Three Bags* and *Match or No Match* extend the *Tiles in the Bag* lesson. *Spinner Puzzles* and *Spinner Sums* extend the two *1-2-3 Spinner Experiment* lessons.

The menu activity *High or Low* is an outgrowth of the menu activity *Roll Two Dice* and gives children additional ways to think about the probability of sums from rolling a pair of dice. In *Shake and Spill*, students use Two-Color Counters to conduct an experiment and later compare the results from small samples with those from larger samples.

The menu has several benefits in the classroom. It solves the classroom problem of what students can do when they finish activities more quickly than others. It responds to students' individual needs by allowing them to work at their own pace. The menu also helps children learn to make choices and manage their time. In addition, when children are working independently, the teacher can work with individuals, pairs, or small groups and initiate discussions that give valuable insights into students' thinking, reasoning, and understanding.

An assortment of materials is used for some of the menu activities. In the *Spinner Sums* menu activity, students use the spinners they made in the two *1-2-3 Spinner Experiment* lessons. Color Tiles are needed for making predictions in *Tiles in Three Bags* and *Match or No Match*. Children use dice or number cubes in *Roll Two Dice, Testing Pig Strategies,* and *High or Low*. They use Two-Color Counters in *Shake and Spill*.

### The Importance of Class Discussions

While the menu activities provide experiences with probability ideas, class discussions are essential for cementing and furthering student learning. Class discussions help students express their ideas, learn about others' ideas, and develop and strengthen their understanding. These discussions also provide teachers with opportunities to receive feedback about activities and assess what students have learned.

A class discussion is most beneficial after students have had time to interact with a menu activity and engage with the probability ideas. The "From the Classroom" section for each menu activity contains valuable suggestions for leading class discussions. The situations described in these sections will not, of course, be the same in other classrooms, but they are representative of what typically occurs, and the teacher's responses are useful models for working with students during menu time.

### Classroom Suggestions

The "Notes about Classroom Organization" section on pages 5–8 includes information about organizing the classroom for menus. Following are additional suggestions.

Because the menu activities relate to previous instruction in whole class lessons, students are somewhat prepared for them. However, menu activities need to be introduced carefully so that children understand what you are asking them to do. When children are clear about what is expected of them, they're more able to function as independent learners. Specific teaching directions are provided in the "Getting Started" section of each menu activity.

Also, it's best to introduce just one or two activities at a time during the unit. "A Suggested Daily Schedule" on pages 8–12 offers one plan for introducing menu activities and structuring menu time for the unit.

Giving clear directions is not sufficient for helping children learn to work independently. Additional time and attention are required. Children might need to be reminded from time to time that information about a menu activity is available to them on the written menu tasks. Also, you might need to review directions several times on several different days to be sure that the children understand and remember what to do. For example, blackline masters for menu activities that require students to work in pairs are marked with a *P* in the upper right-hand corner; those that can be done individually are marked with an *I*.

### Providing Ongoing Support

From time to time, before the children begin work on menu activities, you might want to have a discussion about working with partners. Have the children talk about how they are helpful to each other. Ask them to bring up problems they've encountered and either describe how they resolved them or ask the class for suggestions. You may want to report what you've observed about children working independently and cooperatively. These discussions are invaluable for helping the children become productive learners.

Although students are encouraged to make choices and pursue activities of interest to them during menu time, they also should be required to try all of the menu activities. Be aware, however, that children will respond differently to activities. Not all children get the same value out of the same experiences; children will engage fully with some activities and superficially with others. This is to be expected and respected. Also, each activity can be revisited several times, and the menu gives children the opportunity to return to those activities that especially interest them.

## MENU ACTIVITY

### Overview

### Roll Two Dice

*Roll Two Dice* builds on students' experiences with playing Pig. The activity gives children the opportunity to think about the probability of the sums generated when rolling two dice and also provides practice with basic addition facts. After listing the possible ways to roll each sum (2 to 12), the children work individually to roll the dice and record the combinations on a chart, continuing until one sum reaches the "finish line." Then they post their winning sums on a class chart.

---

235

# Roll Two Dice

**You need:** Two dice
Roll Two Dice recording sheet

1. Roll two dice and record the addition sentence under the correct sum. (See the sample below.)

2. Continue rolling until one number gets to the Finish Line.

3. Mark a tally on the class chart to show your winning number.

| 2 | 3 | 4 | 5 | 6 | 7 | 8 | 9 | 10 | 11 | 12 |
|---|---|---|---|---|---|---|---|----|----|----|
|   |   | 1+3 | 3+2 | 3+3 | 1+6 | 5+3 |   |   |   |   |
|   |   |   |   | 4+2 | 5+2 | 2+6 |   |   |   |   |
|   |   |   |   |   | 5+2 |   |   |   |   |   |
|   |   |   |   |   |   |   |   |   |   |   |
|   |   |   |   |   |   |   |   |   |   |   |
|   |   |   |   |   |   |   |   |   |   |   |
|   |   |   |   |   |   |   |   |   |   |   |
|   |   |   |   |   |   |   |   |   |   |   |
|   |   |   |   |   |   |   |   |   |   |   |

🏁 Finish Line

**Before the lesson**

Gather these materials:
■ Dice, two per student
■ Roll Two Dice recording sheet (See Blackline Masters section, page 236.)
■ One sheet of chart paper, entitled horizontally "Sums from Two Dice"
■ One sheet of chart paper, entitled vertically "Roll Two Dice"
■ Blackline master of menu activity, page 235

**Getting started**

■ Ask students the smallest and largest sums that can come up when two dice are rolled. Then ask what other sums can come up. Post the sheet of chart paper entitled "Sums from Two Dice" and list the numerals from 2 to 12 across the top:

Sums from Two Dice

2   3   4   5   6   7   8   9   10   11   12

■ Ask the students what numbers they would have to roll to get the sums listed on the board. As they make suggestions, record each combination below its sum. You should eventually have a chart like the one below. (Note: The order of the combinations for each number most likely will differ from this chart.)

Sums from Two Dice

| 2 | 3 | 4 | 5 | 6 | 7 | 8 | 9 | 10 | 11 | 12 |
|---|---|---|---|---|---|---|---|----|----|----|
| 1+1 | 1+2 | 2+2 | 3+2 | 3+3 | 4+3 | 4+4 | 5+4 | 5+5 | 6+5 | 6+6 |
| | 2+1 | 3+1 | 2+3 | 4+2 | 3+4 | 5+3 | 4+5 | 6+4 | 5+6 | |
| | | 1+3 | 4+1 | 2+4 | 6+1 | 3+5 | 6+3 | 4+6 | | |
| | | | 1+4 | 5+1 | 1+6 | 6+2 | 3+6 | | | |
| | | | | 1+5 | 5+2 | 2+6 | | | | |
| | | | | | 2+5 | | | | | |

Total Ways: 1   2   3   4   5   6   5   4   3   2   1

■ Talk with students about why reversed combinations (e.g., 3 + 4 and 4 + 3) count as two different ways to get a sum. Use different colored dice to show, for example, that 2 can come up on one color die and 3 on the other and vice versa. If a student raises the question, explain that doubles cannot be reversed because the same number comes up on each color die; therefore, each double is written only once under its sum.

■ Write the following statements on the board and ask students to explain why each one makes sense:

With two dice, 11 sums are possible.
There are 6 possible ways to get the sum of 7.
There are 3 possible ways to get the sum of 3 or 10.
There are 36 possible ways to get all of the sums.

■ Post the other sheet of chart paper entitled "Roll Two Dice," and list the numerals 2 to 12.

### Roll Two Dice

2
3
4
5
6
7
8
9
10
11
12

■ Show students the enlarged copy of the menu activity. (See page 235.) Hold up the *Roll Two Dice* recording sheet and explain to the students that they will work individually to roll dice and record the two numbers that come up under the sum on the recording sheet. The students keep rolling the dice until one sum reaches the "finish line." Then they put a tally mark next to that number on the *Roll Two Dice* class chart.

■ Continue the introductory discussion by asking students to share their ideas about what sums they think will come up most often and what they think the chart will look like after they have entered their data.

■ After students have done *Roll Two Dice* for several days, initiate a class discussion about the data on the class chart. Ask: "What do you notice?" After students have shared their ideas, ask: "If we continue to collect data, what do you think the results will be?" Encourage children to repeat the activity and add additional data to the chart.

## FROM THE CLASSROOM

"I'm going to teach you an activity called *Roll Two Dice,*" I said to the class. This was the first menu task I was introducing. I knew the activity would be easy for the children to learn because they were comfortable using dice. Also, some of the children had been in my class as second graders last year, and we had done the activity then during our probability unit.

Thinking about the probabilities of the sums when rolling two dice presents a challenge for young children. The idea is complex, and children require a good deal of experience and many opportunities to talk about their thinking in order to develop understanding. Last year, in second grade, most of these children had focused on data they had collected as individuals or as a class. This time I was interested in seeing if I could help the students think more about the reasons why some sums are more likely than others.

Before explaining the activity, I posted a sheet of chart paper entitled "Sums from Two Dice" and initiated a discussion about the possible sums.

"If I roll these two dice and add the numbers that come up," I said, "what's the smallest sum that's possible?"

"Two," several children said. This seemed obvious to many of the students. A few said 1 but quickly corrected themselves when they realized I was talking about rolling two dice.

"What's the largest sum possible?" I asked.

"Twelve," many answered in unison.

I wrote the numbers from 2 to 12 across the chart paper and asked, "Do you think it's possible to get all of the sums between 2 and 12 from rolling and adding two dice?" Most of the children nodded.

"What would you have to roll to get 2?" I asked. More than half the students raised their hands. I called on Lisa.

"Two 1s," she said.

I wrote *1 + 1* under the number *2*.

"How do you get 12?" I asked. I called on Alan.

"You get a 6 on both of them," he said. I wrote *6 + 6* under the *12*.

"Let's list all the ways we could get the other sums," I said. As the children reported addition facts, I listed what they said under the correct sum. The children seemed to enjoy reporting facts for each number.

From time to time, someone offered an addition combination that was not possible for the two dice. For example, after children had offered a few ways to get 8, Elliot suggested 7 plus 1.

"You can't get 7 on a die," Lee Ann pointed out.

"Oh, yeah," Elliot said. I could tell he felt embarrassed, so to give him a chance to be successful, I called on him as soon as he raised his hand again.

Students volunteered combinations with the numbers reversed as different possibilities—2 + 3 and 3 + 2, for example. I accepted their suggestions and recorded them, but I didn't think they were thinking about why reversed addends counted as different combinations when rolling two dice. I thought they were just recalling facts. I decided to explain to the class why I thought the reversed addends counted as different ways. I held up one blue die and one white one and pointed out that getting a 2 on the blue die and a 3 on the white die was different from getting a 3 on the blue die and a 2 on the white one.

Even though I showed the children what I meant with the dice, I knew that not all of them followed my reasoning. I learned long ago that I can't count on teaching-by-telling to help all children learn. I presented the information with a light touch, not as something for all the students to learn but as something of interest I thought they might consider.

**NOTE** It often takes time for students to make sense of a new idea and teaching-by-telling doesn't guarantee learning. While explanations may be helpful, children have to process the information, connect it to what they already know, and construct understanding for themselves.

After I had listed all of the combinations, we counted to see how many possibilities there were for each sum. I listed these numbers under each column. Eventually, I had constructed the following chart:

### Sums from Two Dice

| 2 | 3 | 4 | 5 | 6 | 7 | 8 | 9 | 10 | 11 | 12 |
|---|---|---|---|---|---|---|---|----|----|----|
| 1+1 | 1+2 | 2+2 | 3+2 | 3+3 | 4+3 | 4+4 | 5+4 | 5+5 | 6+5 | 6+6 |
| | 2+1 | 3+1 | 2+3 | 4+2 | 3+4 | 5+3 | 4+5 | 6+4 | 5+6 | |
| | | 1+3 | 4+1 | 2+4 | 6+1 | 3+5 | 6+3 | 4+6 | | |
| | | | 1+4 | 5+1 | 1+6 | 6+2 | 3+6 | | | |
| | | | | 1+5 | 5+2 | 2+6 | | | | |
| | | | | | 2+5 | | | | | |

| Total Ways | | | | | | | | | | |
|---|---|---|---|---|---|---|---|---|---|---|
| 1 | 2 | 3 | 4 | 5 | 6 | 5 | 4 | 3 | 2 | 1 |

The children noticed patterns. "Look," Seth said, "there's one less than each number." He was looking at the number of possibilities for each sum. "Oops," he corrected himself, "it only works up to 7."

"It's like a triangle pattern," Lori said.

"Oooh, I thought of another one for 8," Kristin called out. "You have to write 4 plus 4 again."

"Explain why you think that," I said.

Kristin answered, "Because you get 4 on the blue one and 4 on the white one. Then you switch them." Kristin was responding to the explanation I had given about why 2 + 3 and 3 + 2 counted as different combinations. Her idea is one I frequently hear from children and adults when they're first thinking about the probability of the sums from rolling two dice.

"What do you mean by switching them?" I asked.

"You just switch them around, so you have the white one first and the blue one second," she answered. "Just slide them."

"Oh, I see what you mean," I responded, and I demonstrated with the dice. Kristin nodded.

"But even though I slide them, the same number is still on both dice," I then said. "Each die shows the same 4, no matter where it is. So it's still the same possibility. For the other combinations, like 5 and 3, there can be a 5 on the blue die and a 3 on the white die. Sliding them in different places on the desk doesn't change the possibility. But I can change the dice to a different possibility by showing a 5 on the white die and a 3 on the blue one. So there are two different ways to roll the dice to get a sum of 8 with 5 and 3. With 4 and 4, they may land in different places on the desk, but the combination is always the same."

This long-winded explanation seemed to challenge Kristin's thinking—and her attention span. She nodded, but I wasn't sure she was convinced. Also, I suspected others in the class were also unsure about this situation. But I knew we'd have more opportunities to talk about it.

I continued with the discussion. I said to the children, "I'm going to write a sentence on the board, and I want you to explain why it makes sense." I wrote:

> With two dice, 11 sums are possible.

I waited a few moments to give children time to think, and then I called on Erin.

"There are 11 numbers if you count from 2 to 12," she said.

"I have a different way," Charlie said. "If you went from 1 to 12 that would be 12, but you left off 1 so it's only 11."

I had the children count aloud the numbers from 2 to 12 on the board to prove that there were 11 possible sums.

"I'm going to write another sentence on the board," I then said. "See if you can explain why it makes sense." I wrote:

> There are six possible ways to get the sum of 7.

Again I waited. I called on Lisa. "We have six ways under the 7," she said, and read them off.

"I'll write another sentence," I said, and wrote:

> There are three possible ways to get the sum of 3 or 10.

I called on Abby. "Can I come up and show?" she asked.

"Yes," I said, and Abby came up and pointed out the three possibilities for each of the two sums.

"One more," I said. "This one is tricky." I wrote:

> There are 36 possible ways to get all of the sums.

As I waited to give the children time to think, I noticed several of them counting all the combinations listed. "Yes!" Doug said to himself when he finished counting, raising his fist in a salute of triumph. Several others got to 36 at about the same time. I counted the possibilities aloud with the class. I was interested to see if the children would use the information on the chart when I introduced the activity.

"Why do you think I listed the numbers from 2 to 12?" I asked. I waited until more than half the students had raised their hands, then called on Amanda.

"Because that's what you can get on the dice," she answered, in a tone that indicated the question was trivial for her.

"Why didn't I start my chart with 1?" I pursued. I noticed an expression of doubt flicker across Amanda's face. The class was quiet for a moment. Then hands shot up. I called on Erin.

"You can't get 1 with two dice, only with one," she said.

**NOTE** When learning something new, students' understanding is often fragile and easily challenged. It's important that children have opportunities to think about ideas in different ways to help them develop understanding.

"Yeah," Tom added. "When you get 1s, you have to add them, and that gives you 2."

Other children nodded. Amanda looked relieved.

I then began to explain the activity. I showed the children the enlarged version of the activity and a *Roll Two Dice* recording sheet.

Roll Two Dice

| 2 | 3 | 4 | 5 | 6 | 7 | 8 | 9 | 10 | 11 | 12 |
|---|---|---|---|---|---|---|---|----|----|----|
|   |   |   |   |   |   |   |   |    |    |    |
|   |   |   |   |   |   |   |   |    |    |    |
|   |   |   |   |   |   |   |   |    |    |    |
|   |   |   |   |   |   |   |   |    |    |    |
|   |   |   |   |   |   |   |   |    |    |    |
|   |   |   |   |   |   |   |   |    |    |    |
|   |   |   |   |   |   |   |   |    |    |    |
|   |   |   |   |   |   |   |   |    |    |    |
|   |   |   |   |   |   |   |   |    |    |    |
|   |   |   |   |   |   |   |   |    |    |    |

Finish Line →

"This is an individual activity," I began. "You roll two dice and record the two numbers that come up under the correct sum. Keep rolling until one number gets to the finish line. Then you make a tally mark on the class chart to show your winning number." I posted another sheet of chart paper entitled "Roll Two Dice" and listed the 11 possible sums.

## Roll Two Dice

2
3
4
5
6
7
8
9
10
11
12

"Can we work together?" Lisa asked.

"You may work side by side," I answered, "but you each need to roll dice and record your own data." There were no other questions.

"What do you think our class chart will show after you enter your data?" I then asked. The class was silent. Then a few children raised their hands. I called on Charlie.

"I think it will have most on 7 because of the chart," he said, referring to the chart of combinations I had written on the board.

Elliot had a different idea. "They'll be spread out," he said. "Any number can win."

"I don't think so," Seth called out. "It would be hard for 2 to win."

"Hold your idea," I said to Seth. "First I want Elliot to explain his."

"Well, it's just chance," Elliot said, "so anything can happen."

Seth countered, "But you can hardly get 2. They're not equal chance."

"But you could," Elliot insisted.

I called on Emelia next. She said, "I think 7 will get a lot, but 6 and 8 will get some, too. They're not too far behind on the chart."

"What do you mean?" I probed.

"See, there are six ways to make 7, and five ways to make 6 and 8. That's pretty close," she said.

"I think that the big numbers will get more," Lisa said.

"Why do you think that?" I asked.

"I don't know," Lisa shrugged. "It just seems like you should get big numbers more."

This conversation revealed the different ways children think and the different understandings they have. I was curious to see what effect their experience with the activity would have on their perceptions. I ended the discussion and told the children they could either try *Roll Two Dice* or play Pig. About two-thirds of the children chose to do *Roll Two Dice*.

Lori was surprised by her results because she thought all the sums should come up at least once.

| 2 | 3 | 4 | 5 | 6 | 7 | 8 | 9 | 10 | 11 | 12 |
|---|---|---|---|---|---|---|---|----|----|----|
|   |   | 1+3 | 3+2 | 3+6 | 1+6 | 5+3 | 5+4 | 6+4 |   | 6+6 |
|   |   | 2+2 |   | 3+3 | 5+2 | 3+5 | 5+4 | 6+4 |   |   |
|   |   |   |   | 4+2 | 5+2 | 2+6 | 4+5 | 5+5 |   |   |
|   |   |   |   | 3+3 | 4+3 | 4+4 |   |   |   |   |
|   |   |   |   |   | 4+3 | 5+3 |   |   |   |   |
|   |   |   |   |   |   | 4+4 |   |   |   |   |
|   |   |   |   |   |   | 6+2 |   |   |   |   |
|   |   |   |   |   |   | 5+3 |   |   |   |   |
|   |   |   |   |   |   | 6+2 |   |   |   |   |
|   |   |   |   |   |   | 6+2 |   |   |   |   |
|   |   |   |   |   |   | 5+3 |   |   |   |   |
|   |   |   |   |   |   | 5+3 |   |   |   |   |

Finish line ↗

### Observing the Children

The children enjoyed this activity. Over the next several days, many of them completed several sheets and entered their data on the class chart.

I watched to see how the children figured the sums when they rolled the dice. I noticed a variety of approaches. Some children seemed to know the sums and after rolling the dice quickly recorded the combination in the correct column. Other children seemed to know some facts automatically, such as doubles and when to add 1, and counted to verify others, such as 5 + 3 and 2 + 6. The children who counted also had different methods. I noticed that Carrie and Maura used their fingers to find totals. Joseph used his pencil to touch the dots. Except for Mercedes, the children who counted didn't count all of the dots but counted on, typically starting with the larger number and counting on the smaller amount. We had spent time earlier in the year talking about the addition facts and about different ways to figure sums other than counting. However, even with repeated experiences adding in various situations, some children resorted to counting with some or all of the facts.

Before collecting data, Amanda wrote a star in hopes that 9 would win. But 7 got to the finish line first.

| 2 | 3 | 4 | 5 | 6 | 7 | 8 | 9 | 10 | 11 | 12 |
|---|---|---|---|---|---|---|---|----|----|----|
| 1+1 | 1+2 | 3+1 | 3+2 | 5+1 | 4+3 | 5+3 | 6+3 | 4+6 | 6+5 | 6+6 |
|  | 1+2 | 3+1 | 3+2 | 3+3 | 5+2 | 6+2 | 5+4 | 4+6 | 6+5 | 6+6 |
|  | 1+2 | 2+2 | 3+2 | 5+1 | 1+6 | 6+2 | 6+3 | 6+4 |  |  |
|  | 2+1 | 2+2 | 1+4 | 4+2 | 5+2 | 5+3 | 6+3 | 4+6 |  |  |
|  | 1+2 | 1+3 | 4+1 | 1+5 | 4+3 |  | 6+3 | 6+4 |  |  |
|  | 2+1 | 2+2 | 2+3 | 4+2 | 6+1 |  | 5+4 | 9+6 |  |  |
|  |  | 2+2 | 3+2 | 4+2 | 6+1 |  | 5+4 | 6+4 |  |  |
|  |  |  |  | 5+1 | 4+3 |  | 4+5 | 6+4 |  |  |
|  |  |  |  |  | 1+6 |  | 6+3 |  |  |  |
|  |  |  |  |  | 6+1 |  |  |  |  |  |
|  |  |  |  |  | 6+1 |  |  |  |  |  |
|  |  |  |  |  | 4+3 |  |  |  |  |  |

Finish line ⟶

As I circulated, I initiated conversations with children who were counting. For example, I sat down with Maura. "What do you think of this activity?" I asked.

"It's fun," Maura answered. "This is my second sheet. I had 6 win on the first one." She showed me her paper. I scanned it and noticed that she had written all the combinations in the correct columns.

"Everything is right on your paper," I confirmed. Maura smiled.

"When you roll the dice, how do you figure out where to record?" I asked.

"What do you mean?" she asked.

"When you rolled 2 and 1," I said, pointing to where she had written *2 + 1* on her paper, "how did you know to write it in the 3 column?"

"I just knew," she said. "It's easy."

"What about if you roll a 5 and a 3?" I asked.

Maura turned her gaze up to the ceiling and nodded her head gently three times. "It's 8," she said.

"How did you figure?" I asked.

"I went 5, then 6, 7, 8," she answered.

"What about 3 and 3?" I asked.

"That's an easy one," she said. "It's 6."

From similar conversations with other children, I've learned that knowing some facts and not others is typical for children this age. Also, some students have a keener number sense than others do. Alan, for example, said, "I know 5 and 4 because 5 and 5 is 10, so 5 and 4 is 9. It's just 1 less."

Lee Ann, who knows all the sums without having to figure, said, "I just know them. But it's harder with bigger numbers, like 27 and 35 and stuff."

The question I raise for myself is how and when to push children to memorize the facts. It seems to me that many of the efforts teachers traditionally have made to help children learn their facts—flash cards, worksheet drill, and oral drill, for example—work for some children and not for others. Learning the addition facts seems to result from a combination of timing, interest, and experience, and the combination differs from child to child. I'm convinced that the more experiences students have, the more familiar they become with the number facts. An activity such as *Roll Two Dice* can help provide such experience.

## A Class Discussion

About a week later, I began class one day by discussing the results on the *Roll Two Dice* class chart. All of the children had completed the activity at least twice. I asked the children to look at the data.

### Roll Two Dice

2 |
3 |
4 | |
5 𝍷𝍷𝍷 | |
6 𝍷𝍷𝍷 | | |
7 𝍷𝍷𝍷𝍷 𝍷𝍷𝍷𝍷 𝍷𝍷𝍷 𝍷𝍷𝍷𝍷
8 𝍷𝍷𝍷𝍷 𝍷𝍷𝍷 𝍷𝍷𝍷 𝍷𝍷𝍷𝍷
9 | |
10 | |
11
12 )

"What do you notice?" I asked. I waited until more than half of the students had raised their hands. Then I called on Charlie.

"Seven has the most marks," Charlie said.

"That's because it has the most ways to get it," Lee Ann added.

"What are the ways?" I asked.

"There's 4 and 3, and 3 and 4," she began. "Then 6 and 1, and 1 and 6." Lee Ann faltered, losing her train of thought.

"I know," Lisa said, "you can do 5 and 2, or 2 and 5."

"That makes six ways," Charlie said.

"And 8 came in second," Doug said. Others nodded.

"All your ideas are correct," I responded, "but please raise your hand when you have an idea to share." The children were eager to respond, and although I enjoy spontaneity, I wanted to bring some order into the discussion. I called on Lori.

"There's only one mark for 12 and 2," she said. "Those are the hard ones."

"Why do you say they're the hard ones?" I asked.

"You have to get doubles to get them, and doubles are hard," Lori answered.

About 10 children had raised their hands. "Who has something else to say about Lori's comment?" I said in order to help me decide whom to call on next. I called on Elliot.

"But you get 8 with doubles, and it has a lot of tallies," he said.

"Any ideas about this?" I asked.

"That's because 8 has other ways to get it, too," Andrew said, "not just doubles."

"What other ways?" I asked.

Andrew answered, "5 and 3, 3 and 5, 6 and 2, 2 and 6."

"Some people say that when you roll two 4s, you get 8 the hard way," I said. "Why do you think people say that?"

I called on Emelia to answer. "Because there's only one way to get 4 and 4," she said, "and two ways to get the others."

"That doesn't make sense," Doug said. "Oh, sorry," he added, realizing that he had blurted out. He raised his hand.

"Let's hear your idea, Doug," I said.

"There's the same chance of rolling a 4 on one dice as any other number," he said. "So I don't think it's harder to get 4 and 4."

Emelia, Charlie, Andrew, and Elliot raised their hands to respond. I called on Emelia since she had begun the explanation.

"Doug's right," she said, "but there are two different ways to get a 3 and a 5, and only one way to get a 4 and a 4."

Doug remained confused, but I could tell he was thinking about what Emelia had said.

"Does anyone have another way to explain this?" I asked. I called on Charlie.

"It's like when you have blue and white dice," he said. "Then you get a 5 on the blue one or the white one. That's how you get two different ways." Doug still wasn't convinced.

I was impressed by the sophisticated reasoning of a few of the students. I knew that not all of the children understood the probability of the sums, but I felt that hearing different ideas was valuable for them. However, I wanted to ask other questions and see if more of the students would participate in the discussion.

"Suppose we continue collecting data on our chart," I said. "What do you think will happen?" I waited to give the children time to consider my question. I looked around to see which volunteers hadn't yet had a turn. I called on Amanda.

"It's just chance," she said. "You could get anything. You don't know."

I called on Tomo next. "You probably would get something on the 11," he said. Tomo had noticed that on our chart the 11 had no tally marks next to it.

"I still think we wouldn't get very many on 2 or 3," Kristin added. "Those are hard to get."

Eric spoke next. "I think that you might get some more on the 6," he said. "I don't think 8 should have more than 6."

"Can I say something about Eric's idea?" Andrew asked. I nodded.

"I think that you will still get the big numbers more than you get the small numbers, like on our chart," he said. There were murmurs of agreement and a few of disagreement. Hands shot up. I called on Abby.

"There's no reason for that," she said. "You don't get 12 more than 2. They each have only one way."

I looked at Andrew. Abby's tone had been confident, almost insistent, but Andrew held on to his opinion. "But I think it's different for 8, and I bet you'd get 12 more if we did more," he said.

"So you think that 12 would come up more often than 2 if you rolled the dice many times?" I asked.

"It did on my papers," Andrew said. "It didn't win, but it came up more."

Conversations broke out among the children at several tables. Clearly, there was some disagreement about this issue. I didn't respond to Andrew's idea at this time because it was time for recess. I ended the discussion and dismissed the class.

Erin's chart showed a close finish between 5 and 7.

| 2 | 3 | 4 | 5 | 6 | 7 | 8 | 9 | 10 | 11 | 12 |
|---|---|---|---|---|---|---|---|----|----|----|
| 1+1 | 1+2 | 2+2 | 4+1 | 3+3 | 5+2 | 4+4 | 6+3 | 6+4 | 6+5 | 6+6 |
| | 1+2 | 2+2 | 4+1 | 4+2 | 3+4 | 6+2 | 4+5 | 6+4 | 5+6 | 6+6 |
| | 2+1 | 3+1 | 2+3 | 5+1 | 5+2 | 5+3 | 6+3 | 5+5 | 6+5 | |
| | | 3+1 | 3+2 | 6+1 | 6+1 | 4+4 | 6+3 | 6+5 | 6+5 | |
| | | 2+2 | 4+1 | | 6+1 | 5+3 | 3+6 | 5+6 | | |
| | | 2+2 | 3+2 | | 4+3 | 5+2 | 6+3 | 5+5 | | |
| | | 3+1 | 3+2 | | 5+3 | | 6+3 | | | |
| | | 2+2 | 4+1 | | 4+3 | | | | | |
| | | 2+2 | 4+1 | | 5+2 | | | | | |
| | | | 4+1 | | 6+1 | | | | | |
| | | | 3+1 | | 5+3 | | | | | |
| | | | 1+3 | | | | | | | |

Finish line ⟶

I thought about what I might do to give the children more experience to test the notion that larger sums would come up more often. I thought about making a huge chart on which the children would post all the combinations they rolled, not just the sum that reached the finish line first. However, a few days later, Andrew came to me and suggested a more interesting and manageable way to investigate the issue based on a different activity that he had invented with two dice.

In the meantime, I encouraged children to collect additional data from rolling two dice. Many found the activity to be satisfying and were eager to complete more papers. When we discussed the new data they had collected, Andrew pointed out that the high numbers still had come up more times.

"But they're practically the same," Charlie said, a bit exasperated.

I decided to add Andrew's game to the menu. (See the *High or Low* menu activity, page 152.)

## MENU ACTIVITY

### Tiles in Three Bags

**Overview**

*Tiles in Three Bags* extends the whole class lesson *Tiles in the Bag*. (See page 54.) This activity gives students additional experience making predictions based on a sampling of information. The children are told the assortments of Color Tiles in three bags but not which bag contains which assortment. Working in pairs, they choose a bag, take samples, record data, and then analyze their data to predict how many tiles of each color are in the bag.

---

237

### Tiles in Three Bags

You need: One paper bag with tiles—A, B, or C

1. Record which bag you took—A, B, or C.

2. Without looking inside, take out one tile. Record its color. Put it back in the bag, and shake the bag to mix the tiles. Take 12 samples this way.

3. Repeat step 2 two more times.

4. Still without looking inside the bag, look at your data and predict whether the tiles in the bag are:

      6 red, 3 blue, 3 yellow   OR
      2 red, 8 blue, 2 yellow   OR
      1 red, 2 blue, 9 yellow

Write about why you made your prediction.

5. Check your prediction by looking inside the bag. Write about what you learned from looking in the bag.

6. Repeat steps 1 to 5 with the other bags.

From *Math By All Means: Probability, Grades 3–4* ©1995 Math Solutions Publications

---

## Before the lesson

Gather these materials:
■ Color Tiles
■ Nine lunch bags, three labeled *A*, three labeled *B*, and three labeled *C*
■ Blackline master of menu activity, page 237, enlarged and posted

## Getting started

■ Fill the bags with Color Tiles so that they have the following assortments of tiles:
Bag A: 1 red, 2 blue, 9 yellow
Bag B: 6 red, 3 blue, 3 yellow
Bag C: 2 red, 8 blue, 2 yellow

■ Show the class the bags labeled A, B, and C and the enlarged menu task. Explain that each bag has one of the assortments of tiles listed on the task, but do not tell the students which bags have which assortments of tiles. Also tell the students that all the A bags have the same assortment, all the B bags have another assortment, and all the C bags have a third assortment.

■ Explain to the students that this menu activity is similar to the *Tiles in the Bag* whole class lesson. Students will work with a partner to choose one bag and draw 12 samples, recording the colors they draw. After drawing three sets of 12 samples, students predict which assortment is in the bag. They write down their prediction, look to see what assortment is actually in the bag, and then write about what they learned.

## FROM THE CLASSROOM

To introduce the activity, I posted an enlarged version of the menu task and showed the children the nine bags I had assembled. I pointed to the information on the enlarged menu task about what was in the bags:

6 red, 3 blue, 3 yellow OR
2 red, 8 blue, 2 yellow OR
1 red, 2 blue, 9 yellow

"Each bag has one of these assortments of tiles," I explained.
"Are they in order?" Charlie wanted to know.
"What do you mean?" I asked him.
"Do they go A, B, and C?" he said.
"No," I answered. "I purposely mixed them up to make a guessing game. In this activity, you predict what's in each bag. You'll do this by taking samples and recording data, the same way we did when we did *Tiles in the Bag.*" The children enjoyed guessing games and seemed interested in hearing more about the activity.
"Oh, good, it's for partners," Lisa said, noticing the P in the corner of the task.
"To do this activity, you pick one bag," I continued. "Don't peek inside. You'll be able to look later, but first follow the directions to see if you can predict what's in the bag you chose."

Seth had a question. "Do both partners take a bag?" he asked.

"No," I answered, "you need just one bag for the two of you. You should agree first on which one you'll try." Seth nodded.

"Once you have your bag," I continued, "take samples the same way we did before. Without looking inside, reach in, take out one tile, record its color, and put it back in the bag. Then shake the bag to mix the tiles." I took one of the bags and demonstrated for the class.

"Take three sets of 12 samples," I continued. "When you've done the three trials, predict what you think is in the bag. Write down your prediction and explain why you made it. Then look in the bag and write about what you learned."

I referred the children again to the enlarged task and reviewed the directions once more. Then I had them begin work on the menu.

### Observing the Children

Over the next several days, I observed the different ways that pairs organized themselves and shared the work. Lisa and Erin, for example, were careful to take turns drawing tiles from the bag and recording the tally marks. Janos, however, was happy to reach into the bag and pick out the tiles and let Eric do all the recording. I didn't interfere with either pair.

However, when I noticed that Abby seemed to be doing all the work for her and Mercedes and that Mercedes seemed listless and uninvolved, I was concerned. Mercedes is a passive child who rarely asserts herself. I approached the girls. Abby looked up, and, from the look on her face, I could tell that she knew what concerned me.

"She didn't want to do the writing," Abby said, defensively. Mercedes didn't respond.

"Is it all right with you to do the recording?" I asked Abby.

"I don't mind," she answered.

"But you're also doing all the drawing of the tiles," I said. "Remember that you both have to contribute to the activity."

"Okay," Abby said and then turned to Mercedes. "Here, you pick the next one." Mercedes reached into the bag. I watched as they took turns drawing tiles. I felt that Mercedes was beginning to get engaged.

"Remember that you're to discuss the data and make the prediction together," I said and left the girls to work.

Tom rushed over, excited. "Look!" he said, waving his paper in front of me. "We got the same as the last one."

"Explain to me what you mean," I said.

"We got 9, 2, 1—just like the last one on the board," Tom said. "That must be it!"

I walked Tom back to his partner, Charlie. "Can we peek now?" Charlie asked.

"How many draws did you take?" I asked.

"Twelve," the boys answered in unison.

"And it has to be 9 yellow, 2 blue, and 1 red," Charlie added.

"It has to be," Tom confirmed. "It's the only one with more yellow."

"Do you think it's possible that even though you got these results there could be more red or blue tiles in the bag?" I asked.

"Not very," Charlie answered.

"It could be," Tom said, "but I don't think so. I *really* don't think so."

"The reason that I asked you to take 12 samples three times is to help you be sure of your prediction," I said. "Do another set of samples and let me know what comes up." I left the boys to do more draws.

Lori and Erin had finished their experiment and were writing their results. Lori was writing, and Erin was helping her decide what to write. When they finished, I asked Lori to read aloud what she had written. She read: *"We took bag letter B. We think six red 3 blue and three yellow because in the first sample there were eight reds three blues and three yellows. In the second sample there were 14 reds 7 blues and 13 yellows. The second one the same thing hapened."*

"Oops," Erin interrupted, "we have to change that sentence."

"Oh, yeah," Lori said, and made the correction. She then read: *"In The third one the same thing hapened. We were Right!"*

The girls seemed pleased with themselves.

Lori and Erin collected their data, then wrote their results on a separate sheet of paper.

| RED | BLUE | | Yellow |
|---|---|---|---|
| ₩ (tally) III — 8 | III — 3 | | III — 3 |
| RED ₩ ₩ IIII — 14 | BLUE ₩ II — 7 | | YELLOW ₩ ₩ III — 13 |
| YELLOW ₩ ₩ III — 23 | RED ₩ ₩ ₩ ₩ — 30 | | BLUE ₩ II — 12 |

Tiles in a Bag

We took bag letter B.
We think six red 3 blue
and three yellow because
in the first sample there
were eight reds three blues
and three Yellows. In the
second sample there were
14 reds 7 blues and 13
Yellows. In The third one the
same thing hapered. We were
Right!

Lisa was working with Ajani, who had just finished writing up their results. Ajani read them to me: *"In bag B we estimat that there are three blues, three yellows and six reds. We grabed the same thing we estimated. We dumped the whole bag out. We counted how many yellows, reds and blues. That how we played* Tiles in a Bag. *The End."*

"Let me see your statistics," I said. On their first set of trials, they had gotten 4 of each color. On the second set, they had drawn 6 red, 3 yellow, and 3 blue. On the third, they had 6 red, 2 yellow, and 4 blue.

"It had to be 6 reds," Ajani said. "That's what we grabbed most."

At that point, Tom and Charlie rushed up. They were very excited. "This was amazing!" Charlie exclaimed.

"Look what happened!" Tom said. After drawing 9 yellow, 2 blue, and 1 red on their first trial, they had drawn 4 yellow, 5 blue, and 3 red. But on the third trial, they had drawn 10 yellow and 1 each of blue and red.

"What was amazing to you?" I asked.

"The second time," Tom said. "It was so weird."

"It didn't match any of the others," Charlie said, referring to the list on the board. "But the third one helped us make up our minds for sure. We predicted 9, 2, and 1."

"Finally!" Tom said, rolling his eyes. "And we were right."

They went back to repeat the activity for another bag.


**The Children's Writing**

I didn't hold a class discussion about this activity. I had a chance to talk with most of the children as they worked on the activity, and it didn't seem necessary to discuss their results because they had verified them by looking in the bags. Also, from reading the students' work, I could see that all of them were able to complete the activity successfully.

For example, when Amanda and Kristin did the activity for all three bags, they based their predictions on the data they collected. For bag A, they wrote: *We pridict that there is: 1R, 2B, 9Y because there is so many yellows!* For bag B, they wrote: *We pridict that there are more red, because there were alot of reds!* For bag C, they merely wrote their prediction: *2R, 8B, 2Y.* (Their work appears on the following page.)

"You didn't explain your reasoning for bag C," I commented.

"You don't need to," Amanda said with confidence. "It's the only one left."

Tom and Charlie had also investigated all three bags. When I looked at their work, however, I realized that they hadn't explained how their predictions related to their data. But I had talked with them, so I knew they had considered the data. Therefore, I didn't have them revise their work. (Their work appears on the following page.)

Not all children tried all three bags. Seth and Lee Ann, for example, did the activity just with bag B. They wrote: *Our estimate is that there is six reds four blues and two yellows because red always got five and blue and yellow got lower.*

There are 12 in each bag.

A.

| Red | Blue | Yellow | |
|---|---|---|---|
| 2 | 2 | 7 | =12 |
| 2 | 1 | 9 | =12 |
| 1 | 3 | 9 | =12 |

We pridict that there is: 1R, 2B, 9Y because there is so many yellows!

Answer: 1R, 2B, 9Y.

B.

| 8 | 4 | 0 | =12 |
|---|---|---|---|
| 10 | 1 | 1 | =12 |
| 11 | | | =12 |

We pridict that there are more red, because there were alot of reds!

Answer: 6R, 3B, 3Y.

C. Answer: 2R, 8B, 2Y.

---

| Samples | blue | red | Yellow |
|---|---|---|---|
| | 2 | 1 | 9 |
| | 5 | 3 | 4 |
| | 1 | 1 | 10 |

A. We think there are 9 yellows, two blues and 1 red in bag A.

| blue 3 | red 6 | yellow 3 |
|---|---|---|
| 2 | 5 | 5 |
| Blue | red | yellow |
| 3 | 6 | 3 |
| Blue | red | yellow |
| 3 | 6 | 3 |

B. We think there are 3 Blues, 6 reds and 3 yellows.

C. We know there are 2 red, 8 blues and 2 yellows.

---

(left) Amanda and Kristin collected data on two of the bags, then assigned tiles to the third bag based on process of elimination.

(right) Tom and Charlie's work showed that they had kept careful statistics but didn't explain the reasoning for their predictions.

# MENU ACTIVITY

## Overview

## Shake and Spill

In the activity *Shake and Spill*, children toss six Two-Color Counters and record how many land with the red side up and how many land with the yellow side up. Each child does this six times, then posts the data on a class chart. The activity gives children experience with comparing and contrasting their own small samples with a larger class sample and challenges them to think about what is most likely to occur in this experiment.

---

238

# Shake and Spill   $\boxed{\text{I}}$

You need: Six Two-Color Counters
          Shake and Spill recording sheet

1. Shake and spill six Two-Color Counters. Record what colors come up by coloring one section of the recording sheet.

2. Shake and spill five more times to fill the recording sheet.

3. Cut out the six sections on your recording sheet. Post them on the class graph in the correct rows.

From *Math By All Means: Probability, Grades 3–4*   ©1995 Math Solutions Publications

---

**Before the lesson**

Gather these materials:
■ Two-Color Counters, six per student
■ Shake and Spill recording sheet (See Blackline Masters section, page 239.)
■ Red and yellow crayons or markers
■ Blackline master of menu activity, page 238

**Getting started**

■ Show students Two-Color Counters and explain that they will individually conduct an experiment, then share the results with the class.

■ Model for the students how to conduct the experiment. Spill six counters, then color circles in a section of a *Shake and Spill* recording sheet. For example, if four counters come up red and two come up yellow, color the corresponding number of circles in those two colors on the first section of the recording sheet.

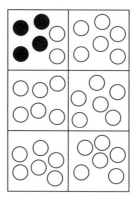

■ Spill the counters a second time and color in another section. Tell the children that each of them will spill the counters and record six times.

■ Have the students discuss the color combinations that could come up. As they suggest a new combination, color in the corresponding number of circles on a recording sheet. (Note: There are seven possibilities. Each record sheet has only six sections, so you will need two recording sheets for this demonstration.)

■ When all seven combinations have been described and recorded, cut apart the sections. Post them vertically on the chalkboard or bulletin board, starting with the section in which all circles are colored red, then the section with five reds and one yellow, four reds and two yellows, and so on. Ask the students if they think they know the pattern you are using to order the sections and can predict what you will post next.

■ To model how students will post their work, cut out the two sections you colored after spilling the counters and post them next to the sections on the board that show those color combinations. Explain that each student will post his or her work the same way after completing six spills.

■ When all students have finished the experiment, discuss the results. Ask students what they notice about the data.

■ Follow this menu activity with the writing assignment described in the assessment *Results from Shake and Spill.* (See page 119.)

## FROM THE CLASSROOM

"In this activity," I told the class, "each of you will do the same experiment and post your results on a class graph. Then we'll talk about the data."

I showed the children the Two-Color Counters and the recording sheets they would use. "You need six counters," I explained. "Shake and spill them and see how many land with the red side up and how many land with the yellow side up."

I spilled six counters and commented, "Try to spill the counters carefully so they land right in front of you on your desk." Four of the counters I spilled landed with the red side up and two with the yellow side up. In one section of a recording sheet, I colored four circles red and two yellow to model for the children how to record.

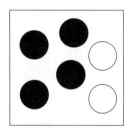

I shook and spilled the counters again. Again, four red and two yellow sides were showing, and I colored a second section on the sheet.

"Do you think it's possible for all six counters to land with the red side up?" I asked. Most of the children murmured yes.

"But it would be almost impossible," Seth said.

"It's not very likely," Erin added.

"How come?" I asked. The children were quiet for a moment. Often they have an intuitive notion about something but don't have a way to explain their thinking. Finally, Tom raised his hand.

"I think they should come up three red and three yellow," he said.

"Why do you think that?" I asked.

"Because they're like coins," he said, "and either side could come up the same amount. I think three and three."

"But Ms. Burns got four reds and two yellows two times," Lee Ann said. "She didn't get three and three." Lee Ann's comment confused Tom, and he seemed to lose confidence in his idea. At this age, empirical evidence is compelling for children, often more powerful than their theoretical notions. I shifted the direction of the discussion.

"What are the different possibilities that could come up when you spill six counters?" I asked. The children were confused by my question, so I elaborated.

"When I spilled the counters," I added, "I got four reds and two yellows twice. That's one possibility." I took an unused recording sheet and colored in a section to represent this possibility.

"Another possibility is six reds," I continued, "even though some of you think it's not very probable." I colored six reds on another section of the paper. "What else could come up?"

Several children understood the question and called out responses. "Six yellow." "Three red and three yellow." "Two and four."

I called on students one by one and colored the possibilities they suggested. There are seven possibilities, so I had to use part of a second recording sheet to record them all. Then I cut the sections apart.

I posted the section in which I had colored all six circles red. I planned to post all the sections in a vertical line down the left side of the bulletin board in order to organize the bulletin board for collecting the data the students were going to generate.

"See if you can figure out the pattern I'm using to post these possibilities," I said, posting the section with five reds and one yellow and then the one with four reds and two yellows. The children caught on quickly and called out what I was to post each time. Finally, I had posted all seven possibilities.

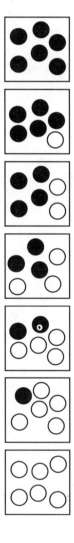

"When you've done the experiment six times," I said, "cut your recording sheet apart and post each section in the correct row." I cut out the two sections from my first two *Shake and Spill* examples and posted them.

"Who can explain why I posted my first samples here?" I asked. I waited to see who understood. About half of the children raised their hands. I called on Lisa.

"You put them next to the one you had colored with four red and two yellow," she explained. I pointed out the colors Lisa was referring to.

"I get it now," Timmy said. He hadn't raised his hand before.

I then asked, "If you each do the experiment six times and post your results, how many papers will be on our graph?" There were 27 children in the class, and they had studied multiplication just before beginning this unit.

"Can I get a calculator?" Doug asked.

"Tell me what you would press," I responded.

"I'd do 6 plus 6 plus 6 27 times," he answered.

"I know another way," Lori chimed in. "I'd press 6 times 27 and then equals."

"Or you could do 27 times 6," Charlie added.

"I think you could add 27 six times," Linsey said.

"I know," Amanda said, "you could press 6 then plus then equals, equals, equals, 27 times." In the multiplication unit, the children had learned how to use the calculator for repeated addition.

"I think the answer is 162," Emelia said.

"How did you figure?" I asked.

"Well," she said, "I added 14 and 14 in my head and that gave me 28. And then I added another 14, and that gave me . . . ," Emelia stopped, having forgotten the sum, and added again in her head. "That gives me 42," she concluded.

"What does that have to do with 27 times 6?" Andrew challenged. I was wondering the same thing but was more patient than Andrew with trying to understand Emelia's thinking.

"Because three 14s is the same as six 7s," she answered. I then realized that Emelia was adding 27 six times by starting with the 1s place.

"Oh, I get it," Tomo blurted out.

"Let Emelia finish," I said.

"Okay," she said, "then I did 20, 40, 60, 80, 100, 120 and 120 and 40 is 160 and 2 more is 162."

I was impressed. Andrew also seemed impressed. But most of the other students didn't seem to understand what Emelia was doing.

"Can I get the calculator now?" Doug asked.

"In just a moment," I answered. "When you start your menu work, you can check the answer to this problem."

I reviewed with the children the choices they now had for the menu. "You can choose from *Roll Two Dice, Tiles in Three Bags,* or *Shake and Spill,*" I said.

"*Shake and Spill* is the second individual activity on the menu," Tomo commented. He often likes to work alone and was pleased that it was okay to do so on this task.

"Can we do more than one sheet of *Shake and Spill?*" Abby asked.

"I'd rather you do just one sheet now," I replied. "Then we'll see if we need more data to think about the results." I set this restriction for several reasons. One was that I wanted to have a reasonable amount of data to count. Another was that I wanted to leave open the opportunity of repeating the experiment and comparing results, and I didn't want the children to become bored with it. Third, the space on the bulletin board was limited.

"Can we play Pig?" Elliot wanted to know.

"Not unless you've completed all three menu activities," I said. The children got to work.

### Observing the Children

Eric was excited about the discovery he had made after coloring in all six sections on his sheet. "They're both the same," he said.

"Explain what you mean," I said.

"Watch," he said. He counted to show me he had colored 18 red and 18 yellow circles on the entire sheet.

"What do you think about that?" I asked.

"I think it came out just right," he said.

On the way to the bulletin board to post her results, Amanda showed me her papers. "I only got two different kinds," she said. "Four red and two yellow and the other way around."

"What do you think of those results?" I asked. Amanda shrugged.

"Look," Corrine said to me as I wandered by. "I got six yellows on the first try. I don't believe it happened." She returned to coloring.

After a while, a crowd of children stood at the bulletin board. I noticed some helping others find the rows to post their results. For some children, this part of the task was difficult.

"They're always colored different," Janos said.

"What do you mean?" I asked.

"See?" he pointed. "Sometimes the two reds together are colored and sometimes they're apart, so it's hard to tell." I watched as Janos continued to consider each sample to decide where it should go. He posted them correctly, but slowly.

At one point, Kristin reached over Mercedes to post one of her papers and the box of push pins spilled to the floor. The children froze, startled. "You pushed," Mercedes accused Kristin.

Kristin looked frightened. "I didn't," she said, a bit weakly.

"It's not a big deal," I said. "Let's pick them up quickly. Be careful not to stick yourselves." Kristin looked relieved. She, Mercedes, and a few other children hunted for all the pins on the floor.

"Uh, oh," Tom said, "we're running out of room on the line with four reds and two yellows. That's funny, there aren't as many three and threes."

"After all the results are posted," I said, "we'll count to see how many there are."

### A Class Discussion

Two days later, all of the children had posted their data on the class graph. I initiated a class discussion.

"Let's look at the results," I said to the children at the beginning of class one day. "What do you notice?" I gave the children a few minutes to look over the data. Finally, I called on Tomo.

"Three reds and three yellows has the most," he said. Many of the children nodded or called out their agreement.

"All reds and all yellows are about the same," Lori added. We counted to verify her observation. Nine papers had all reds colored and eight had all yellows.

"It looks to me like there are more reds altogether," Lee Ann said. "Look how many four red and two yellow there are in that line."

"How would you check that?" I asked.

"You could count all the red circles and all the yellow ones," Lee Ann answered.

Tom had a different view. "I think that about half are yellow," he said, "because the bottom half is mostly yellow and the top half is mostly red."

"I noticed a pattern," Doug said. "The top is six reds, then it goes five reds, then four reds, three reds, two reds, one, and none." Doug was commenting on the order in which I had posted the samples.

"She did that purposely," Lori commented. "Remember?"

"Oh, yeah," Doug responded.

"There are a lot of ties," Alan said.

"What do you mean by 'ties'?" I asked.

"They're the same," Alan replied, "like three and three."

"I see different ties," Kristin said. "The lines up there and the ones down there are the same." She came up and showed that four rows had the same number of papers in them: the top row (all reds), the second row from the top (five reds and one yellow), the bottom row (all yellows), and the second row from the bottom (five yellows and one red).

Amanda raised her hand. "I noticed the three middle ones have the most," she said, "the ones with four red and two yellow and three red and three yellow and four and two. They're kind of equal."

"It looks like a crocodile with his tongue sticking out," Janos observed. Children laughed. Timmy asked him what he meant. Janos came up and pointed out how the long lines looked to him like the tongue.

"I don't see a crocodile," Corrine said.

"It looks like a skyscraper on its side," Eric said.

"I think it's like a rocket lying down," Joseph said.

I know how comments like these can move a class discussion away from the mathematics, and I tried to refocus the children. "Let's talk more about what you notice in the data about reds and yellows," I said. I called on Charlie.

"I think there aren't more reds," Charlie said, commenting on the observation Lee Ann had made earlier. "There are a lot of reds in the top and a lot of yellows in the bottom."

Lisa agreed. "It looks the same to me, too," she said.

"It's hard to be sure from looking if there are more reds or more yellows altogether," I said, "but it's easy to see that there are more in the line of three reds and three yellows than in any other line." The children murmured their agreement.

"Why do you think three reds and three yellows came up so often?" I asked. "Think about that for a minute, or talk with your neighbor. Then I'd like to hear your ideas." I allowed some time for the children to formulate their ideas and then had all who volunteered explain their ideas.

"It's like flipping a coin," Lisa said. "It's like half and half."

"I think the same as Lisa," Tom said. "It's like a coin."

"Red and yellow both have a 50 percent chance," Erin said.

"I think it is just chance," Charlie said. "There's no real way to tell."

"The three and three has the most chance because it's in the middle," Kristin said.

"Why does being in the middle make for the most chance?" I asked. Kristin shrugged.

"I know," Amanda said. "It's like the 7 on the dice."

"How is the three and three like the 7 on the dice?" I probed.

"The 7 is in the middle," Amanda said. "It goes 2, 3, 4, 5, 6, 7, 8, 9, 10, 11, 12, and 7 is in the middle."

"I think it's just chance," Lori said. "I mean, when you flip a coin, it's the same chance that heads come up and tails come up. It's just chance." I wasn't sure what Lori meant, but I also wasn't sure what question to ask her. I chose to keep calling on others who wanted to share.

"I agree with what Lisa and Tom said," Seth said. "It's like flipping a coin."

"I think it's chance," Emelia said, "but I also have a reason. I think three and three should come up more because it's easier to get than six reds or six yellows. You hardly ever get those."

The children's comments revealed their different ideas and ways of thinking. Although class discussions are useful for assessing children's understanding, I find that having students write gives me more specific information and allows me to assess how each student thinks. I asked the students to write about the experiment. (See *Results from Shake and Spill* on the next page.)

# ASSESSMENT Results from Shake and Spill

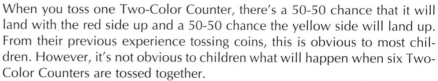

When you toss one Two-Color Counter, there's a 50-50 chance that it will land with the red side up and a 50-50 chance the yellow side will land up. From their previous experience tossing coins, this is obvious to most children. However, it's not obvious to children what will happen when six Two-Color Counters are tossed together.

The class results from the *Shake and Spill* menu activity will typically show that all six counters landing the same way—all red or all yellow—is unusual. It's possible, but unlikely. Class results will also show that most of the tosses produce three of each color, or four of one color and two of the other. Some children have an intuitive sense that these results make sense, while others will be surprised by them.

At this grade level, the goal of the *Shake and Spill* menu activity is not to teach children how to calculate the probabilities of the experiment. However, asking children to think about the results and talk about why they occurred is a beginning step to helping them formulate ideas about probability. Having students write after a discussion helps you assess the class's overall understanding and provides you with specific information about each child's thinking. This assessment is appropriate after you've discussed the results from *Shake and Spill*. (See pages 117–118.)

For the assessment, pose two questions to the children. (It's helpful to write the questions on the board for the children to read.)

1. Why did 3 and 3 come up more often than the other combinations?
2. Why did all red (or all yellow) come up least?

There's no need to discuss the children's papers afterward because you've already had a class discussion. Use the students' writing to help you better understand their thinking.

A mathematical note: *Shake and Spill* is similar to predicting the sex of siblings. It's just about an equally likely chance to conceive a boy or a girl, 50 percent for each. The same chance exists for successive pregnancies; each time, there's an equally likely chance of having either a girl or a boy. Each pregnancy is independent of another. When you toss six counters, it's as unlikely for all of them to come up the same way as it is for a family to have six children all of the same sex. As a matter of fact, the distribution of the tosses of six counters on a class graph should resemble a bell curve.

## FROM THE CLASSROOM

To introduce the assessment, I referred the children to our discussion of the class graph. "When we talked about the results on our *Shake and Spill* graph," I said, "we noticed that all reds or all yellows hardly came up, while three of each color came up more often than any other possibility."

"I know why that happened," Emelia said.

"I think it was just chance," Lori said.

"I'm interested in what you think about the results on our graph," I said, "so I'd like each of you to write about it."

"What do we write?" Seth said, always wanting to be sure what to do.

"I'll write two questions on the board," I said, "and I'd like you to answer both of them." I wrote on the board:

1. Why did 3 and 3 come up more often than the other combinations?
2. Why did all red (and all yellow) come up least?

I called on students to read the questions aloud and then let the children get to work.

The students' work revealed that most of their understanding was fragile and partial. Some of their papers blended some mathematical thinking with notions of how the counters behave. For example, to answer the first question, Abby wrote: *Three red and three yellow come up more often because the counters have red on one side and yellow on the other side and there is 50 percent of a chance yellow will come up and 50 percent of a chance red will come up. Another reason three and three came up the most is that the counters flip around in the air and twist and twirl on the table so they land on the table three red and three yellow.* For the second question, she wrote: *Each two-colored counter uasually lands on difrent colors so all red and all yellow came up fewer times.*

Emelia's answers were concise. She wrote: *I think 3 and 3 came up most because one side is red and the other side is yellow. There is a 50% chance it will be red and a 50% chance it will be yellow. 2. I think all red and all yellow came up least because if you spill the counters they should come up even so it is not likely that it would come up all reds or all yellows.*

Emelia based her responses on her understanding of 50 percent chance.

Substantial Evidence

I think 3 and 3 came up most because one side is red and the other side is yellow. There is a 50% chance it will be red and a 50% chance it will be yellow.

2. I think all red and all yellow came up least because if you spill the counters they should come up even so it is not likely that it would come up all reds or all yellows.

Lori had a unique response to the second question.

Lori wrote a unique answer to the second question: *I think all yellow and all red came up so few because it is hard for them all at the same time to flip to the same side.*

> 1. I think 3 and 3 came up the most because there is more of a chance.
>
> 2. I think all yellow and all red came up so few because it is hard for them all at the same time to flip to the same side.

Some students did not concern themselves with the mathematics involved. For example, Joseph wrote: *1. I think the most was red and Yellows beause my hand got stiky and the counters stuk to my hand but some did not stik so thay came to that number. 2. All the Yellows and all the Reds came up few beause that was hard to throw.*

*(below, left)* Joseph was not able to think about the questions mathematically.

*(below, right)* In order to make sense of the second question, Amanda thought about what happened to the counters.

> 1. I think the most was red and Yellows beause my hand got stiky and the counters stuk to my hand but some did not stik so thay came to that nomber.
>
> 2. All the Yellows and all the Reds came up few beause that was hard to throw.

> There is a fifty-persent chance that it's going to land on red and a fifty-persent chance it's going to land on yellow.
>
> All yellow and all red came up least because when you shake them they bounce up and down and when they hit the the top or the bottom of your hand they flip and they have a ten-persent chance their going to come up all red or all yellow.

## MENU ACTIVITY

### Overview

## Spinner Puzzles

*Spinner Puzzles* extends the two whole class lessons with 1-2-3 spinners. (See pages 24 and 67.) In this activity, children design spinner faces to match statements about what should happen if the spinners are used for experiments similar to those done in the whole class lessons. The activity asks children to consider how different spinner faces can affect outcomes. Students later solve one another's puzzles.

---

240

## Spinner Puzzles  I

You need: One sheet of 9-by-12-inch paper divided into six sections, with a circle traced in each section.

1. In each circle, draw a spinner face with five sections: <u>a</u>, <u>b</u>, <u>c</u>, <u>d</u>, and <u>e</u>. Design one spinner face to fit each of the following statements:

    1. <u>a</u> is certain to win.
    2. <u>a</u> can't possibly win.
    3. <u>a</u> is likely to win.
    4. <u>a</u>, <u>b</u>, <u>c</u>, <u>d</u>, and <u>e</u> are all equally likely to win.
    5. <u>a</u> or <u>b</u> will probably win.
    6. <u>a</u>, <u>b</u>, and <u>c</u> have the same chance to win, and <u>d</u> and <u>e</u> can't possibly win.

2. To make your spinner faces into puzzles for others to solve, draw them in mixed-up order and do not number them.

3. Fill in an answer sheet for your puzzle. Have someone check your answers and write his or her name at the bottom of the sheet.

4. Solve other students' puzzles.

From *Math By All Means: Probability, Grades 3–4*   ©1995 Math Solutions Publications

---

**Before the lesson**

Gather these materials:
- 9-by-12-inch white paper, one sheet per student
- Circular objects, about 3 inches in diameter, for tracing circles
- Statements for Spinner Puzzles, enlarged and posted (See Blackline Masters section, page 241.)
- Spinner Puzzles Answer Sheet, one per student (See Blackline Masters section, page 242.)
- Spinner Puzzles Solutions recording sheet, one per student (See Blackline Masters section, page 243.)
- Blackline master of menu activity, page 240

**Getting started**

- Direct students' attention to the six spinner statements on the enlarged blackline master.

1. a is certain to win.
2. a can't possibly win.
3. a is likely to win.
4. a , b, c, d, and e are all equally likely to win.
5. a or b will probably win.
6. a , b, and c have the same chance to win, and d and e can't possibly win.

- Explain that students are to work individually to draw six spinners, each one matching one of the six statements.

- Demonstrate how to fold and measure paper for drawing spinners. Fold a 9-by-12-inch sheet of white drawing paper in half lengthwise. Open it and show students how to draw a line with a ruler on the fold line. Explain that you will divide the paper into three sections the other way so there will be six sections altogether. Ask students how you can use a ruler to measure three equal sections. Measure and draw lines to create six sections. Draw a circle in each section by tracing around a can or other circular object.

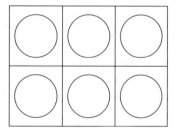

- Model the activity by drawing a spinner face in one section of your paper. Ask students to match your spinner to one of the six statements.

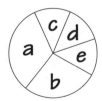

■ Repeat with another spinner face.

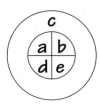

■ If you feel it's needed, draw a third spinner face.

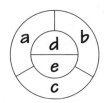

■ Explain that students must create a spinner for each statement, and each spinner must have sections marked <u>a</u>, <u>b</u>, <u>c</u>, <u>d</u>, and <u>e</u>.

■ Hold up a Spinner Puzzles Answer Sheet. Explain that the boxes on this sheet correspond to those on the *Spinner Puzzles* sheet. Demonstrate how to write in the first box the number of the statement that your first spinner matches, in the second box the number of the statement the second spinner matches, and so on. Remind students not to do the statements in order because their spinner faces will become puzzles for others to solve.

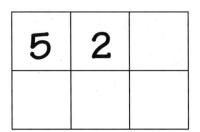

■ Tell the class that before turning in spinner puzzles and an answer sheet, each student must have a partner check his or her work and sign the paper.

■ As you review students' work, separate the puzzles from the answer sheets. Create a booklet with just the answer sheets for later use.

■ Initiate a class discussion. Ask:

What happened when you made your puzzles?
Did you have any problems?
Did you get help from someone else?
Did you learn something new?

■ Show students a Spinner Puzzles Solutions sheet and tell them to solve one another's puzzles. They should write their name at the top of the sheet, then another student's name above one of the solution boxes. Then they should look at the six spinners on the other student's sheet and write in the solution box what statements they think the spinners match. They can check their work by looking in the booklet of answer sheets. If they disagree with answers, they should talk to the student who created the spinners. Each student should guess the answers to eight students' spinner puzzles.

## FROM THE CLASSROOM

I gathered the children on the rug to introduce *Spinner Puzzles*. I posted the enlarged statements and duplicated copies of the menu task so each child would have the six statements while drawing spinners. Following are the statements:

1. <u>a</u> is certain to win.
2. <u>a</u> can't possibly win.
3. <u>a</u> is likely to win.
4. <u>a</u>, <u>b</u>, <u>c</u>, <u>d</u>, and <u>e</u> all are equally likely to win.
5. <u>a</u> or <u>b</u> will probably win.
6. <u>a</u>, <u>b</u>, and <u>c</u> have the same chance to win, and <u>d</u> and <u>e</u> can't possibly win.

"For this activity you're going to design spinners to match the six statements on the chart," I said, directing the children's attention to the statements. I had students read each statement aloud.

"I don't get it," Lee Ann said.

"Don't worry," I said. "I'll explain. On a sheet of paper, you'll draw six circles and draw a spinner face in each circle. Each of your spinners must match one of the statements." I could tell that the children still didn't understand, but I knew a demonstration would help.

"First, you need to divide your paper into six sections," I continued. I folded a sheet of 9-by-12-inch white drawing paper in half lengthwise, opened it, and used a ruler to draw a line on the fold.

"Now I'll divide the paper into three sections the other way," I said, pointing to show the children what I meant. "Then there will be six sections altogether." I measured the length of the paper with a ruler.

"The paper is 12 inches long," I said to the children. "How long should each section be so I have three sections the same size?" The children had studied multiplication, but it wasn't immediately obvious to them that their multiplication learning was applicable here.

"Three inches?" Elliot guessed.

"If there are three sections, and each is 3 inches, how long would that be altogether?" I asked.

"Nine inches," several children called out.

"But the paper is 12 inches long," I said, "so that's not enough."

The class was silent for a minute. Then several children raised their hands. I called on Lisa.

"I think 4 inches," she said.

"Why do you think that?" I asked.

"Because 4 and 4 is 8," she answered, "and then 8 and 4 more is 12, and that fills up the whole paper."

"I did it a different way," Charlie said. "I know three 4s make 12, so that has to be it."

No one else volunteered to comment, and I wasn't sure that all of the children understood Lisa's or Charlie's explanation or agreed with them. But when they partitioned their own papers, I'd be able to help those who were confused. I could have duplicated papers for the children to use and avoided the confusion I knew would arise from their doing the measuring, but I thought the experience was a good one. I look for situations with real purpose to give the children practice measuring.

I measured and drew lines to make six sections. Then I used a can to trace a circle in each section. "When you've prepared your paper like this, you can begin to make your puzzles," I said.

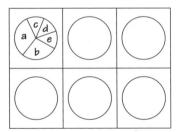

"First, I'm going to look at the statements and pick one to illustrate with a spinner," I explained. "I've chosen one, but I won't tell you which one it is."

I drew a spinner face on one of the circles and held up my paper for the children to see.

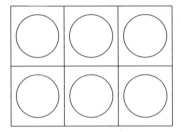

"Suppose you used this spinner for the kind of experiment we did with the 1-2-3 spinners," I said. "Raise your hand when you think you know which statement my spinner face matches." I waited until about two-thirds of the class had raised their hands, and then I called on Erin.

"It's number 5," she said. "a or b will probably win."

"I agree," I said. "Why do you think that?"

"Because a and b take up about the same space," Erin said, "and the others only have a little bit."

"Does anyone have another way to explain why my spinner face matches statement 5?" I asked. I called on Doug.

"Even if you put together <u>c</u>, <u>d</u>, and <u>e</u>," he said, "it's not even as much as <u>a</u> or <u>b</u>. So they probably won't win."

"That makes sense to me," I said. "Any other ideas?" There were none, so I ran my fingers down the list of statements, then drew a spinner face on the next circle.

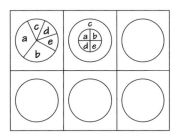

"Which statement do you think this matches?" I asked. I waited until more than half of the children had raised their hands. I called on Kristin.

"It has to be number 2," she said, "because it says that <u>a</u> can't possibly win, and it can't. It's in the middle."

"But <u>b</u> and <u>d</u> and <u>e</u> can't come up either," Abby pointed out.

"Oh," Kristin said, now uncertain of her reasoning. She looked over the statements again. I waited, not commenting or reacting.

"But nothing else fits," Seth said.

"It should be '<u>c</u> has to come up,'" Lee Ann said.

"But that's not on there," Amanda said. The class fell quiet.

"It has to be number 2," Charlie insisted. "It's the only one."

I finally interjected. "Statement 2 says that <u>a</u> can't possibly win," I said. "Is that true for the spinner I drew?" Most of the children nodded.

"I know you could write other statements that also are true for this spinner face," I said, "but statement 2 is the only one on the list that describes what I drew."

I showed the children the answer sheet I had prepared. "So far, I've done spinner faces for statements 5 and 2. I'll record these on an answer sheet." I did so.

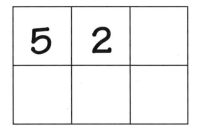

"Who can explain why I wrote the numbers 5 and 2 in these spaces?" I asked. It was obvious to most of the children that the spaces on the answer sheet corresponded to the sections on the drawing paper.

**NOTE** Having children make materials that they will use later in another activity helps them take part in the process of classroom learning. The children become producers as well as consumers of the curriculum.

"I purposely chose statements out of order for drawing my spinners," I said, "so that when I finish my paper, it will be a puzzle, and others can figure out which spinner face matches which statement."

"Oh, I think I get it now," Lee Ann said.

"I'll do one more," I said. I drew a spinner face on the third circle.

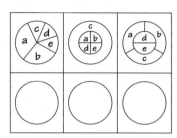

Children's hands shot up more quickly this time, as more of them understood the activity. I called on Lori.

"It's number 3," she said, "*a* is likely to come up." This wasn't the statement I had intended, but I understood why Lori thought that it could fit.

"Explain your idea," I said to Lori.

"Because it looks like *a*, *b*, and *c* are all likely," she said, "so *a* can be likely."

"I don't think so," Tomo said.

"What do you think?" I asked.

"I think it's number 6," he answered, "because *d* and *e* are trapped in the middle."

"I think they both work," Abby said.

"If you have a situation like this," I said, "then you'll have to look at the rest of the spinner faces. You should be able to use all six statements. It may be that two statements work for one spinner face, but you may need one of the statements for another spinner. So when you do your paper, be sure to draw a spinner face for each statement."

"Can we put other letters on them, too?" Eric asked.

"No," I said, "use just the letters *a, b, c, d,* and *e,* and use all of them. Be sure to draw your puzzles in mixed-up order. Don't just do the statements 1 to 6 in order. After you've drawn your spinners, fill in the numbers *1, 2, 3, 4, 5,* and *6* in the correct places on an answer sheet." I showed them a blank Spinner Puzzles Answer Sheet.

I added a few more directions. "Be sure to remember to put your name on your spinner puzzles and on your answer sheet. Then ask a partner to try your puzzles and check your answers, then sign his or her name." I showed the children the space on the answer sheet for the checker to write his or her name.

"Then put your spinners and answer sheet in the In box," I said. "After I check everyone's work, I'll put the puzzles out, and you can try to match spinners and statements."

I reviewed once more how the children were to set up their papers, draw the spinner faces, and record on the answer sheet. "If you decide to do this task today," I added, "take a sheet of statements and a piece of paper. I'll put them on the supply table for those of you who will need them later." I pointed out the last direction on the menu task: "Solve other students' puzzles."

"Don't worry about this direction now," I said. "You'll do that after everyone has made puzzles." I dismissed the students by groups to return to their tables and begin work on the menu.

## Observing the Children

Watching the children gave me information about their measuring skills—or lack of measuring skills. Most children struggled, and some needed help from me or a classmate. Maura, for example, came to me for assistance.

"I messed up," she said. She had folded the paper the long way, and the line she drew on the fold was very messy.

"Let me hold the ruler in place for you," I said. I held the ruler firmly as she drew another line.

"Now what do I do?" she asked.

"You have to draw lines the other way to make three sections," I said.

"They're each 4 inches, aren't they?" Maura asked. I nodded. Maura hadn't a clue how to use the ruler to measure. She carefully placed the 4 on the ruler at the edge of the paper and looked at me, confused. I showed her how to line up the beginning of the ruler with the edge of the paper and make a mark at 4 inches. I held the ruler while she drew the line.

Maura then turned the paper upside down to place the end of the ruler at the other edge. She made a mark at 4 inches and asked me to hold the ruler so she could draw the line. She was pleased to see that her paper was now ruled into six sections.

Antonio had taken a ruler marked only in centimeters. He had marked off 4 centimeters twice and wound up with two skinny sections and one big section. He was perplexed about what to do and came to me for help. I showed him a ruler marked in inches and suggested he use it. He went off and successfully divided his paper.

Tomo avoided using a ruler altogether and tried to partition his paper by folding. I watched as he folded his paper in half the long way and then folded it in half the short way. When he opened the paper, he counted the four sections. "I've got to do it again," he murmured to himself. He folded the paper again on the two folds he had already made and then folded it in half once more. He opened up the paper and counted again. "Oh, no," he exclaimed, "there are eight now!" He was amazed. He looked around and saw me. "Look," he said, "I got eight. I thought it would have to be six because 3 times 2 is 6, and I folded it three times."

"Maybe you ought to try using the ruler," I suggested. Tomo nodded and went off to get one.

Charlie also tried folding but had more luck. "My grandma showed me how to fold a letter," he said, "and I did it that way." After folding the paper in half the long way, Charlie had successfully folded the paper into thirds.

After about 10 minutes, all of the students had ruled their papers and drawn circles.

"Look at what I drew," Elliot came and showed me his first spinner face.

"Which statement does it match?" I asked. I didn't see a match with any of the statements.

"None of them," he said in a surprised voice. "I made up my own."

"That's a good idea," I said, "but right now I want you to draw spinner faces that match the statements I wrote."

"Rats," Elliot said, and returned to his seat.

Corrine came up to show me her spinner face for statement 5. "Mine is different than yours," she said.

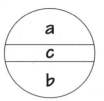

"I agree," I responded, "and it's true that <u>a</u> and <u>b</u> are equally likely. But you have to figure out a way to put <u>d</u> and <u>e</u> on it as well."

Corrine looked at her drawing quietly. Then her face broke into a grin. "I know how," she said. She returned to her seat and quickly made an alteration.

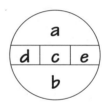

Abby was standing in front of the enlarged menu task, her partially completed puzzle sheet in hand. "I don't think this one works for number 6," she said.

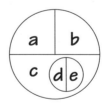

"What's the problem?" I asked.

"I got the '<u>d</u> and <u>e</u> can't possibly come up' part," she said, "but I have a problem with the <u>a</u>, <u>b</u>, and <u>c</u>."

"How would you explain the problem?" I probed.

"There's too much room for <u>c</u>," she said.

"Do you know how to fix it?" I asked.

"Yes, but I like it this way," she said. I didn't respond. Abby sighed. "But I'll change it," she said and returned to her desk.

Some children worked quickly, drawing spinner faces with impressive ease. Doug was one of these students. He got stuck, however, trying to divide one of the circles into five equal pie-shaped pieces. "This is hard," he said. "Every time I make one bigger, another one is too small."

"Do you want help?" I asked, knowing that it was hard to divide a circle into five equal segments.

"No," he said, "I think I can do it." He came back a little while later. "I got it," he said. I could tell he felt good.

Later, I checked the spinner puzzles that children had put in the In box. Several hadn't had a partner check their work, and I returned their puzzles and answer sheets to them. Others had turned in papers with errors, even though someone had checked them, and I returned these as well for students to find their errors. A few hadn't put their names on their spinner puzzles, and I reminded them to do so. By the next week, I had a complete set of spinner puzzles and answer sheets.

Alan's puzzles were similar to other students' spinners.

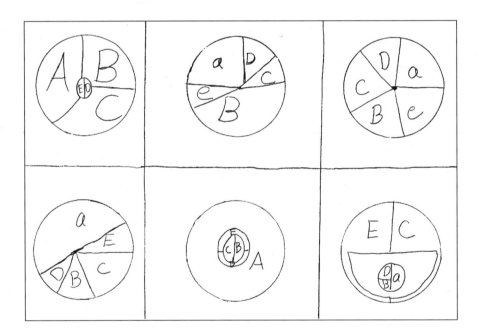

**A Class Discussion**

One day at the beginning of class, I gathered the students together. I had separated the puzzles from the answer sheets and duplicated Spinner Puzzles Solutions sheets for them to use for recording answers.

"The spinner puzzles are ready for you to solve," I said. "But before I explain how you'll do that, I'm interested in hearing about what happened when you made your puzzles. Did you get stuck? Did you get help from anyone else? Did you learn something new? Who has something to share?"

I waited to give the students time to think. After about seven or eight raised their hands, I called on Charlie. I often find that after one or two students say something, others are encouraged to share as well.

"Tom helped me," Charlie began. "I drew one that I thought would be right for '<u>a</u> is certain to win,' but then Tom showed me that there was a teeny chance for <u>c</u> and <u>e</u> to come up."

"What did you do?" I asked.

"I moved them into the center so they can't be reached," he answered.

Abby shared next. "I had a hard time trying to figure out how to draw spinners for the sentences," she said, "and I had to do it over again. Then I got it. But it was hard to find one spinner for each. Maybe older kids would like it, too."

I called on Amanda. "Lee Ann was my partner," she said, "and she found one wrong, so I had to change it. But all the other ones fit the sentences."

Seth reported something he had learned. "I used to think that if a section on a spinner is bigger, you have a better chance of spinning it. But bigger is not always better. Sometimes smaller is better."

"Can you show an example of what you mean?" I asked. Seth came up to the board and drew a spinner face to explain.

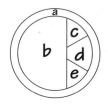

"This fits '<u>a</u> is sure to win,'" he said, "but <u>b</u> has the bigger space." Several other children called out that they did the same.

"That's what I did to make hard ones," Andrew said.

I called on Mercedes. "I didn't do hard ones," she said. "I think I made mine too easy."

"Me, too," Lisa chimed in.

"Well, you can find out if your puzzles are easy or complicated after other students try to guess them," I responded.

Emelia tried to make her spinner puzzles difficult for others to solve.

I then initiated a discussion about the various solutions students had found for statement 4: "a, b, c, d, and e are all equally likely to win."

"I noticed that a lot of solutions looked somewhat the same for this statement," I said. "I counted, and 17 of you did it like this." I made a sketch on the board of the typical spinner face.

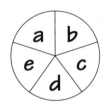

"That one was hard to do," Tom said.

"What was hard about it?" I asked.

"It was hard to get them all the same," he answered. "I had to erase a lot." Others nodded.

"Five of you made a spinner face like this," I said, making another sketch.

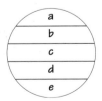

The class was quiet while children thought about this. "Discuss at your tables whether you think this works for statement 4," I said. Animated conversations broke out. After a few minutes, I called the students back to attention.

"It can work," Seth said, "but you have to draw it right."

"It's kind of hard," Eric said, "because you have to have double space on the line for <u>a</u> and <u>e</u> because the others have two." He came up and showed what he meant.

"I think your sketch is pretty good," Abby said, "but it could be better."

"How could I measure to make it better?" I asked. I was curious how the children might think about this problem. They had several suggestions.

"Get a piece of string," Lisa said, "and measure around and then . . ." She faltered, unsure of what she would do next.

"I know," Amanda said. "You'd then divide the string into five parts. Maybe that would work."

"Eight parts," Andrew called out. "No, ten," he added.

"You need a ruler that bends around," Doug said.

"Maybe like the one my mom uses to sew," Kristin added.

"You mean her tape measure?" I asked. Kristin nodded.

"Can you use a compass?" Andrew asked. He knew what a compass was, but only how to use it to draw circles.

"Yes, a compass would help," I answered, "and so would another tool called a protractor. When you get to middle school, you'll learn about how to use these tools to solve math problems."

Lee Ann sliced her spinner with parallel lines for statement 4. (See lower right-hand corner.)

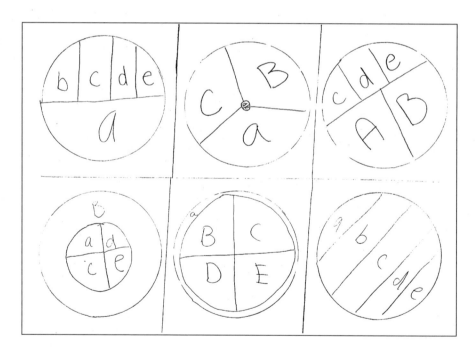

I then explained to the children how they could solve one another's puzzles. I showed them the Spinner Puzzles Solutions sheet for recording their answers. "Check your answers in the answer booklet," I said. I showed them how I had made a booklet of their answer sheets, stapling them inside a cover of construction paper.

"If you disagree with any of the answers," I added, "then talk to the person who made the spinner."

"Is this for the menu?" Lisa wanted to know.

"Yes, you can choose to do this at menu time," I answered.

"Can we do more than one sheet?" Tomo asked.

"Yes, you have to do at least eight puzzles and fill one sheet," I answered, "but you can do more."

There were no other questions, so the students went to work on the menu.

The class thought that Eric's spinners were the most unusual.

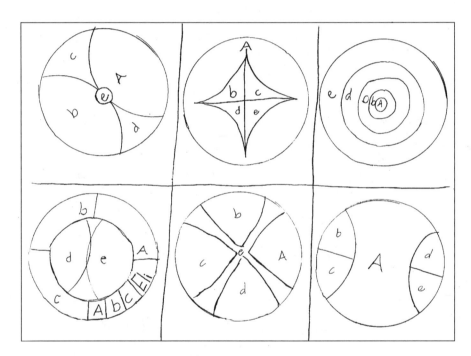

# ASSESSMENT  Spinner Statements

A good deal of vocabulary is linked with this probability unit—*probable, improbable, possible, impossible, likely, unlikely,* and so on. Understanding of and comfort with new vocabulary is best developed through hearing the terminology and using it in a variety of contexts. Therefore, the unit strives to integrate the language of probability into all lessons and activities. This assessment focuses on children's interpretation of probability terminology in the context of analyzing a spinner.

In this assessment, children work in small groups to examine a spinner face and come to consensus about which of 17 statements are true and which are false. Listening to the students' discussions provides valuable insights into how the children are thinking about and using the language of probability. As with all assessments, the benefit is instructional as well. Through their discussions, students have the opportunity to think out loud, clarify their ideas, extend their thinking, and hear other points of view.

Introduce the assessment by presenting a situation similar to the one the class will work on. On the board, draw the following spinner face:

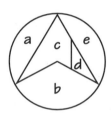

Have the students discuss the statements listed below. Begin by writing just the first statement on the board and asking the class to decide whether it is true or false for the spinner face you drew. Write the second statement and discuss. Continue in this way for all five statements.

1. <u>a</u>, <u>b</u>, and <u>e</u> are equally likely to win.
2. <u>c</u> and <u>d</u> can't possibly win.
3. <u>b</u> is certain to lose.
4. <u>c</u> has a 0% chance of winning.
5. <u>a</u> has a 50% chance of winning.

After you have discussed all five statements, distribute a Spinner Statements sheet to each student (see Blackline Masters section, page 244) and post an enlarged copy. Tell the students that they will first examine the statements individually and circle those they think are true. Then they'll compare their sheets in small groups and try to agree as a group which are true and which are false.

As groups discuss, observe and listen to assess students' comfort with using the vocabulary of probability, their ability to relate the vocabulary to the spinner, and their understanding of the probability of each of the five sections on the spinner.

After groups have had time to discuss the statements, start a class discussion. The following questions are discussion guidelines:

What differences in opinions were there when you shared your ideas? How did you settle your differences?

Are there any statements that your group couldn't agree on?

Finally, you may want to have students write about the experience. To help them think about what to write, post questions to spark their thinking. It's not necessary that the students answer each question in detail, but they should use them as guidelines to include as much information as possible about their experiences.

1. How did your group work to make decisions about the statements?
2. What arguments did you have?
3. How did you feel when convincing someone else or being convinced?
4. What are you still not sure about?

## FROM THE CLASSROOM

"I have an a, b, c, d, e spinner that I'd like you to think about," I said to the class to introduce the assessment. I drew the spinner face on the board.

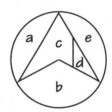

The children had all drawn spinner faces during the *Spinner Puzzles* menu activity, and they began to talk among themselves about the spinner face I drew.

"Ooooh, b has a big space," Amanda said.

"But it doesn't count so much," Seth responded. "Look at the edge."

"I'd bet on b anyway," Elliot said.

"You can't get c or d," Lori said.

"Maybe you can if the line touches exactly on one of those spots," Timmy said.

"No way," Doug commented. "There's no space."

As the children talked, I wrote on the board:

1. a, b, and e are equally likely to win.

I interrupted the students' conversation and focused them on the statement I had written. "I'm interested in whether you think the statement I wrote is true or false," I said. "Imagine doing an experiment as we've done for the other spinners, where we keep track of what comes up and see which gets to the top of the sheet first. What do you think about the statement I wrote?" Almost half the class raised their hands.

"I think it's right," Lee Ann said. "Even though <u>b</u> has a bigger space, it has the same amount on the edge, and that's what counts."

"You mean this edge?" I asked Lee Ann, tracing the circumference of the circle. She nodded. "It's called the circumference," I added, writing the word on the board.

"I don't think they're exactly the same," Doug said.

"What do you mean?" I asked.

"It looks like <u>b</u> has a little more space," he said.

"I think <u>a</u> looks like it's bigger," Lisa said.

"I tried to draw it so they were all equally likely," I said, "but I didn't measure exactly. Besides, measurement is never exact. Maybe I should edit my statement." I inserted *about* into the statement so it read:

　　　1. <u>a</u>, <u>b</u>, and <u>e</u> are about equally likely to win.

That seemed to satisfy Doug and Lisa.

"So is it true or false?" I asked. More than half the class answered "True" in unison.

I then wrote a second statement:

　　　2. <u>c</u> and <u>d</u> can't possibly win.

Before I even turned around to face the class, most of the children called out "True." I looked over at Timmy, but he didn't seem interested in pursuing the idea he had stated earlier. Peer pressure, I suspect, had had its effect.

Next I wrote:

　　　3. <u>b</u> is certain to lose.

Conversation buzzed among the children. After a minute, I interrupted them and asked for a verdict. I called on Ajani.

"False," he said, with confidence. "You can't tell that because it could win. It has the same chance as <u>a</u> and <u>e</u>." Others nodded their agreement.

I wrote another statement:

　　　4. <u>c</u> has a 0% chance of winning.

"True!" the children called out.

"So does <u>d</u>," Erin added.

"One more statement," I said to the children, and wrote:

　　　5. <u>a</u> has a 50% chance of winning.

There were mixed responses. I called on Andrew.

"It can't be true," he said, "because there are three that have the same chance. It's like the *1-2-3 Spinner Experiment*. It's $33\frac{1}{3}$ percent chance for each." Andrew was remembering the discussion we had had during *The 1-2-3 Spinner Experiment, Part 2* whole class lesson. Andrew has a good deal of status in the class for his math understanding, and although some of the children probably didn't understand his explanation, no one argued.

I then explained the activity. I posted an enlarged copy of the Spinner Statements sheet. (See Blackline Masters section, page 244.) "This spinner face is different from the one I drew on the board," I said, "and there are more statements. I'm going to give each of you a sheet. Read it quietly to yourself and circle the statements you think are true. Then, when everyone at your table has read the statements, talk about them together and see if you agree. If you disagree about a statement, talk about it and try to see if you can come to agreement. Later, we'll talk as a class about the results."

The students were curious about the statements and interested in getting started. I distributed the papers, and the room became quiet as the children read and thought about the statements. After several minutes, conversations began at tables, and after about 10 minutes, all of the children were discussing the papers.

Charlie kept track with check marks as his group agreed.

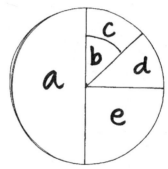

**Spinner Statements**

√ 1. a has a 50% chance of winning.
√ 2. d is twice as likely to win as c.
√ 3. e is twice as likely to win as c.
√ 4. It is probable than d won't win.
√ 5. c can't possibly win.
√ 6. It's just as likely for e to win as c and d together.
√ 7. d has more than a 25% chance of winning.
√ 8. It is certain that a will win.
√ 9. It is possible for c to win.
√ 10. It is possible for e to win.
√ 11. c has the same chance of winning as b.
√ 12. The probability of e winning is 25%.
√ 13. The probability of d coming up when you spin is a little more than 10%.
√ 14. b can't possibly win.
√ 15. b has a 0% chance of coming up.
√ 16. It is uncertain which letter will win.
√ 17. It is unlikely for c to win.

I circulated and listened to conversations. There was consensus among the children about many of the statements, but there were also some differences.

Joseph, Antonio, and Janos disagreed about statement 8. Carrie, also at their table, sat quietly listening.

"It can't be true," Janos was saying. "You can't tell for sure."

"But, look," Antonio countered, "you know <u>a</u> will win."

"Yeah," Joseph said, "it's got the best chance."

"But that doesn't mean it will win for sure," Janos insisted. "Certain means for sure, not maybe."

I didn't intervene but made a note to myself to be sure and talk about statement 8 with the entire class.

I then noticed Elliot in a heated discussion with Amanda. I went over to listen. They were talking about statement 2. Elliot was arguing that <u>d</u> was twice a big as <u>c</u> and therefore had twice the chance of winning. Amanda was exasperated.

"It's just like <u>a</u> and <u>b</u> on the spinner on the board," she said, practically shouting. Amanda was referring to the spinner face I had used to introduce the activity.

"I'd still bet on the bigger space," Elliot insisted.

Alan circled the statements he thought were true.

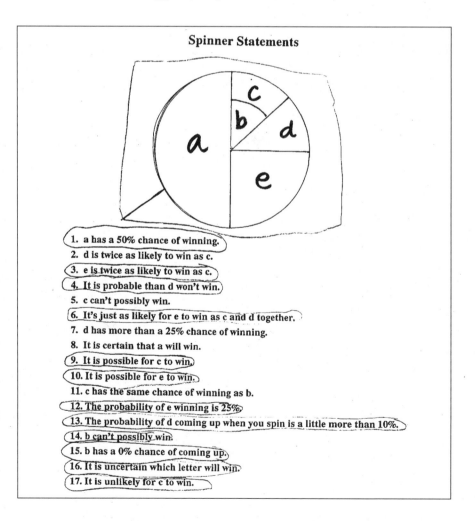

**Spinner Statements**

1. a has a 50% chance of winning.
2. d is twice as likely to win as c.
3. e is twice as likely to win as c.
4. It is probable than d won't win.
5. c can't possibly win.
6. It's just as likely for e to win as c and d together.
7. d has more than a 25% chance of winning.
8. It is certain that a will win.
9. It is possible for c to win.
10. It is possible for e to win.
11. c has the same chance of winning as b.
12. The probability of e winning is 25%.
13. The probability of d coming up when you spin is a little more than 10%.
14. b can't possibly win.
15. b has a 0% chance of coming up.
16. It is uncertain which letter will win.
17. It is unlikely for c to win.

"You're so stubborn!" Amanda exclaimed in almost a shriek.

"You're not right," Eric said quietly to Elliot. Kristin nodded her agreement with Eric. Elliot just shrugged.

"Let's do the next one," Eric suggested.

Tom came into the room at that point. "Oh, no," Charlie exclaimed. "Just when we finished agreeing." Lisa and Erin also groaned.

"Do you think you can explain the activity to Tom?" I asked Charlie, Lisa, and Erin. The three of them nodded, and I gave a sheet to Tom. A few minutes later, I noticed Charlie and Tom deep in discussion; Lisa and Erin were playing a game of Pig.

At the next table, Lee Ann, Lori, Seth, and Doug were in hot discussion about statement 17. The girls felt it was false and the boys felt it was true. They were animated and involved. I made a note to have them report to the class.

### A Class Discussion

As groups finished, the children chose menu activities to do. When all the groups had completed their discussions, I initiated a class discussion. I began by referring to the conflicts I had overheard. I had Janos and Joseph present their differences about statement 8 and let others respond.

"Certain is like 100% chance," Emelia said in support of Janos.

"There's no chance with certain," Abby added. "It's for sure."

Janos seemed pleased to receive support from others. "I'm glad I stuck to my guns," he commented.

Amanda reported on her frustration with Elliot. "He just won't admit he's wrong," she said. Elliot's face colored.

"Okay, okay," he said. Elliot sometimes takes a stance and sees changing his mind as losing face.

"Remember, you have to be able to explain why your idea makes sense," I said, making a general comment that I hoped Elliot would embrace. "Also, it's fine to change your mind when something convinces you. That shows you're thinking and learning."

"We didn't have to change our minds much," Erin reported. "We all agreed except for number 2, and it was easy."

"What about when Tom came in and joined you?" I asked.

"I helped him," Charlie said. "He agreed, too."

"Can we tell about our argument?" Seth asked. I nodded.

"Lee Ann would make a good lawyer," he began. "She argues and doesn't give in. But Doug and I still don't think she's right."

"Which statement were you arguing about?" I asked.

"Number 17," the four children said in unison.

"Lori and I think d and c have the same chance," Lee Ann reported.

"But that has nothing to do with the statement," Seth countered. "They're both unlikely. So it's true."

All four children started talking at once. I interrupted them and asked them to share their ideas one at a time. The girls finally gave in to the boys, and the issue seemed resolved.

The final class consensus was that the only false statements were 2, 5, 7, 8, and 11. The conversations indicated that most of the children were able to think about and use the language of probability.

To end the lesson, I asked the children to write about the experience. I listed some questions to help them get organized and started:

1. How did your group work to make decisions about the statements?
2. What arguments did you have?
3. How did you feel when convincing someone else or being convinced?
4. What are you still not sure about?

This writing assignment seemed easy for the children. I think this was because they had been so involved discussing their ideas, and therefore they had something to write about.

Elliot described his confusion. Still, he felt the activity was fun.

> **Spinner Statements**
> We worked good. Some people dicigred with some people. They dicigread with 2 and then they comvinced me it was not true. I agread with 4 and everyone dicigread with me then we had a argument with them and they still didn't agreay with me. Then I said," It's True!". When they convinced I felt conphased becagse they screamed at me. I'm sure there right. it was really really FUN!

Abby wrote about the process at her table.

## Spinner Statements

We each did are own paper and when we we were done I read outloud like I said "number one is right" and if most of us agreed that is what it is. We disagread on number 17 because the rest of the table thought that unlikely meant not possible but finaly they figured it out. I was never convined my table always agreed with me. and some of them did not understand some questions like 17. We are pretty sure everything is right. I think this is very fun and mabie you should try it on second graders.

## Spinner Statements

When we started descussing about the questions we went down the list and to my suprise all of them we agreed on except one. It was number two. D is twice as likely to win as c. But it didn't take a long time to decide. I felt much better when I agreed with my table. I don't know why. But the good thing is we're all sure about the sentences at our table. When I did it by myself I went very slowly to think about each one. I still knew I would get convinced to change one though I was the last one to finish doing it by myself. I thought this activity was fun because I could think hard.

*(top)* Lisa described her thinking and the process of her group.

*(below, right)* Mercedes listed the statements she still wasn't sure about.

## Spinner Statements

My group worked to decide esay because we we're expaning why we thought it was right or why we thought it was rong. We had no arguments because we all agreed with each other. I felt ok convincing with my table but I'm still not sure about 2,5,7,8,11 and 17. I think this activity is easy and fun because I like discucsing this kind of stuff.

## MENU ACTIVITY

### Overview

## Testing Pig Strategies

This activity extends the children's experience from the whole class lesson *The Game of Pig* (see page 38) and focuses the students on the effectiveness of various strategies. The children again play Pig, this time choosing a strategy and sticking with it for a series of 10 games. After discussing what they learned from the experience, the students write about what strategy they think is best.

---

245

# Testing Pig Strategies

You need: Two dice
List of Pig strategies

1. Choose a Pig strategy from the list. You and your partner should each pick a different strategy.

2. Play Pig 10 times. Use the strategy you picked for all 10 games.

3. Look at your scores. What did you learn about the different strategies? Would you pick another strategy if you were to play again? Discuss your thoughts with your partner.

From *Math By All Means: Probability, Grades 3–4* ©1995 Math Solutions Publications

---

## Before the lesson

Gather these materials:
- ■ Dice, two per pair of students
- ■ List of strategies for playing Pig (Use the strategies generated by your students in the whole class lesson *The Game of Pig* or use the ones listed below.)
- ■ Blackline master of menu activity, page 245

## Getting started

■ Post the list of strategies the class generated during the whole class lesson *The Game of Pig*. If you prefer, use some or all of the following to supplement your students' ideas:

1. Roll once and stop.
2. Go for it.
3. Roll three or four times and stop.
4. Roll high enough so your friend is behind.
5. Use a combination and pay attention to your partner's score.
6. When you get 15 or 20, stick.

■ Tell the students that they will play Pig again with a partner, but this time they will choose one strategy from the list and use it for 10 games. Their partner should choose a different strategy. After playing 10 games, they can choose different strategies and play 10 games again.

■ Initiate a class discussion after all the students have had a chance to test strategies. Ask:

What do you think about the different strategies for playing Pig?
What strategy do you think is best? Why?

■ After the discussion, ask the students to write about what they learned about the different strategies and which one they think is best.

## FROM THE CLASSROOM

"In this activity, you play Pig again," I said to introduce the new menu task to the class. Pig was the favorite activity for many of the students, and several children cheered.

"But you'll play in a slightly different way," I continued. "This time, you'll test the strategies you've been thinking about." I posted the list of strategies the children had generated and reviewed the strategies:

1. Roll once and stop.
2. Go for it.
3. Roll three or four times and stop.
4. Roll high enough so your friend is behind.
5. Use a combination and pay attention to your partner's score.
6. When you get 15 or 20, stick.

I then explained the directions for the activity. "You'll each choose one of the strategies to use," I said, "and play 10 games with someone who chooses a different strategy. The goal of this activity is to find out if some strategies work better than others."

Lisa raised her hand. "I have an idea," she said.

"What is it?" I asked.

"I think that if strategy 2 plays strategy 3 for 10 games, it will be a 5-5 tie," she said.

"Which of those strategies would you choose to play?" I asked.

"Number 3: 'Roll three or four times and stop,'" she said.

"I'll play you," Doug said. "I like to go for it."

I gave one last direction. "After you test two strategies with 10 games," I said, "you can try two other strategies and play 10 games again. We'll talk about what you've found out after everyone has had the chance to do the activity." Many of the children chose partners and began to play.

### Observing the Children

As I circulated, I reminded children about recording the number of the strategy they were using and staying with the same strategy for 10 games.

Maura came to me and complained that Corrine wasn't really playing the go-for-it strategy. Corrine was right behind her. "She tried to stop at 30," Maura said, "but doesn't she have to keep rolling to 65 or 70?" I looked at Corrine.

"I know," she said, "but I want to stop."

"So you're not so sure that 'Go for it' is the strategy you want to use?" I asked. Corrine nodded.

"Remember that this is an experiment to test the strategies and see what you can learn," I said. "I think you should follow the strategy you chose for 10 games and then decide if you'd like to change the strategy and how. You may lose, but you may learn something." The girls returned to their desks to continue.

Andrew was playing with Eric. "I think his combo strategy works good," Eric said. "He's really winning."

"Remember to play 10 games, so you'll have enough evidence to be convinced," I said.

"'Go for it' isn't working today," Timmy said. "I lost three games already. I want to switch." Timmy was playing with Alan, who was successful in using Eric's strategy of trying to stay ahead of Timmy each round.

"Which strategy would you switch to?" I asked.

"Kristin's strategy of stopping when you get 15 or 20," Timmy said. "It's kind of like 'Go for it' but safer."

Timmy often has difficulty sticking with an activity. He becomes frustrated and discouraged easily, and I often encourage him to stay focused. This time, I allowed him to switch, deciding that he would stay more involved if he had the chance to make another choice. I realized that I was making a different decision for Timmy than I had for Corrine. This is an example of one of the myriad decisions to make when teaching.

"Is it okay with you if Timmy switches?" I asked Alan.

Alan nodded. "I think I'll still win," he said with confidence.

"Start again," I told the boys, "but this time play 10 complete games." The boys nodded and began to play.

The children continued to play over the next several days. As always, they enjoyed the game, and they also stayed interested in testing the strategies. One day, Erin and Emelia brought to me the results from their 10 games. Erin had used strategy 2: "Go for it," and Emelia had chosen strategy 4: "Roll high enough so your friend is behind." Both girls were grinning.

"Look, it was a tie," Emelia said.

"Our score was 5-5," Erin added.

"What do you think about these two strategies?" I asked.

"You get a lot of zeros with 'Go for it,'" Erin said. "Look at this." She showed me the results of their first three games. She had won the first game, but in the second and third games, she had gotten mostly zeros.

"That's why I think 'Go for it' isn't as good, even though Erin won five games," Emelia said.

"Explain what you mean," I said.

"Well, it's too risky," she answered. "You just get too many zeros."

"How do you explain the tie, then?" I asked. The girls shrugged.

These are the results from Emelia and Erin's first three games. Their 10 games, however, resulted in a tie.

"There's always luck," Emelia commented.

Lee Ann shared Emelia's opinion about "Go for it." She brought the scoresheet she and Amanda were keeping. Amanda had won the first five games they played.

"It's no good," Lee Ann said. "It's just no good. It's terrible." She showed me the results of several games in which she never scored more than zero.

"What do you think?" I asked.

"That's not a good strategy to pick, for sure," she answered, emphatically.

In one of her games with Amanda, Lee Ann never scored a point.

### A Class Discussion

The next week, I initiated a class discussion. "I'm curious about what you think now about the different strategies for playing Pig," I said. Hands shot up. The children's interest was still high. I called on Lisa.

"I like the combo," she said, "because it gives you a choice of how far you want to go or how little."

"What do you mean?" Amanda wanted to know.

"What I mean is with combo you can look at your opponent. If you're way behind, you can go for it. If you're ahead by like 15 numbers, then it's best to stick. You get to choose, and that's better."

"I disagree," Doug said. "I think combo isn't so good because you could go really overboard and not stop in time, and then you lose."

"What strategy do you think is best?" I asked him.

"'Roll three or four times and stop,'" he said. "You get a good average of points."

Doug stuck with his defense of the strategy of rolling three or four times and then stopping.

> ## Pig Strategy
> I think that the second strategy three or four roles and stop is a good strategy because it gets you a good number of points and even if you get a one you dont loose that much points. The problem with a combination is you might go overboard and use Go for It and you might loose a lot of points. But three or four roles and stop it prevents you from going overbourd. So you won't loose a lot of points if if you get a one.

Andrew had a comment about Doug's idea. "I have a reason why 'Roll three or four times and stop' isn't as good as the combo," he said. "Because if you just got a double 1 and your opponent has a lot, like 81 points, then you'd probably lose because you couldn't catch up."

"I agree with Andrew," Seth said. "But before I started using the combination, I thought that 'Roll three or four times and stop' was the best because you stayed out of danger but you increased your score. But now I think it's second best."

"I kind of agree with everyone so far," Lee Ann said. "I thought that combo was the best one, but now I'm thinking about what Doug said. I think he's right, and you might get very greedy with combo and lose all your points."

Tom expressed confidence in his own judgment. "I think that the combination is best because you can let your own self let you make your own choices. I think that's best for winning."

Alan favored Doug's choice ("Roll three or four times and stop"). "It's more likely you won't get a 1 with it," he said.

The discussion continued for a while longer, with almost all of the children expressing opinions. When the children wrote later, 17 indicated that they thought the combination strategy was best. Six children chose "Roll three or four times and stop." Tomo, who didn't say anything in the discussion, wrote about why "Roll once and stop" was best. He wrote: *Even though it's slower then the other strategys it's better thaen losing all.*

Amanda's preference for the combination strategy reflected the thoughts of most other students.

I would use combination. I would because you could do any of the other 5. It is just what you want to do. you don't have to keep track of how many rolls you do. or keep going and going. you can do three rolls and stop. or go till your friend is beihnd you or just anuff to get to onehoundred. The combination is the best for me!

Emelia gave specific reasons for choosing the combination strategy.

I think the comboo is best for winning. The reason is, you aren't restrickted by your stratagy.

If your way behind and your uootnent is getting lots of high numbers, go for it.

If you're about twenty ahead three or four rolls and stop.

If you're way ahead one roll and stop

## MENU ACTIVITY

## High or Low

### Overview

*High or Low* gives students another way to think about the probabilities of the sums from rolling two dice. Andrew, one of the third graders in my class, initially suggested the activity as a variation of *Roll Two Dice.* (See page 92.) I added Andrew's game to the menu then in progress, and it was a successful extension. The children enjoyed having a new approach to something they already understood and liked. Also, the activity sparked lively discussion among them, continuing their investigation about the probabilities of two-dice sums. This menu leads into the assessment *Which Number Wins?* (See page 162.)

---

246

# High or Low

You need: Your papers from Roll Two Dice
Two dice
Roll Two Dice recording sheet

1. Count the number of low sums, the number of 7s, and the number of high sums on each Roll Two Dice paper.

2. Write these numbers on the class chart. Circle the number that shows whether a low sum, 7, or high sum won.

3. When you play Roll Two Dice, do you think you are more likely to get a high sum or a low sum? Find a partner who thinks differently from you and play Roll Two Dice again.

4. Post your results.

---

**Before the lesson**

Gather these materials:
- ■ Dice, two per pair of students
- ■ Student papers from the *Roll Two Dice* menu activity
- ■ *Roll Two Dice* recording sheet (See Blackline Masters section, page 236.)
- ■ One sheet of 12-by-18-inch paper
- ■ Blackline master of menu activity, page 246

**Getting started**

■ Start a class discussion by reminding students of the *Roll Two Dice* menu activity. Ask: "When you roll two dice, do you think you will more likely get high sums or low sums, or do you think the chance is the same for both?" Invite student responses.

■ Hold up one student's *Roll Two Dice* recording sheet. Suggest that one way to answer the question is to collect data from student papers. Explain that the "low sums" are 2, 3, 4, 5, and 6, and the "high sums" are 8, 9, 10, 11, and 12. The middle sum is 7, and when it wins, neither the high nor low sum wins.

■ Have the class count the number of times low sums, 7s, and high sums came up on the student's paper. At the top of the paper write the total number of times the sums in each category came up.

| | | 9 | | | 12 | | 34 | | | |
|---|---|---|---|---|---|---|---|---|---|---|
| 2 | 3 | 4 | 5 | 6 | 7 | 8 | 9 | 10 | 11 | 12 |
| | | 3+1 | 4+1 | 5+1 | 5+2 | 5+3 | 5+4 | 6+4 | 6+5 | 6+6 |
| | | 3+1 | 4+1 | 4+2 | 5+2 | 5+3 | 6+3 | 5+5 | 6+5 | |
| | | 2+2 | | 3+3 | 3+4 | 5+3 | 6+3 | 6+4 | 6+5 | |
| | | | | 4+2 | 4+3 | 6+2 | 4+5 | 5+5 | 6+5 | |
| | | | | | 3+4 | 6+2 | 5+3 | 6+4 | 6+5 | |
| | | | | | 6+1 | 4+4 | 6+4 | 6+4 | 6+5 | |
| | | | | | 5+2 | 5+3 | 6+4 | | 6+5 | |
| | | | | | 6+1 | 5+3 | 6+3 | | 6+5 | |
| | | | | | 5+2 | 5+3 | | | | |
| | | | | | 4+3 | 5+3 | | | | |
| | | | | | 5+2 | 4+4 | | | | |
| | | | | | 5+2 | | | | | |

■ Post vertically a sheet of 12-by-18-inch paper. Rule three columns and label them "Low Sums," "7," and "High Sums." Record the results from the student paper by writing in the Low Sums column how many sums there were that totaled 2–6, in the 7 column how many sums there were that totaled 7, and in the High Sums column how many sums totaled 8–12. Then circle the numeral that indicates where the *Roll Two Dice* winner was. For example, in the paper shown above, 7 won, so you would circle 12.

■ Tell students that they are to get their papers from *Roll Two Dice* and determine how many low sums, 7s, and high sums there were. They should record the totals at the top of their papers and on the posted 12-by-18-inch paper. They should also circle the number that tells what kind of number (low, 7, or high) won.

■ Ask students to think about what kind of number they think will win most often and find a partner who thinks differently. They should play additional games of *Roll Two Dice* and post those results.

■ After a few days, call the students together for a class discussion. Add the numbers in each column and write the total at the bottom. (It makes sense for students to use calculators to total the numbers in each column.)

■ Discuss the data. Ask students their thoughts now about whether low sums or high sums come up most often. Remind them that data alone can't prove or disprove theories.

■ Follow this menu activity with the writing assignment described in the assessment *Which Number Wins?* (See page 162.)

## FROM THE CLASSROOM

**NOTE** Children need many experiences in order to learn and cement their understanding of new ideas. Offering opportunities to examine their thinking from different perspectives challenges children to question their understanding; encourages them to reconsider, extend, and revise their thinking; and helps them strengthen their understanding.

I gathered the children on the rug at the beginning of the math period and asked, "When you roll two dice, do you think you're more likely to get high sums or low sums, or is it the same for both?" We had already examined the different ways to get each sum and had collected data from rolling two dice. I raised the question in response to the conjecture Andrew had made when we were discussing the *Roll Two Dice* menu activity. (See page 92.)

The question sparked a heated discussion. The children's responses reminded me of children's fragile understanding and the benefit of giving students repeated experiences with the same ideas.

About a third of the students raised their hands. The issue had been raised the week before when we were discussing the results from *Roll Two Dice*, so the children had had time to think about the question. I find that returning to discussions about issues is useful since it gives students the chance to think over time about their ideas.

To start the discussion, I called on Emelia. "I've been thinking about what Andrew said last time," she began, "and I think he's wrong that the big numbers come up more. The 2 is the same as the 12, and the 3 is the same as the 11, like that. So they have to have the same chance."

Andrew raised his hand to respond. "I know the big sums come up more," he said. "Can I get my papers?" I nodded, and Andrew ran to his desk to get his folder. He fished out the papers he wanted to show.

"Look," he said. "Timmy and I did *Roll Two Dice* together, and I was rooting for the low numbers and he was rooting for the high numbers."

"What about 7?" I asked, interrupting him. "Did you count it as a high sum or a low sum?"

"It didn't count," Timmy chimed in. "It's like if 7 wins, then the computer wins."

"Yeah," Andrew concurred. "I took from 2 to 6, and Timmy had from 8 to 12."

"So how many sums did you each have?" I asked. Andrew counted quickly on his fingers.

"Five," he said. "We each got five sums, and the computer got one."

"What computer are you talking about?" I asked.

"Well, not really a computer," Andrew answered.

"It was just pretend," Timmy added, "so it didn't count for Andrew or me."

Andrew and Timmy had the attention of the entire class. "So, who won?" Elliot asked.

"We played three games," Andrew said, "and we're in the middle of the fourth. I won the first because 6 won, then the computer won the next because 7 won, then Timmy won because 8 won, and now Timmy is almost winning the next game." He held up each paper to show the class.

"It doesn't make sense that you think high numbers win," Amanda said. "One time a low number won and one time a high number won and the computer won once. It came out even."

"But then I counted how many combinations I wrote," Andrew said, getting excited.

"What do you mean?" Alan asked.

"Look," he said. "On this paper, 6 won, but there are only 28 combinations for the numbers from 2 to 6 and there are 33 combinations from 8 to 12."

At the top of his sheet, Andrew recorded the number of combinations he wrote for low sums, 7, and high sums.

| 2 | 3 | 4 | 5 | 6 | 7 | 8 | 9 | 10 | 11 | 12 |
|---|---|---|---|---|---|---|---|----|----|----|
| 1+1 | 2+1 | 1+3 | 3+2 | 2+4 | 3+4 | 5+3 | 6+3 | 6+4 | 5+6 | |
| | 2+1 | 1+3 | 3+2 | 1+5 | 2+5 | 3+5 | 5+4 | 5+5 | 5+6 | |
| | 2+1 | 3+1 | 3+2 | 2+4 | 2+5 | 4+4 | 6+3 | 6+4 | 5+6 | |
| | 1+2 | | 2+3 | 2+4 | 2+5 | 6+2 | 6+3 | 5+5 | 5+6 | |
| | 1+2 | | 1+4 | 5+1 | 5+2 | 5+3 | 4+5 | 6+4 | | |
| | 1+2 | | 2+3 | 4+2 | 4+3 | 3+5 | 4+5 | 4+6 | | |
| | | | | 4+2 | 3+4 | 6+2 | 4+5 | 4+6 | | |
| | | | | 1+5 | | 6+2 | 5+4 | 6+4 | | |
| | | | | 1+5 | | 2+6 | 6+3 | 5+5 | | |
| | | | | 1+5 | | 4+4 | 6+3 | | | |
| | | | | 5+1 | | | | | | |
| | | | | 1+5 | | | | | | |

"I think those numbers are pretty close," Lee Ann said.

"Not really," Doug said, "they're kind of far apart."

"And look here," Andrew continued. "On this paper, 7 won, but big numbers came up 34 times and low numbers only 9 times.

In this game, high sums came up much more often than low sums.

| | | | | 9 | | 12 | | | 34 | |
| --- | --- | --- | --- | --- | --- | --- | --- | --- | --- | --- |
| 2 | 3 | 4 | 5 | 6 | 7 | 8 | 9 | 10 | 11 | 12 |
| | | 3+1 | 4+1 | 5+1 | 5+2 | 5+3 | 5+4 | 6+4 | 6+5 | 6+6 |
| | | 3+1 | 4+1 | 4+2 | 5+2 | 5+3 | 6+3 | 5+5 | 6+5 | |
| | | 2+2 | | 3+3 | 3+4 | 5+3 | 6+3 | 6+4 | 6+5 | |
| | | | | 4+2 | 4+3 | 6+2 | 4+5 | 5+5 | 6+5 | |
| | | | | | 3+4 | 6+2 | 6+3 | 6+4 | 6+5 | |
| | | | | | 6+1 | 4+4 | 5+4 | 6+4 | 6+5 | |
| | | | | | 5+2 | 5+3 | 5+4 | | 6+5 | |
| | | | | | 6+1 | 5+3 | 6+3 | | 6+5 | |
| | | | | | 5+2 | 5+3 | | | | |
| | | | | | 4+3 | 5+3 | | | | |
| | | | | | 5+2 | 4+4 | | | | |
| | | | | | 5+2 | | | | | |

"Timmy won the third one. High numbers came up 38 times and low numbers 29. So high numbers came up more," Andrew concluded.

"That could just be chance," Abby said.

"I think high numbers win more, too," Eric said. "When I played Pig, I rolled 6s more than 1s, and if you roll a 6 on one of the dice, you have to get a high answer."

"I kind of think both ways," Seth said. "When a 6 comes up, you get a high number, but if a 1 comes up you can only get a low number."

"What do you think we might do to investigate this further?" I asked.

"We need more data," Charlie said.

"What sort of data could we collect?" I asked.

"Oh, I know!" Doug blurted out. "We could each fix our papers like Andrew and Timmy did."

"What do you mean?" Lisa asked.

"Put those numbers on top to show how many boxes we filled in for high numbers and low numbers," he answered. "Then we could write those on a chart."

"I think we should count how many times 7 came up, too," Lori said. "It wins the most."

"Make three rows," Andrew said, "for low, high, and 7."

I posted a sheet of 12-by-18-inch paper and ruled three columns. I labeled the columns "Low Sums," "7," and "High Sums."

"Let me record the results from Andrew and Timmy's three papers, and then we'll decide if we think this chart gives us the information we need," I said. I recorded the results Andrew had reported:

| Low Sums | 7 | High Sums |
|----------|----|-----------|
| 28 | 7 | 33 |
| 9 | 12 | 34 |
| 29 | 11 | 38 |

"But you can't tell what won," Kristin said.

Seth's hand shot up. "Put a circle to show what won each time," he said.

"What do I circle for the first one?" I asked.

Seth turned to Andrew. "Which number won?" he asked.

Andrew referred to his paper. "It was 6," he said.

"So circle the 28," Seth said, "because 6 is a low number."

"Oh, I get it," Erin said. "That's a good idea, Seth."

"I know that on the next line I have to circle the 12," I said. "Who can explain how I know that?"

The students were silent. Finally, Emelia raised her hand. I waited a moment more, but no one else volunteered. I called on Emelia.

She said, "It takes 12 spaces to get to the finish line. So if 7 has 12, then it had to get to the finish line first." Others commented: "Oh, yeah." "That's right." "I get it."

"But I can't tell what to circle on the third row," I said.

Andrew looked at his papers. "Circle the 38, because 8 won," he said. I did so.

I then gave the students directions. "Go back over the papers you did for *Roll Two Dice*," I said. "Count the combinations and post your data the way we did for Andrew and Timmy's papers. Then play the game with a partner and record additional data."

Lori had a suggestion. "I think that people who think high numbers will come up more should be partners with people who think low numbers will win," she said. Others nodded.

"That's fine," I said. "Everyone who thinks that high sums come up more often stand up." About 10 students stood up, all boys. Five boys and all of the girls remained seated. Ajani, who was standing, quickly figured out that he'd most likely have to pair up with a girl if he remained standing. That was unthinkable for him, and he quickly sat down and asked Antonio, who was standing, to be his partner. I didn't comment. The students got to work.

## Observing the Children

Over the next several days the children entered data from their *Roll Two Dice* papers and from new games they played with partners. From time to time, students came to me and reported their results. Interest remained high. Some students held to their original views; others changed their minds; others still weren't sure; some didn't engage with the question at all but focused only on rolling the dice and recording the combinations. I didn't give my opinion to the children but listened to what they had to say. I decided to wait until a good amount of data was posted and then talk with the class about the results.

### A Class Discussion

At the beginning of class one day, I initiated a class discussion. More than 50 entries were on the chart, and I asked the children to look at the data.

"What do you notice?" I asked, my usual first question when I want students to examine data.

"Seven won a lot," Lisa said.

"It looks like high numbers won a lot," Elliot said.

"Let's count and see," I said. Together we counted and found that low sums had won 20 times, 7 had won 16 times, and high sums had won 17 times.

"That shows that low numbers come up more," Alan said.

"No it doesn't," Andrew said. "You have to add up all the numbers to see how many times they came up."

"Oh, yeah," Alan responded.

"That's a lot to add," Lisa said.

"Yes," I answered. "Even using a calculator, it's a lot of adding. Those of you who are interested can do the adding, and the rest of you can choose something else from the menu."

Eight students got calculators and gathered around the chart to add. "Check your results with one another to make sure you agree," I said. "You may want to do the adding more than once to be sure you pressed the correct calculator keys."

The next morning, I again started class by having the students look at the data. I had posted the sum for each column.

"I have some more data," Amanda said. "Can I add it on?"

"Me, too," Elliot said.

"Let's discuss what we have," I said. "Then if you'd like to add additional data, we can see what that does to our results."

I pointed to the sums I had written at the bottom of each column. "These are the totals from each column," I said. "So during your experiments of rolling two dice, low sums came up 1,249 times, 7 came up 494 times, and high sums came up 1,346 times. What do you think?"

"How come the answer for 7 is so much littler than the other two numbers?" Joseph wanted to know.

"Who would like to answer Joseph's question?" I asked. I called on Seth.

"It's because 7 is only one number and there are five numbers for the other two," he said.

"Does that make sense, Joseph?" I asked. He shook his head.

"Can anyone explain it a different way?" I asked. I called on Erin.

"Can I come up to the chart?" she asked.

"Yes," I answered.

Erin came up and pointed to each total as she explained. "The 1,233 is the number of times that Andrew's numbers came up," she said, "and he had 2, 3, 4, 5, and 6. That's what Seth means by 'five numbers.' And then Timmy had five: 8, 9, 10, 11, 12. And the 7 was for the computer."

"Oh, I get it," Joseph said.

Tomo raised his hand, and his comment was predictable. "It makes 3,089 altogether," he said.

"And what does that number tell you?" I asked.

"What do you mean?" he asked. Tomo is always more interested in computing with numbers than thinking about their meanings in contexts.

"I think I know," Lee Ann said.

"Let's hear your idea," I responded.

"It means that if we count up all the times everyone in the class rolled the dice, it was 3,089 times," she said.

"Wow, that's a lot of times," Kristin commented.

"It shows the benefit of all of us pooling our data," I said. "Each of your samples contributes to this large amount of information."

"I notice something weird," Charlie said. He changed the subject. "On the Low Sums side, there are two weird numbers. Look, there's a 41, and down below it there's a 4."

"Why do you say those are weird?" I asked.

Charlie answered, "I don't know, but 41 is awfully big and 4 is awfully small."

"I got the 41, and it *was* weird," Doug confirmed. "All the numbers kept coming up."

"Can you show us your paper?" I asked. Doug fished it out of his folder and held it up for the class to see.

This game took Doug many rolls to complete.

|  | 41 |  |  |  | 11 | 38 |  |  |  |  |
| 2 | 3 | 4 | 5 | 6 | 7 | 8 | 9 | 10 | 11 | 12 |
|---|---|---|---|---|---|---|---|---|---|---|
| 1+1 | 2+1 | 3+1 | 4+1 | 4+2 | 6+1 | 6+2 | 6+3 | 5+5 | 5+6 | 6+6 |
| 1+1 | 1+2 | 2+2 | 3+2 | 5+1 | 6+1 | 6+2 | 5+4 | 5+5 | 5+6 |  |
|  | 1+2 | 1+3 | 4+1 | 5+1 | 6+1 | 6+2 | 6+3 | 5+5 | 5+6 |  |
|  | 1+2 | 2+2 | 3+2 | 4+2 | 2+5 | 3+5 | 3+6 | 5+5 | 6+5 |  |
|  | 1+2 | 1+3 | 1+4 | 2+4 | 5+2 | 4+4 | 6+3 | 5+5 | 6+5 |  |
|  | 2+1 | 3+1 | 3+2 | 5+1 | 6+1 | 5+3 | 4+5 | 6+4 |  |  |
|  | 2+1 | 2+2 | 2+3 | 3+3 | 6+1 | 6+2 | 4+5 | 6+4 |  |  |
|  | 1+2 | 2+2 | 5+1 | 5+1 | 6+1 | 5+3 | 4+5 | 5+6 |  |  |
|  |  | 3+1 | 3+2 | 5+1 | 4+3 | 6+2 | 5+4 | 5+5 |  |  |
|  |  |  | 4+1 | 4+2 | 5+2 | 5+3 | 5+4 |  |  |  |
|  |  |  | 1+4 | 4+2 | 6+1 | 6+2 | 5+4 |  |  |  |
|  |  |  |  |  |  |  | 5+4 |  |  |  |

"I kept rolling and rolling, and it took a long time for something to win," he said.

"The most you could get is 56," Andrew said.

"What do you mean?" I asked.

"Well, it would be like almost a tie," he explained. "All of them would have 11, and 5 times 11 is 55, and then one would win, and that would make 56."

"That would be very unusual," Emelia said, "and very unlikely."

"What do you think the paper looks like that had 4 in the Low Sums column?" I asked.

"It couldn't win," Elliot said.

"There's not enough for any of them to get to the bottom," Ajani added.

"Something else must have zoomed ahead," Janos said.

"That was mine," Amanda said, having fished her paper from her folder. "Eight won. It just left the other numbers in the dust."

"Let's see," Abby said. She was sitting on the other side of the room from Amanda. Amanda held up her paper.

Amanda's results were unusual.

| 2 | 3 | 4 | 5 | 6 | 7 | 8 | 9 | 10 | 11 | 12 |
|---|---|---|---|---|---|---|---|----|----|----|
|   | 2+1 | 2+2 | 3+2 |   | 3+4 | 6+2 | 6+3 | 6+4 | 5+6 |   |
|   | 2+1 |   |   |   | 4+3 | 5+3 | 6+3 | 5+5 | 5+6 |   |
|   |   |   |   |   | 5+2 | 6+2 | 6+3 |   | 6+5 |   |
|   |   |   |   |   | 5+2 | 6+2 | 6+3 |   |   |   |
|   |   |   |   |   | 5+2 | 5+3 | 5+4 |   |   |   |
|   |   |   |   |   | 5+2 | 5+3 | 6+3 |   |   |   |
|   |   |   |   |   | 5+2 | 5+3 |   |   |   |   |
|   |   |   |   |   | 6+1 | 5+3 |   |   |   |   |
|   |   |   |   |   |   | 6+2 |   |   |   |   |
|   |   |   |   |   |   | 6+2 |   |   |   |   |
|   |   |   |   |   |   | 6+2 |   |   |   |   |
|   |   |   |   |   |   | 5+2 |   |   |   |   |

"I'm interested in your ideas about the probability of high sums versus low sums," I said, trying to bring the conversation back to the issue of Andrew's original conjecture. I called on Lisa.

"Well, according to the chart," she said, "high sums came up more. But I don't think that proves anything."

"How come?" I asked.

"Well, it could be chance, and the numbers are pretty close," she answered.

"They're 97 apart," Tomo said. He had done the subtraction with paper and pencil.

"That's what I got, too," Andrew said.

"That's not much apart for all those rolls," Lee Ann said. "I think that they're pretty close and the chance is about the same for both."

"Me, too," Seth agreed.

"I'm still not changing my mind," Andrew said. "I'll stick with what the chart says."

"Me, too," Alan added. "I'll go with the chart."

I often remind children that data don't prove or disprove a mathematical conjecture. However, this concept is difficult for children at this age, especially when their ideas about the mathematical theory are weak. Data can confirm or challenge thinking, but data alone are not sufficient to provide convincing evidence that an idea is true or not. A convincing argument is also necessary. Engaging children in discussions such as this one gives them beginning experiences with formulating mathematical proofs.

The discussion went on a bit longer, and then I stopped it and had the children write about their ideas. Through this assignment I would learn about each student's thinking. (See *Which Number Wins?* on the next page.)

# ASSESSMENT Which Number Wins?

This assessment draws from children's experience with the *High or Low* menu activity. (See page 152.) Students write about the probabilities of getting high sums (8–12) and low sums (2–6) when rolling a pair of dice. The assessment is appropriate after the students have collected a large sample of data for *High or Low* and have had opportunities to examine the data and discuss the results. A good time to have children write is just after a class discussion. Verbalization always helps children express themselves in writing. (See pages 158–161 in the menu activity *High or Low* for information about the kind of class discussion that might precede this assessment.)

"I'm interested in knowing more about what you think about rolling high sums or low sums with two dice," I said to the class after we looked at the data they had recorded for *High or Low*.

"Look at the chart," Andrew said. "You can see the high numbers are winning."

"That doesn't have to count," Charlie responded. "It's just chance."

"Wait, wait!" I said. "I don't want to discuss it more now. Instead, I want each of you to write about whether you think it's more likely for high sums to come up, for low sums to come up, or if high sums and low sums are equally likely."

With a little prodding, the children got to work. Their papers revealed a mixture of certainty, partial understanding, and confusion. There were 25 students present that day, and 12 of them wrote about why they thought high sums and low sums were equally likely. Lori, for example, wrote: *I think 2–6 and 8–12 are equally likely because they all have same cominations like 12 and 2 have only 1 combination and 5 and 9 have only 4 combinations. So it doesn't really matter which one you root for.*

*(left)* Lori explained why she thought high sums and low sums were equally likely.

*(right)* Tomo's reasoning was similar to Lori's.

---

Which Number Wins?–Andrew's Version

I think 2-6 and 8-12 are equally likely because they all have same cominations like 12 and 2 have only 1 combination and 5 and 9 have only 4 combinations. So it doesn't really matter which one you root for.

---

Which Number Wins? Andrew's version

I think 2-12 and 10-4 are equally likely because there is only 1 way to get a 2 and a 12 and there is 3 ways to get a 10 and a 4 and so on.

Abby referred to the chart we had made that listed the possible ways to get each sum. (See page 96.) She explained why she wasn't convinced by the class data showing that high sums came up more often. She wrote: *I think that it is equaly likely for the smaller and the bigger numbers to win because on the chart there is proofe for them to be equaly likely because both of them have the same chances to come up. I am sure that it is equaly likely fore them to come up. On the data paper it looks like the bigger number should win but I still think that it is equally likely for eather one to win because of the chart. The data could just be donig that because it is a chance game.*

Charlie also commented on the chart and the class data. He wrote: *there is no logicall explination that high numbers won by about 100 rolls except chance. When I look at the chart the high and low numbers both have the same amount of combinations which I think should result in <u>equall</u> chance.*

Charlie referred to the data on the class chart.

> Which number wins? Andrews version
> there is no logicall explination that
> high numbers won by about 100
> rolls except chance. When I
> look at the chart the high and
> low numbers both have the same
> amount of combinations which
> I think should result in <u>equal</u>
> chance.

Eight students wrote about why they thought high numbers would win. Andrew based his reasoning on the class data. His statistics differed slightly from Charlie's. He wrote: *I think the high numbers (8–12) are more likely because I added up all the games and higher numbers had 97 more rolls then lower numbers and had 364 more rolls than 7. All together we rolled 1252 times.*

*I think there is a reason that the higher numbers are winning but I don't know what it is.*

Andrew wrote about why he thought higher sums were more likely.

> Which Number Wins —
> Andrews version (me)
> I think the high numbers (8–12 are more likely becacose I added up all the games and higher numbers had 97 more rolls then lower numbers and had 364 more rolls then 7. All together we called 1252 times.
> I think there is a rcason. that the higher numbers, are winning but I don't know what it is.

Doug didn't have a reason for thinking that higher sums were more likely and felt he needed more data. He wrote: *I think that the hier numbers would win but I can not explane why. I am going to have to play this game a lot more to find out if the hier numbers or the lower numbers is better.*

Two students made a case for the low sums to win. Janos wrote: *I think the low numbers are more likely because I always roll (1) one more than six and 7 is still probably going to win.*

Three students wrote that they weren't sure. Lee Ann, for example, wrote: *I thought that 2–6 had the same chance of winning as 8–12 because if you look at the chart. But I also think the lower numbers have a better chance to win because all of the lower numbers have a one in it and all the higher numbers have a 6 in it. I think that you have a better chance to get a one than a 6.*

Janos thought lower sums were more likely.

> Wich Number wins
> Andrews version:
> I think the low numbers are more likely because  I alwaxs roll (1) one more than six.
> and 7 is still probably going to win.

# MENU ACTIVITY

## Overview

## Spinner Sums

*Spinner Sums* gives children the opportunity to think about what happens when they spin two spinners and add the numbers that the spinners land on. Using the spinners from two whole class lessons (see pages 24 and 67), children try three versions of the experiment, post their data on a class chart, and later compare the results. See "A Mathematical Note" on page 175 for an explanation of the probabilities of the sums for each version.

---

247

## Spinner Sums   I or P

**You need: Two spinners—version #1, #2, or #3**
**Spinner Sums recording sheet**

#1     #2     #3

1. At the top of the recording sheet, write your name and the Spinner Sums version number you chose. In the two circles, draw the two spinners.

2. Predict what sum will win.

3. Spin both spinners and add the two numbers that come up. Write the addition sentence in the correct column on the recording sheet.

4. Repeat until one column on the recording sheet is filled in. Make a tally mark on the class chart to indicate which sum won.

5. Write about which sum you predicted would fill the column first and what happened.

**Before the lesson**

Gather these materials:
- ■ Spinners from the whole class lessons *The 1-2-3 Spinner Experiment, Part 1* and *Part 2*
- ■ Spinner Sums recording sheet (See Blackline Masters section, page 248.)
- ■ One sheet of chart paper, entitled "Spinner Sums"
- ■ Blackline master of menu activity, page 247

**Getting started**

■ Set up the chart paper as shown to use as a class chart:

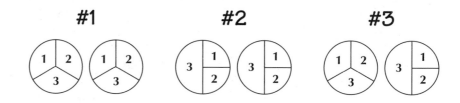

■ Using spinners from the whole class lessons *The 1-2-3 Spinner Experiment, Part 1* and *Part 2*, post three pairs as shown:

**#1**       **#2**       **#3**

■ Ask the students what sums can come up if they spin two spinners and add the numbers. Write the numerals 2 through 6 on the board and have the children tell the different ways the spinners can produce each sum. Record the combinations:

| 2 | 3 | 4 | 5 | 6 |
|---|---|---|---|---|
| 1+1 | 2+1 | 2+2 | 2+3 | 3+3 |
|  | 1+2 | 3+1 | 3+2 |  |
|  |  | 1+3 |  |  |

■ Explain to the students that in this activity they will choose one pair of spinners and draw them on the Spinner Sums recording sheet. Then they will spin the spinners, add the numbers they land on, and record the combination. They stop recording when one column is full.

■ Ask students what sum they think is most likely to win. Discuss.

■ Demonstrate the procedure with one pair of spinners. Be sure to show the students how to record the version of the experiment they are doing (#1, #2, or #3) and to draw the spinner faces.

■ Post the class chart and tell the students to make tally marks to indicate which sums won. Demonstrate.

■ Tell students that after they do *Spinner Sums,* they are to write about what sum they predicted would win and what happened.

■ After students have reported on the class chart, lead a discussion about what they notice from the data.

## FROM THE CLASSROOM

To introduce this activity, I used the two different spinners that the children had made for the two earlier whole class lessons. I taped spinners to the board to show the three different combinations of pairs.

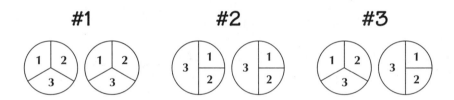

"I've paired the spinners in different ways," I said to the class, "and I have a new activity for you to do with them. In this activity, you choose a pair of spinners, spin both of them, and add the numbers that come up."

"Like with the dice?" Erin asked.

"Yes," I replied, "but there are fewer numbers to add, so there aren't as many sums possible."

"The most you can get is 6," Andrew said, quick to analyze the situation.

"And 2 is the smallest," Charlie added. "You have to get two 1s to get a 2."

I wrote a *2* on the left side of the board and underneath wrote *1 + 1.* I wrote a *6* farther to the right on the board and said to the class, "What would you have to spin to get a sum of 6?" Several children answered "3 and 3" in unison.

"Are the numbers between 2 and 6 also possible sums?" I asked. I wrote *3, 4,* and *5* on the board.

2      3      4      5      6

1+1                    3+3

I turned to the class. About half of the children had their hands raised. I called on Lori.

"If you spin 2 on both of them, you get 4," she said. I wrote *2 + 2* underneath the *4.* I called on Eric.

He said, "2 and 1 makes 3, or you can do 1 and 2. There are two ways."

I recorded *2 + 1* and *1 + 2* underneath the *3.* Because I wasn't sure all of the children understood why the two ways were different, I explained.

"Look at this pair of spinners," I said, pointing to the pair with one of each type. "You could spin a 2 on the equally likely spinner and a 1 on the other, or a 1 on the equally likely spinner and a 2 on the other. So there are two different ways to spin a sum of 3." I looked around the room and noticed some children nodding and some just listening. I returned to the chart I was constructing on the board.

"What else could I write?" I asked. Hands shot up again. I called on Kristin.

"You can get a 5 two ways, just like 3," she said. "You do 2 and 3 or 3 and 2." I wrote these two combinations under the *5.* I had now recorded the following:

| 2 | 3 | 4 | 5 | 6 |
|-----|-----|-----|-----|-----|
| 1+1 | 2+1 | 2+2 | 2+3 | 3+3 |
| | 1+2 | | 3+2 | |

"Have we listed all the possible ways to spin the spinners?" I asked. Some children nodded and others were quiet.

Then Doug raised his hand.

"You can get a 3 and a 1, so that makes two more," he said.

Several other children concurred, as I added these two combinations to the board.

"Oh, yeah," Seth said.

"Ooooh, I forgot that one," Lee Ann added.

"Good work," Charlie congratulated him.

| 2 | 3 | 4 | 5 | 6 |
|-----|-----|-----|-----|-----|
| 1+1 | 2+1 | 2+2 | 2+3 | 3+3 |
| | 1+2 | 3+1 | 3+2 | |
| | | 1+3 | | |

"Are there any other combinations?" I asked. The children scanned the list and agreed that I had written them all.

"It seems finished," Lisa said, "because it has a point, just like we had when we did it with the dice." She was referring to the chart I had constructed earlier showing the possible combinations for the sums from rolling two dice. (See page 96.)

"But what do spinners have to do with dice?" I asked. There was silence, so I asked the children to talk among themselves about the similarities between probability experiments with dice and those with spinners. After a few minutes, I called the class back to attention.

"What do you think?" I asked.

**NOTE** Making connections between activities is important for helping children learn to think mathematically. Asking children to consider how two activities relate is a way to help them think about connections among the mathematical ideas they're studying.

Abby answered first. "We thought they're kind of the same," she said, "because they both give you numbers. You just spin on one and roll on the other."

Charlie had something to add. "They're not exactly the same because there are less numbers on the spinner," he said, "but you could have more numbers on a spinner, like 1 to 6, the same as the dice."

"I don't think they're the same," Amanda said. "The dice are all the same, but the spinners are different even though they have the same numbers. Look, that one has a big space for 3 and the other kind doesn't."

"But they still both give you numbers and you add them," Seth countered.

"Lisa thinks the chart I wrote on the board is like the chart I posted about the dice," I said. "How are they alike?" I waited for several children to raise their hands and called on Emelia.

"The 7 was in the middle on the dice chart, and it had the most possibilities," she said. "And the 4 is in the middle of the spinner chart, and it has the most, too."

Seth had a different observation. "There's only one way to get a 2 on both charts."

"And only two ways to get a 3," Ajani added.

"And the 4s match, too," Abby added. "There's three ways to get them on both charts."

"But then it's different," Andrew said. "Look, on the dice chart there are four ways to get a 5. But with the spinners, there are only two ways."

"Why do you think that's so?" I asked. The children were quiet.

"What combinations are on the dice chart for 5 that aren't on the spinner chart?" I asked, to give a hint. After a moment, several hands were raised. I called on Tom.

"4 plus 1 and 1 plus 4," he reported.

"Oh, I get it," Charlie said. "You can't get those with the spinners because there aren't any 4s. They only go up to 3s." I heard murmurs of agreement.

"So the spinners and dice are alike in some ways and different in others," I said. "The charts have the same shape, with the number in the middle having more possible ways. But they are also different because there are more numbers on the dice and, therefore, more possible sums."

I then showed the children the recording sheet they would use for the *Spinner Sums* activity. "In this activity," I said, "you choose a pair of spinners, write down what pair you selected, and draw the spinner faces in the circles. Then you do the experiment the way you did with the dice, spinning both spinners and recording each combination in the correct column. Stop when one column is full, and make a tally mark in the correct place on the class chart to record the sum that won." I posted the chart I had prepared. (See page 166.)

"Any questions?" I asked. There were none. The children were familiar with collecting data in this way, so the directions were easy for them to understand.

"Before you start, I have a question that I'd like you to consider," I then said. "What sum do you think is most likely to win?" I purposely didn't specify one of the spinner versions, but was interested in what the students thought in general. Several had comments.

"It will be like the dice," Emelia said. "The 4 should win."

"That's what I was going to say," Doug said.

"Me, too," several others added.

"But it doesn't make sense to me that you'll get the same results from different spinners," I said.

"That's what I was thinking," Abby said. "I think that the ones with the big space for 3 would make 6 win." The others were impressed with Abby's observation and most agreed.

"What about the pair with two different spinners?" I asked, pointing to version 3.

"It's got to be different, too," Andrew said. "Maybe 5 will win with them." Others thought that was a good idea.

"We'll talk more about this later," I said, "after you've had time to try the experiments and report data for each of the three versions."

I reviewed the written directions. Then I did the activity for the first version to model for the children how to record combinations and make a tally mark to report the results in the correct space on the class chart.

### Observing the Children

As I circulated, children reported results to me. Amanda said, "Look, mine worked perfectly." She showed me her results for the first version.

Amanda felt that her results were "pretty perfect."

Spinner Sums #1

| | | | | |
|---|---|---|---|---|
| | | 3+1 | | |
| | | 1+3 | | |
| | | 2+2 | | |
| | | 3+1 | | |
| | | 1+3 | | |
| | | 3+1 | | |
| | 2+1 | 1+3 | | |
| | 1+2 | 2+2 | 2+3 | |
| | 2+1 | 3+1 | 3+2 | |
| | 1+2 | 2+2 | 2+3 | |
| | 2+1 | 1+3 | 3+2 | 3+3 |
| | 1+2 | 3+1 | 2+3 | 3+3 |
| | 2+1 | 1+3 | 3+2 | 3+3 |
| 1+1 | 1+2 | 3+1 | 2+3 | 3+3 |
| **2** | **3** | **4** | **5** | **6** |

"What do you mean by perfectly?" I asked.

"Well, 4 won," she said, "just like on the chart."

"But the chart also shows that 2 and 6 can come up the same number of ways," I said. "But you got 6 more times."

"But it's pretty perfect," she said, getting up to record on the class chart.

Erin brought three recording sheets to me. "This is crazy," she said.

"What's crazy?" I asked.

"I used spinners with the big space for 3, and 4 won three times," Erin said. "Look!"

### Spinner Sums # 2

| 2 | 3 | 4 | 5 | 6 |
|---|---|---|---|---|
| | | 1+2 | | |
| | | 1+3 | | |
| | | 1+3 | | |
| | | 3+1 | | |
| | | 1+3 | | |
| | | 1+3 | | |
| | | 3+1 | | |
| | | 1+3 | 2+3 | |
| | | 3+1 | 2+3 | 3+3 |
| | | 1+3 | 3+2 | 3+3 |
| | 2+1 | 1+3 | 3+2 | 3+3 |
| | 2+1 | 3+1 | 3+2 | 3+3 |
| | 2+1 | 1+3 | 3+2 | 3+3 |
| 1+1 | 2+1 | 1+3 | 3+2 | 3+3 |

Erin was surprised that 4 won three times.

### Spinner Sums # 2

| 2 | 3 | 4 | 5 | 6 |
|---|---|---|---|---|
| | | 1+3 | | |
| | | 1+3 | | |
| | | 1+3 | | |
| | | 1+3 | | |
| | | 1+3 | | 3+3 |
| | | 1+3 | | 3+3 |
| | | 1+3 | 3+2 | 3+3 |
| | | 1+3 | 3+2 | 3+3 |
| | | 1+3 | 3+2 | 3+3 |
| | | 1+3 | 3+2 | 3+3 |
| 1+1 | 1+2 | 1+3 | 2+3 | 3+3 |
| 1+1 | 1+2 | 1+3 | 2+3 | 3+3 |
| 1+1 | 1+2 | 1+3 | 2+3 | 3+3 |

### Spinner Sums # 2

| 2 | 3 | 4 | 5 | 6 |
|---|---|---|---|---|
| | | 1+3 | | |
| | | 1+3 | | |
| | | 1+3 | | |
| | | 1+3 | | |
| | | 1+3 | | |
| | | 1+3 | | |
| | | 1+3 | | |
| | | 1+3 | | |
| | | 1+3 | 2+3 | |
| | | 1+3 | 2+3 | |
| | | 1+3 | 3+2 | |
| 1+1 | 1+2 | 1+3 | 3+2 | 3+3 |
| 1+1 | 1+2 | 1+3 | 2+3 | 3+3 |

"What did you think would happen?" I asked.

"I thought 6 should win, like Abby said," Erin answered. "But it didn't. Maybe it's just chance, but it's goofy." She went over to show her results to Abby.

Charlie and Alan came up to me. Charlie looked perplexed, but Alan was laughing. "What's up?" I asked.

"He's upset," Alan said, nodding his head at Charlie. "He was sure that 5 would win, but it didn't even come out close." Charlie showed me his paper. He had done version 3, which had one of each spinner; 4 had won, and 5 had come up only once.

Charlie had predicted that 5 would win, and he was perplexed by the results.

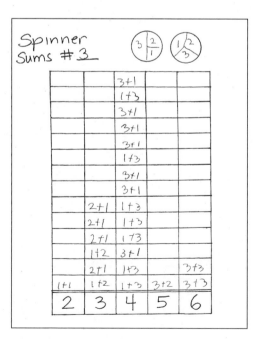

### Spinner Sums # 3

| 2 | 3 | 4 | 5 | 6 |
|---|---|---|---|---|
| | | 3+1 | | |
| | | 1+3 | | |
| | | 3+1 | | |
| | | 3+1 | | |
| | | 3+1 | | |
| | | 1+3 | | |
| | | 3+1 | | |
| | | 3+1 | | |
| | 2+1 | 1+3 | | |
| | 2+1 | 1+3 | | |
| | 2+1 | 1+3 | | |
| | 1+2 | 3+1 | | |
| | 2+1 | 1+3 | | 3+3 |
| 1+1 | 1+2 | 1+3 | 3+2 | 3+3 |

"It just doesn't make sense," Charlie said, shaking his head.

Alan laughed again. "I told him," he said, "but he won't listen."

"What did you tell him?" I asked.

"Well," Alan said, "the way I figure is that this is almost like the first experiment with the equal 1, 2, 3, except the 3 has just a little bigger space. But that's not enough to matter. It's just a little bit bigger, and the 1 and 2 have the same space."

"They can't be the same," Charlie argued. "You can't have two different things be the same. It doesn't make sense."

"Remember," I said, "when you look at data, you need to look at a large sample to have confidence about the results. How about reporting what happened, and then we'll see how the class data shape up." That was okay for Charlie, and he went to record on the class chart.

On her way back to her desk after recording on the class chart, Erin commented to me. "It worked for Abby. On hers, the 6 won. I don't get it."

Abby reported the results that Erin was hoping to get.

> Spinner Sums #2
>
> Today I played Spinner Sums it came out pretty much how I expected. I predicted that number six would win because we used the spinners that three got half of the space and two and three only got a quarter of the spinner. I expected that the spinners would both get three a lot and that would make six and six would win and just as I expected six won. It ended up like this, two got three, three got four, four got eight, five got twelve and six got fourteen.

**A Class Discussion**

After the children had had time to try the activity and write about their experiences, I began class one day by calling their attention to the data they had recorded. I asked what they noticed.

"The 2s and 3s hardly won at all," Emelia said. "That was just what I suspected."

"The 2s did worst of all," Elliot added.

"I think it's weird how the 4s did the best on all of them," Seth said.

"Maybe we didn't do it enough times," Lee Ann said.

"The 6 didn't do so good," Alan said.

"It won for me," Abby said.

"But not a lot for the whole class," Kristin said.

"It did okay on version 2," Ajani pointed out.

"When I did it, I got a lot of double 1s and 3s," Amanda said. "It was very surprising."

"That's not about the chart," Lori chided her.

"I know," Amanda responded breezily, "but it happened."

Amanda wrote about what happened and what surprised her.

> Spinner Sums #3
>
> Today I played spinner sums #3 I had the 1 spinner and the secont spinner. I spun a 2 and a 3 on my first roll. I got a lot of 2 and 3. at first I thoght 5 would win but 5 didn't 4 did. I was suprised that dobl ones came up 4 times and doble 3's came up 5 times. In order of hou came up to the top first gose like this 4, 3, 5, 6, 2. I was soprised that 4 had 3 dabl 2's, not just all 3 and 5s. I conted all the doubles and all the dods of 4, 2 and 6 are 12 dobls, I relley thoght that 5 would win and even be a hed of 3.

"I think it's all chance," Lisa said. "You really can't tell what will happen. It depends how you spin. If you spin hard, you can get different things than if you spin easy."

"You're supposed to spin hard," Charlie said. "You're not supposed to try and get some number. It's not fair then."

"But it's still chance," Lisa insisted.

"I have an idea," Andrew said. "I think that the middle number still has power, even though the spinners look different."

"But 6 got more on experiment 2 with the bigger space for 3," Abby answered, "so the spinners do count."

I didn't pursue the mathematics further. It's not trivial to analyze the probabilities of the spinners in these experiments, and assigning probabilities to the possible sums is beyond the reach of most third or fourth graders. However, the experience of doing the experiments and then discussing the data provided another opportunity for the students to think about probability.

Andrew described his results from *Spinner Sums* version 1.

> Probability – Spinner Sums 1
>
> Today I played Spinner Seems 1. When I was playing 4 was ahead of all the other numbers But 3 was catching up. But all the time I thought 4 was going to win. Then at the end both 3 and 4 were at the second to the last square. I thought 4 still was going to win. I thought this becacese 4 had more possibilitys then 3. I spun a 2 and a 2.

Writing is laborious for Tom, but he took the time to reproduce his results.

> Spinner sums #1
> Today I played spinner sums #1 here are the relsets. can you belefe that 1+1 and 2+2 and 2+1 got a 10+! 4 won 5 was a little bit behided.

Tomo's paper shows that he was thinking about the probabilities, but points to his partial understanding.

> ### Spinner Sums #1
>
> Today I played Spinner Sums #1. #4 won. I think It's most likely that #4 wins because there is 3 ways too get a 4, 2 ways too get 3 and 5, and 1 way too get 2 and 6. I think 3 and 5 has the equal chance of winning. And I think 2 and 6 has the equal chance of winning. I think the lower numbers has a little bit more of chance of winning then the higher numbers. But I don't know why.

## A Mathematical Note

There are several ways to analyze the probabilities. I do not recommend presenting any of these methods to the students; they will learn more about them when they study probability in higher grades. However, understanding the probabilities helps prepare teachers to respond to children's questions and ideas. Knowing the mathematics is essential for posing questions to help students think about a situation, confirming students' ideas, or suggesting a challenge to push students' thinking further.

For version 1, the chart I recorded on the board (see page 168) displays the nine different possibilities and makes it possible to calculate the probabilities. Because the sums of 2 and 6 can each come up only one way, they each have a 1/9 probability. The sums of 3 and 5 each have a 2/9 probability, and there's a 3/9 chance for 4 to come up. This information can be written as follows:

$$P(2) = {}^1/_9$$
$$P(3) = {}^2/_9$$
$$P(4) = {}^3/_9$$
$$P(5) = {}^2/_9$$
$$P(6) = {}^1/_9$$

Adding 1/9, 2/9, 3/9, 2/9, and 1/9 produces 1, a check that we have accounted for all of the possibilities. Another way to represent the data is on a small addition chart that shows the sums for the numbers 1, 2, and 3. Of the nine sums, 2 and 6 appear once each, 3 and 5 twice each, and 4 three times.

| + | 1 | 2 | 3 |
|---|---|---|---|
| 1 | 2 | 3 | 4 |
| 2 | 3 | 4 | 5 |
| 3 | 4 | 5 | 6 |

Analyzing version 2 requires making an adjustment to account for the fact that, on each spinner, 3 has twice as much of a chance to come up as does 1 or 2. The way that has helped me to think about this is to imagine each spinner divided into four parts, so that each section is equally likely, as are the three sections for version 1. Writing a 3 in two sections makes it possible to construct an addition table that accurately represents the situation.

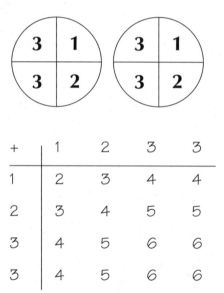

| + | 1 | 2 | 3 | 3 |
|---|---|---|---|---|
| 1 | 2 | 3 | 4 | 4 |
| 2 | 3 | 4 | 5 | 5 |
| 3 | 4 | 5 | 6 | 6 |
| 3 | 4 | 5 | 6 | 6 |

The addition table shows the 16 equally likely ways for the sums to come up. By counting, you can arrive at how many of the 16 ways are possible for each sum:

P(2) = 1/16
P(3) = 2/16
P(4) = 5/16
P(5) = 4/16
P(6) = 4/16

This indicates that the sum of 4 has just a slightly better chance than does the sum of 5 or 6. A large sample size is typically needed to reflect these probabilities.

To analyze version 3, I suggest making an addition table as follows and then figuring the probabilities to show that once again the sum of 4 is most likely with a probability of 4/12.

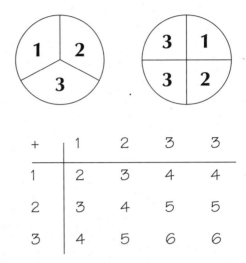

| + | 1 | 2 | 3 | 3 |
|---|---|---|---|---|
| 1 | 2 | 3 | 4 | 4 |
| 2 | 3 | 4 | 5 | 5 |
| 3 | 4 | 5 | 6 | 6 |

Caution: If you haven't had the chance to study much about probability, I encourage you to continue to think about the situation and try to make sense of it for yourself. Your own pursuit of understanding is invaluable for being better able to help your students.

## MENU ACTIVITY

### Overview

## Match or No Match

Children know a variety of ways to decide in a fair manner who gets to choose an activity or go first in a game: tossing a coin, playing Scissors-Paper-Rock, and others. This activity builds on students' experiences with methods of choosing fairly and introduces three ways to choose involving tiles in bags. The children draw tiles, collect data, and analyze which versions are fair games.

See "A Mathematical Note" on page 194 for an explanation of the probabilities for each version.

---

249

## Match or No Match

You need: One paper bag
Color Tiles

1. Choose one version below and put the correct number of tiles of each color inside the bag.

   Version 1: 2 blue and 1 red
   Version 2: 2 blue and 2 red
   Version 3: 3 blue and 1 red

2. Draw two tiles and record a tally mark to show whether you got a "match" or "no match."
   Do 20 samples this way.

3. Decide whether you think this version is fair. You may want to collect more data first before deciding. Write about your thinking.

4. Repeat steps 1, 2, and 3 for the other versions.

5. Record on the class chart the total number of times your draws came up "match" or "no match" for each version.

**Before the lesson**

Gather these materials:
■ Color Tiles
■ Paper bags, about 10
■ One sheet of chart paper, entitled horizontally "Match or No Match"
■ Blackline master of menu activity, page 249

**Getting started**

■ Set up the chart as shown below for students to use to record data:

### Match or No Match

**Version 1**

| Match | |
|---|---|
| No Match | |

**Version 2**

| Match | |
|---|---|
| No Match | |

**Version 3**

| Match | |
|---|---|
| No Match | |

■ Begin a class discussion by asking children about the methods they use to decide how someone goes first in a game or what activity they'll work on next. After everyone who wants to has shared an idea, point out that many methods of choosing give both people the same chance of winning. Mathematicians call this type of method a *fair game* because both people have an equal chance of winning.

■ Tell the students that this new activity will give them an opportunity to decide whether three different methods of choosing are fair. As the students watch, put two blue tiles and one red tile in a paper bag. Explain that you will draw out two tiles. If they are both the same color ("match"), one person wins; if they are two different colors ("no match"), the other person wins. Choose a student to be your partner, and have him or her choose to be the "match" person or the "no match" person.

■ Tell your partner to draw out two tiles. Write *Match* and *No Match* on the board, one underneath the other. Record a tally mark next to *Match* or *No Match* to show what your partner drew.

| Match | |
|---|---|
| No Match | I |

■ Have your partner return the tiles to the bag. Shake the bag and repeat for three or four draws. At this point, students may want to talk about whether match or no match is better. Encourage them to discuss their ideas.

■ Introduce the activity. Explain that there are three versions of *Match or No Match* and write them on the board:

| | | |
|---|---|---|
| Version 1 | 2 Blue | 1 Red |
| Version 2 | 2 Blue | 2 Red |
| Version 3 | 3 Blue | 1 Red |

■ Tell the students that they are to work in pairs, choose a version, put the appropriate tiles in a bag, take 20 samples, and record the data. They record on a class chart the total number of times they got match and no match, and then write about whether they think the game is fair. They should do the experiment with all three versions.

■ Using the data that students have written on the class chart, initiate a class discussion about the experiments. Start with version 1 and ask students what they think about the data and about the fairness of the version. As issues come up, have students talk together in groups, then share their ideas with the entire class. As much as possible, record students' ideas on the board using words and/or pictures.

■ After fully discussing version 1, move on to version 2, then version 3.

## FROM THE CLASSROOM

**NOTE** Relating an activity to children's own experience not only helps to motivate their interest but also builds on their prior knowledge. New learning builds on existing understanding and making the connection to prior experience supports children as they explore new ideas.

Before introducing the menu activity to the class, I talked with the children about what they do when they need to decide among themselves who gets to choose an activity or go first in a game. I think it's valuable to try as often as possible to relate a new activity to children's real-life experiences.

The students reported several different ways of choosing. The most common way was playing Ro-Sham-Bo (their name for Scissors-Paper-Rock). Other methods included tossing a coin and calling heads or tails; one person putting an object in one hand and the other person guessing which hand it's in; and both people showing one or two fingers, with one person winning if there's a match and the other if not.

"Although you have different ways of choosing," I said, "it seems to me that they're all the same in one way. They each give both people the same chance of winning." The children nodded.

I continued, "Mathematicians would call them *fair games* because both people have an equal chance. In this new activity, I'm going to explain three versions of another game you can use for choosing, and you'll investigate whether or not each version is fair."

As the students watched, I put two blue tiles and one red tile into a paper lunch bag. "Suppose you and your partner decide to choose who goes first in an activity by reaching into the bag and drawing out two tiles," I said. "One of you is the match player and the other is the no-match player. When you look at the two tiles you remove, the match player wins if they're the same color, and the no-match player wins if they're different colors."

To demonstrate for the class, I asked Lori to join me at the front of the room. "Would you rather be the match player or the no-match player?" I asked her.

Some children shouted out advice. I quieted them and asked Lori if she had a choice. "Match," she said. Some of the children cheered; others groaned. As much as I try to keep the emphasis on the mathematical investigations and not have the class resemble a TV quiz show, at times I find it hard to contain the children's enthusiasm. I didn't comment about their behavior at this time.

I asked Lori to reach into the bag and remove two tiles. She did so and held them up for the class to see—a red and a blue. Again, there were cheers and groans. I ignored them.

"I'm going to record what happens so we can begin to collect some data," I said. I wrote *Match* and *No Match* on the board, one underneath the other, and made a tally mark next to *No Match.*

I asked Lori to replace the tiles. Then I shook the bag, explaining to the class that I did this to make sure I had mixed up the tiles. Then Lori drew again. Again, she got one of each color. I made another tally mark. We repeated this a third time with the same result.

| Match | |
|---|---|
| No Match | III |

The cheers and groans had increased, and I felt it was time to address the problem.

"The idea of this activity isn't about rooting for who wins," I said sternly, "but about collecting data to use for a mathematical investigation." The children became quiet.

Lee Ann raised her hand. "I think that no match is better," she said.

"But you can't tell yet," Charlie responded. "They only did it three times."

"I still think it's better," Lee Ann said.

"How many times do you think you'd have to draw tiles to have information that you would trust?" I asked Charlie.

"A lot," he answered.

"How many is a lot?" I asked.

"Maybe a thousand," Tom said.

"I think a hundred is enough," Andrew interjected.

"That's too many to do," Amanda complained. "It would take us too long."

"Not if we each did some," Lisa said.

Doug's hand shot up. He had been thinking about what we had done so far and was bursting with an idea. "No match has to win!" he said, excitedly. "The only way you get a match is if you take out those two blues. But it's a better chance to get a no match because you can get a red with either one of the blues."

Doug's idea made sense to me, but only a few of the children had followed his reasoning. "Can you explain that again?" I said. "I want to make sure everyone is listening." I had Doug wait until the class was quiet.

**NOTE** Although a larger sample size provides more reliable information, empirical data are not sufficient to prove a theory. However, the data are useful for corroborating or challenging an idea.

"Look," he said. "You have to pick out the two blue ones to get a match. But you can get the other way two different ways." The children looked confused.

"Look," he said, getting exasperated. "You can pick a blue tile and the red one or the other blue tile and the red one. There are two ways because there are two blue tiles." Doug was emphatic and impassioned, but most of the children seemed disinterested or confused. I didn't push it any further.

"You'll have a chance to test Doug's theory when you collect data with your partner," I told the class, focusing on the activity. "The game that Lori and I were playing is one of three versions that you'll investigate in this activity," I said. "Each version is played the same way, by drawing two tiles out of the bag and seeing if they match or not. The versions are different, however, because of what you put into the bag."

I listed the three versions on the board:

| | | |
|---|---|---|
| <u>Version 1</u> | 2 Blue | 1 Red |
| <u>Version 2</u> | 2 Blue | 2 Red |
| <u>Version 3</u> | 3 Blue | 1 Red |

Conversations broke out at several tables. "Version 2 has to be fair." "I still think version 1 is okay." "Maybe they all work." "No, number 3 can't." The children were definitely interested.

I then presented the directions. I showed the children an enlarged copy of the menu task and explained how they were to work in pairs to choose a version, put the tiles in the bag, and take 20 samples. Then they were to write about whether they thought the game was fair, or take more samples first and then write.

I pointed to the class chart on which they were to record their data. "Count up your tally marks and write the numbers for match and no match on the class chart," I said.

"Do we do all three versions?" Amanda asked.

"Yes," I answered. "But do one version at a time. You don't have to do them all in the same day."

### Observing the Children

By this time in the menu, the children were used to collecting data. I knew that the mechanics of the task would be easy and accessible to all of the children. All could follow the directions and benefit from the experience of generating, recording, and thinking about data. However, I also knew that only some of the students would be interested in and able to think in depth about the mathematical theory.

As I circulated, I noticed that some children drew conclusions from the data they collected, without thinking about the mathematical theory. Mercedes, for example, wrote the following: *I think for version 1 it's fair because we got 10 matches and 10 No matches. We thought it was really werd but thats just what happens. I think for version 2 it's fair also because there were 2 blues and 2 reds and match and no match got 10 and I new that it would be fair because 2 blues and 2 reds sound like they would be*

**NOTE** Not all children get the same experience or benefit from a task. It's important to structure activities so that the students with limited experience and ability can get involved, while students with more experience and aptitude can be mathematically challenged.

*fair. I think for version 3 match is going to win because there are one red and 3 blues and on our sheet it's 9 to 11 and no match wins. My data doesn't make any scents.* When I asked Mercedes why her data didn't make sense, she replied, "That's not what I thought was going to win."

Version 1 Match / No Match
No Match | IIII IIII IIII
Match | IIII IIII IIII
R 1 B 2

Version 2
No Match | IIII IIII
Match | IIII IIII
B 2    B 2

Version 3
B 3 R 1
No Match | IIII IIII I
Match | IIII IIII

Is IT Fair? No Match / Match
I think for version 1 it's fair because we got 10 matches and 10 NO matches. We thought it was really werd but that's just what happens.
I think for version 2 it's fair also because there were 2 blues and 2 reds and match and no match got 10 and I new that it would be fair because 2 blues and 2 reds sound like they would be fair.
I think for version 3 match is going to win because there are one red and 3 blues and on our sheet it's 9 to 11 and no match wins. My data doesn't mak any <u>scents</u>.

Mercedes based her results on her data.

Some children's papers revealed that they wavered between thinking about the mathematics of the situation and relying on the data. Abby, for example, wrote: *V1. No Match definently has an advantage in version one. My data showed that I got five in match and fifteen in no match. I think that it is not fair in version one because in version one you can get two ways of getting no match and one way of getting match. V2. In version two it is fair because there is two ways of getting a no match and two ways of getting the match and that makes it equally likely. V3. In version three I am not quite sure but I think it is fair because in my data it showed that each of them came up ten times.*

Some children reported the data, but relied on their own thinking about the situations. Emelia, for example, wrote: *I think <u>Verson 1</u> no match wins. There are two ways to get no match. The red with one blue or the red*

*with the other. Match only has one way. the two blues. My data was 10,10. It doesn't make sens.*

*I think verson 2 is fair because with the same amount of each color they have the same chance.*

*I think verson 3 is fair. The red can go with any of the three blues to make no match. There are three ways for the blues to go together to make match.*

Verson #1 Match/No Match
NM ||||||||||| 10
M ||||||||||| 10
R1 B2

Verson #2
NM |||||||||| 10
M |||||||||| 10
B2 R2

Verson #3
B3 R1
NM |||||| 9
M |||||| 11

---

Is It Fair?
Match\No Match
I think Verson 1 nomatch wins There are two ways to get no match. The red with one blue or the red with the other. Match only has one way. the two blues. My data was 10,10. It dosn't make sens.
I think verson 2 is fair because with the same amount of each color they have the same chance.

I think verson 3 is fair. The red can go with any of the three blues to make no match. There are three ways for the blues to go together to make match.

Emelia clearly explained why version 3 was a fair game.

In his paper, Andrew at first based all of his opinions on the data he and Timmy had collected. However, then he reconsidered the situations and changed his mind on two of them. At the end of his paper, he wrote: *First I was describing what was more likely by looking at the data but then I realized that I shouldn't have done that and I went back and changed everything. It would have been a catastrofie if I had kept going like that because their are exceptions. Note None of the data matched my theroys.*

When I talked to Andrew about what he had written, he told me, "The data is just chance and you have to think about it. Chance doesn't always count." When I read Andrew's explanation for version 1, however, I realized that his thinking was erroneous. He had written: *I think for Version 1 it is fair. Because you know that you will pick at least one blue every time and so it is 50% you will pick another blue and 50% that you will pick the red.*

While reading the other students' papers, I noticed that Charlie and Tomo thought about version 1 the same way Andrew did. I planned to discuss this activity in a few days, and I began to think about how to present information that would allow the three boys to rethink their ideas. I wondered especially about Andrew. It's hard for him to back down from an idea, even when he seems to realize it's not correct.

### A Class Discussion

After the students had explored all three versions of the game, I initiated a class discussion. I began with version 1, and an argument broke out immediately. Andrew was adamant that the game was fair. He reiterated what he had written.

"You know that you'll get a blue every time," he said, "so you have the same chance that it will match with a red or a blue." Hands shot up to contradict him. I called on Abby.

"What you say makes sense," Abby began diplomatically, "but it can't be right. No match definitely has an advantage because the only way you get a match is to pick both of the blue tiles. But there are two ways to get no match. You just pick the red one and then one of the two blue ones."

Tomo supported Andrew's position. As he does in most instances, he tried to quantify the situation. "It's 100 percent chance that you will get a blue," Tomo began. "Then there's a red and a blue left, and it's 50 percent chance that you will pick either. So it has to be fair."

Lee Ann countered. "You have a blue every time, but it doesn't have to be the same one that matches with the red," she said. "There are two blues, so there are two ways." About seven or eight students voiced their support for Lee Ann. Tomo looked a bit uneasy, but Andrew emphatically shook his head no.

"I can prove I'm right," Andrew said. "Suppose I pick out a blue tile, okay? Then there's a red and a blue left, and it can match with either one."

"Let me see if I can record Andrew's idea," I interjected. To illustrate what was in the bag, I drew three squares on the board and labeled them $B_1$, $B_2$, and $R$.

"Just so we can keep the two blue tiles separate," I explained, "I've labeled one $B_1$ and the other $B_2$. Okay, Andrew, explain your idea and I'll record it."

"Suppose you pick out a blue tile," he began.

"Which one?" I asked.

"It doesn't matter," he said.

I drew a square and labeled it $B_1$. Andrew nodded.

"Now you could get either $B_2$ or R," he said. I drew the two possibilities.

"But what about if you took out $B_2$?" Doug challenged.

"It's the same thing," Andrew said. "You get either $B_2$ and $B_1$ or $B_2$ and R. It's still 50-50." I added the two new possibilities to the board.

The class became quiet. Andrew looked smug. All of a sudden, Seth's hand shot up.

"I got it," he said. "Look, you've got two the same up there. $B_1$ and $B_2$ is the same as $B_2$ and $B_1$. It's like doubles with the dice." Others agreed. But Andrew had a counterargument.

"No, they're not the same," he said, "because I picked a different one first each time."

"I think Andrew's right," Charlie said.

"He can't be," Doug said. "Something's wrong."

I intervened again. "Let me draw the ideas that Seth, Abby, and Lee Ann have suggested to make sure I understand their thinking," I said. I think it's valuable for children see how I use illustrations to clarify thinking because it shows another way to make sense of a situation. "They say that you can get a match only if you draw out the two blues, but you can get a no match in two ways, by drawing out the red one with either of the two blues." I drew the three possibilities on the board.

They concurred.

"What's wrong with their thinking?" I asked, looking at Andrew and Charlie. "This idea seems to point to no match coming up two times and match coming up just once."

"I'm just confused," Charlie said.

"It kind of makes sense," Andrew conceded, "but my way makes sense, too. I'll stick with my way."

I did what I often do in these sorts of situations. "Talk at your tables about these two ideas," I said, "and in a moment we'll talk some more as a class."

Most of the students got involved in the table discussions. There was a good deal of pointing at and trying to make sense of what I had drawn on the board. Some students, however, remained quiet, either listening

**NOTE** Having students talk among themselves in small groups gives more of them the chance to voice their opinions. While some students are reticent to share in a whole class setting, they usually are more willing to offer their opinions or ask questions with others at their tables.

intently or seeming to drift off. As I walked around, I encouraged children to listen to their classmates. I realized that not all of the children had followed other children's thinking. It's hard to understand other people's reasoning, but I wanted to encourage them at least to listen and stay involved.

I then called the children back to attention. "What ideas do you have now?" I asked. Several students began to call out their ideas.

"Wait, wait," I said. "One at a time. Raise your hand if you have an idea to share." I called on Doug. He looked as if he would burst if I didn't recognize him.

"I figured it out," he said. "Look, Andrew, you forgot that you might not pick out a blue tile first."

"What do you mean?" Andrew said.

"You could pick the red one first," Doug said.

"Yeah," Andrew said. "What would that do?"

"Then you have to draw two more ways," Doug directed, "red with blue 1 and red with blue 2." I added Doug's suggestion to the other two Andrew had suggested. Now there were six possibilities.

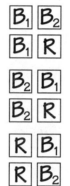

"So, what does that prove?" Andrew demanded. Doug didn't know what to say next. Neither did any of the other students.

"Let's count matches and no matches," I said, and I went down the list of six possibilities, asking the children to decide whether each one was a match or a no match. I labeled them *M* and *NM*.

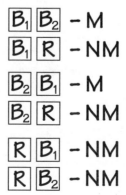

"That does it!" Lee Ann exclaimed.

"That proves it, Andrew," Eric said, gently. "There's two matches and four no matches, so it's double chance for no match." Eric is a sensitive boy and thought that Andrew might have trouble backing down from his position. Andrew is usually right, and it's difficult for him when he's wrong.

"I have to think about this," Andrew said, still not willing to concede—publicly, at least.

I was astounded at the passion in the discussion. I decided not to talk about the other two versions at this time. I worried about those students who weren't following the reasoning and felt that they needed a change of pace.

"I think this is a good time to get to work on the menu," I said. "We'll talk more about versions 2 and 3 on another day. If you want to think about them on your own, you might try making diagrams as I did for version 1. Remember that if you try any of the versions again, add your data to the class chart."

**A Few Days Later**

When I resumed the discussion a few days later, I asked the students to look at the class chart of data.

### Match or No Match

**Version 1**

| Match | 8 | 6 | 5 | 10 | 6 | 10 | 5 | 7 | 9 | 11 | 10 | 18 | 20 | 8 | 16 |
|---|---|---|---|---|---|---|---|---|---|---|---|---|---|---|---|
| No Match | 12 | 14 | 15 | 10 | 14 | 10 | 15 | 13 | 11 | 9 | 10 | 20 | 16 | 12 | 20 |

**Version 2**

| Match | 8 | 10 | 7 | 10 | 9 | 9 | 8 | 8 | 6 | 12 | 10 | 14 | 13 | 6 | 14 |
|---|---|---|---|---|---|---|---|---|---|---|---|---|---|---|---|
| No Match | 12 | 10 | 13 | 10 | 11 | 11 | 12 | 12 | 14 | 21 | 10 | 20 | 20 | 17 | 30 |

**Version 3**

| Match | 6 | 10 | 12 | 7 | 9 | 10 | 8 | 10 | 8 | 10 | 12 | 10 | 20 | 20 | 12 | 20 |
|---|---|---|---|---|---|---|---|---|---|---|---|---|---|---|---|---|
| No Match | 14 | 15 | 8 | 13 | 11 | 10 | 12 | 10 | 12 | 10 | 8 | 10 | 18 | 11 | 8 | 18 |

"What do you notice?" I said. I called on Janos. He doesn't often volunteer in class, and I was pleased to see his hand raised.

He said, "If you take the c out of match, it says math." Some students giggled; others looked impressed. I've learned that Janos usually sees situations in unique ways.

"Yes, that's true," I confirmed. I called on Amanda.

"Everything happened on each of them," she said.

"What do you mean?" I asked.

Amanda replied, "See, sometimes match won, sometimes no match won, and sometimes it was a tie."

"It looks like no match won more in version 1," Abby added.

"Can we add them up?" Tomo said.

"Yes," I answered, "I think that would give us useful information. And I think you should use calculators. Work with a partner so one of you can read the numbers while the other adds, and then switch jobs to check." I had partners count off by 3s and told the ones to do the sums for version 1, the twos to do version 2, and the threes to do version 3.

There were differences when the students reported their results, and it took us a bit of time to agree on the sums. Finally, I wrote the totals on the board.

<u>Version 1</u>
| | |
|---|---|
| Match | 149 |
| No Match | 201 |

<u>Version 2</u>
| | |
|---|---|
| Match | 144 |
| No Match | 223 |

<u>Version 3</u>
| | |
|---|---|
| Match | 184 |
| No Match | 188 |

"What do you think about this information?" I asked.

"Version 1 and version 2 came out about the same," Lisa noticed.

"Both numbers are almost the same for version 3," Alan said. "That can't be right."

"Yeah, that's crazy," Elliot agreed.

"It's 1,099 all together," Tomo said, having calculated the sum of the data I had posted.

"And what does the sum tell you?" I asked. Tomo remained silent.

"I know," Charlie said. "It tells how many times we took tiles out of the bags."

"I still don't get the third one," Elliot said.

"Oooh, I have an idea," Emelia said. As she often does during discussions, she had started working on her own. "I found that there are seven possibilities for what could happen with version 3." The others looked at her with interest. So did I, because I knew that there were only six possibilities. I wondered what she was thinking.

"Wait a minute, Emelia, until I draw a picture of the tiles for version 3," I said. "Then we'll listen to your explanation." I drew four squares on the board and labeled them $B_1$, $B_2$, $B_3$, and $R$. Emelia listed combinations of these four squares taken two at a time, and I wrote down what she said. She had a duplicate, which Seth noticed. Emelia agreed, and I erased one of them, leaving six possibilities:

$B_1, B_2$

$B_1, B_3$

$B_1, B_3$

$B_1, R$

$B_2, R$

$B_3, R$

"What does this list show?" I asked. "Talk at your tables about this."

After a moment, I called the class to attention. Hands were raised from five of the seven tables. I called on Abby.

"It's fair," she declared. "There's three for match and three for no match." There were nods of agreement.

"That seems so crazy," Elliot said. His intuition was challenged by this data.

"What are you thinking?" I asked him.

"It just doesn't seem right," he said, "because there are so many more blues."

"But the data shows it," Lee Ann said to him.

"Remember that the data can't give us enough proof," I said. "Data are just a piece of evidence."

Lori's paper shows a mixture of understanding and misunderstanding that is typical when students are learning something new.

---

**Is It Fair? (Match/No Match)**

Version 1 is unfair because no match has more posibilities than match. Here's how I figured that out [B₁] [B₂] [R] [B₂] [B₁] (that a match) [B₁] [R₁] (no match) [B₂] R₁ (no match) No match has 2 posibilites and match has 1 posibilite. Or if I picked the red one first it's otmaticly a no match. If I picked a blue first it's 50% that it will be a no match and 50% that match will get the tally mark. Also Match is 1/2 and no match is 2/3.

Version 2 is unfair because no match has 4 ways which are [B₁][R], [B₁][R], [B₁][R], [B₂] [R], and match has 2 ways. Another way it's not fair is because match has 2/6 and no match has 4/6. it's totally not fair to me. If I picked a red first it's 50% that match will get it and 50% that no match will get it same with blue.

Version 3 is fair because no match 3 posibillites and same for match. [B₁][R], [B₂][R], [B₃][R], those are all no matchs here are matchs [B₁][B₂], [B₁][B₃],

[B₂] [B₃], thats all for match. Match has 3/6 and no match has 3/6. If red gets picked first it's 100% sure that no match will be picked. Match had 194 wins in version 3 and no match had 188 wins in version 3. Altogether version 1,2 and 3 it is 1099.

"Yeah," Tom said, "because I don't think the numbers make sense for version 2. It should be fair, too."

"To investigate it, I'd have to make a list the way we did for version 3," I said. "If you're interested, work with a partner, figure out all the possibilities, and come and tell me if you think the game is fair or unfair. If you're not interested, then choose another activity from the menu."

I was aware of the disparity in students' understanding and interest, and I didn't think it was essential for all the children to analyze the problem completely.

I asked the children later to write again about the game. Their papers gave me more insight into their thinking. I sorted their papers into three piles: those who were able to analyze the problem completely and correctly (11 children), those whose reasoning was partially correct (10 children), and those who didn't seem to have much understanding at all (4 children). I noticed which children were able to list the combinations and use the information to decide about the fairness of the game; who relied primarily on the data, either on the class chart or from his or her own individual experiments; and who wasn't able to think at all about the mathematics of the situation.

Andrew referred to his previous reasoning to explain how he had changed his mind.

The Class Date
Is it fair

Version 1 is unfair because there are 2 combonations for No Match and 1 combonation for Match:

Before I saw this I thought that it was fair because I knew you had to pick a blue then it would be a 50% chance to get a red and 50% chance to get the other blue. That is why I thought it was fair.

Version 2 is unfair because there are 4 combonations for No Match and 2 combonations for Match.

Before I thought it was fair because it was 25% chance you will pick Blue 1, 25% chance to pick Blue 2, 25% chance to pick Red 1, and 25% chance to pick Red 2.

Version 3 is fair because No Match has 3 combonations and Match has 3 combonations.

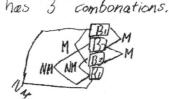

Abby's explanation was clear and succinct.

> **Is It Fair**
> **(Match/No Match)**
>
> **V1** Version one is unfair because there are three possibilitys and in version one and match only has one possibility to win but no match has two possibilitys to win.
>
> **V2** Version two is also unfair because in version two there are six possibilitys to win and no match has four of those possibilitys. That only leaves two possibilitys for match to win.
>
> **V3** Version three is fair because there are six ways to win, and match got three possibilitys and so did no match so it is fair. Our data was very close to what it should be and when I played it match won ten times and no match came up ten times so acourding to my data it should be fair.

Elliot wrote only about version 1 and did not deal at all with the probability aspect of the game.

> **IS It Fair? Match/ No Match**
> I think virsion 1 is not fair because there is a bigger to get red or blue. I think they are the same because when I shake the bag, the red goes on top of the two blues. So I think when I stick my hand in the bag I pick up the red and the blue. But hear is a trick. You can have a red tiel with tow bumpu on it. And then I touch the red and I don't pick it up and so I pick up the two blues. And when I want to get No macht I pick up the the red and the blue,

Version # 1          Is It Fair
                     Match/No Match

2B 1R

M/ |||| ||          7
NM/ |||| ||||| |||   13

V #2    2B 2R

M/ |||| |||          8
NM/ ||||| |||| |||   12

3B 1R

V # 3
M/ |||| |||          8
NM/ |||| |||| ||     12

Charlie's writing described his confusion and
uncertainty.

Is It Fair?
Match \ No Match

I think for Version 1 it is unfair.
David told me no match is more likely
to win and I agree. But what I
dont understand is this. When you
take one blue tile you have an
equal chance of getting red or
blue. But why does red come
out more?
   Version 2 is fair I think
because because there is a
equal chance of picking up a red
or blue and Match is easyer to
get now.

Version 3 I'm not sure about
it isn't as unfair a #1 but it's
also fair like 2. I think this only
from my data but on the chart
it looks unfair so I'm confused.
Also I got the exact same
answer for 3 that I got for 2.
This intrests me alot and want to
find out more about it. I thought
#1 was going to come out even
I guess I was wrong.

## A Mathematical Note

As described in the "From the Classroom" vignette, in class we analyzed the probabilities for each version of *Match or No Match*. I listed all the equally likely outcomes from drawing two tiles and then counted how many of them produced a match and how many produced no match. This reasoning seemed convincing to many of the children.

It's not necessary, however, to list all the equally likely outcomes to analyze the game. Andrew, for example, had a different way of thinking about version 1 of the game (two blue tiles and one red tile). First, he thought about drawing two tiles as drawing one first and then the other. This is actually the same as drawing two tiles together (a brief moment doesn't matter), as long as you don't replace the first tile before drawing the second one. So far so good for Andrew.

Andrew then reasoned that when you draw two tiles, one of them has to be blue. This is true. Still so far so good. But then he reasoned that since there was one red and one blue tile remaining, there was a 50 percent chance to get a match and a 50 percent chance to get no match. There's a flaw in his reasoning. While it's true that there's a 50-50 chance of drawing a red or a blue when there is one of each, it doesn't account for all of what might happen in the game. Andrew didn't think about the possibility of drawing a red tile first, which then results in a 100 percent chance of getting no match since, as Andrew pointed out, one of the two tiles drawn next has to be blue.

A mathematician would represent Andrew's line of reasoning numerically by saying something like this: Let's figure the probabilities of getting a match and a no match. There is a 2/3 chance of drawing a blue tile first. According to the probabilities, half of the time the next draw will be a blue tile and half the time it will be a red tile. So the 2/3 chance gets split—1/3 for match and 1/3 for no match. But, there still is another way to get no match—by drawing a red tile first. There's only a 1/3 chance of drawing a red tile first, since red is one out of three tiles, but drawing a red tile guarantees you no match. So altogether, there's a 2/3 chance of getting no match—1/3 from drawing a red tile first (and either blue next) and 1/3 from drawing a blue tile first (and a red one next). And there's only a 1/3 chance of drawing two blues for a match, as described above.

For me, it's easier to analyze the problem by listing the three possible combinations of drawing two tiles:

$B_1$, $B_2$—match
$B_1$, R—no match
$B_2$, R—no match

This illustrates the 2/3, 1/3 probabilities I explained above. Or, if Andrew were listing all the ways to draw first one and then another tile, he'd list six possibilities:

$B_1$, $B_2$—match
$B_2$, $B_1$—match
$B_1$, R—no match
R, $B_1$—no match
$B_2$, R—no match
R, $B_2$—no match

This still comes down to a 2/3 probability of getting no match and a 1/3 probability of getting a match. Pick your argument, but remember it's always good to be able to defend a mathematical position in more than one way. Try analyzing version 2 all these ways to prove that it's more likely to get no match than match.

Version 3, with three blue tiles and one red tile, can be irritating for some people. It feels counterintuitive for the game to be fair, even if you list the possible pairs of tiles you can draw and see that half of them produce a match and half produce no match:

$B_1$, $B_2$—match
$B_1$, $B_3$—match
$B_1$, $B_3$—match
$B_1$, R—no match
$B_2$, R—no match
$B_3$, R—no match

Some people doubt that the six ways are really equally likely. Some people think that all those blues make a match much more possible. I believe the six possibilities above represent all the ways and that the game is fair, but you'll have to think about it for yourself if you're not yet convinced.

It's also possible to analyze this version by approaching it the way Andrew tried thinking about version 1. See if this helps.

For version 3, there's a 3/4 chance that you'll pick a blue if you pick out one tile. Then, with three tiles left, two blues and one red, 2/3 of the time you should pick another of the blue tiles and 1/3 of the time you should pick the red one. So, of the 3/4 chance, 2/3 of the time you'll get a match, and 2/3 of 3/4 is 2/4. The other 1/3 of the time produces no match, and 1/3 of 3/4 is 1/4. So far, there's a 2/4 (or 1/2) chance of getting a match and a 1/4 chance of getting no match. But there's also another way to get no match—pick the red tile first. And there's a 1/4 chance of that happening, since red is one of four tiles. So, it's a 2/4 (or 1/2) chance to get a match, and a 1/4 + 1/4 or 2/4 (or 1/2) chance to get no match.

What seems clear and obvious to some people is often muddy to others. You need to think about this and convince yourself. Then it helps to explain your thinking to someone else, orally or in writing. Finally, it's good to defend your position before a skeptic. Put yourself through those paces, and your thinking will be strengthened.

# ASSESSMENT Probability Vocabulary

The children in my class did this assessment as a homework assignment. Not only does the assessment provide information about the students' abilities to use probability terminology in the context of spinners, but it also informs parents about their children's math learning.

Duplicate for each child a list of the probability words. (See Blackline Masters section, page 250.) The sheet shows the spinner face from the *Spinner Statements* assessment (see page 136) and gives directions for the assignment. Review the directions with the students.

---

250

## Probability Vocabulary

Use each of the following probability words in a sentence. You may refer to Spinner A in your sentences, draw your own spinner (Spinner B), or refer to any other probability activity we have done.

Underline the probability words as you use them. You may use the words more than once. Also, you may add additional words if you wish.

1. probability
2. likely
3. unlikely
4. chance
5. equally likely
6. certain
7. uncertain
8. probable
9. possible
10. impossible
11. possibility
12. sample
13. data

Spinner A

Spinner B

From *Math By All Means: Probability, Grades 3–4* ©1995 Math Solutions Publications

## FROM THE CLASSROOM

The children were familiar with writing sentences for spelling words, so the directions for this assignment were clear to them.

Eight of the students used Spinner A to write their probability sentences, twelve drew their own spinners, and four referred to different activities. Also, seven students used additional words, including *convince, persuade, percentage, could be, might.*

In general, the children's sentences showed their ability to use probability terminology appropriately and relate the vocabulary to situations with which they were familiar.

Most of Mercedes's sentences referred to real-life situations.

1. There's a probability of rain today.
2. It's likely that "a" is going to win on the spinner.
3. It's unlikely that I'm going shopping today.
4. There's a chance that it's going to be sunny tomorrow.
5. It's equally likely that I won't have candy or chips for lunch.
6. It's certain that I have 4 best friends.
7. It's uncertain if my puppy's outside.
8. It's probable that I'm very good at reading.
9. Possible has a different meaning from probable.
10. I think it's impossible to build a mansion.
11. Possibility means fact or condition of being possible.
12. I had a sample of cake at Safeway today.
13. At school we have a lot of data that we use for probability.

Lori referred to Spinner A, Pig, *Tiles in Three Bags*, and *Match or No Match*. Her paper revealed her erroneous idea that rolling a 1 and rolling double 1s are equally likely.

Spinner A.

A is likely to win. B can't possible win. D and C are probable to be spun. It is certain B can't win. It is chance to which letter will come up. It is unlikely that C will come up a lot. B is impossible to come up because it is like in the middle of the spinner.

Pig

Pig is a probability game because you never know what number will come up on the dice. It is uncertain to which number will come up. It is equally likely that one 1 will come up just as much as double 1s will. There is a small possibility that you will get 2 6's.

Tiles In Three Bags

You need a big sample for Tiles in three bags.

Is It Fair?

You need a lot of data.

Doug used Spinner A for his sentences.

A Spinner

1. It is probable, not certain but probable that "a" will win.

2. It is impossible that "b" will win because if the letter is not tuching the outside at all it cant be spun on. Therefore b cant possibly win.

3. "d" and "c" have the same chance of winning because they both equally grab the same amount of outside space.

4. "e" has twenty five percent chance of winning.

5. "d" and "e" both have a twelve and a half percent chance of winning.

6. "a" has fifty percent chance of winning.

7. It is likely "e" will win.

8. This spiner is probability.

9. It is unlikely for "D" to win.

10. It is certain that "b" wont win.

11. It is uncertain that "e" will win.

12. There is a possibility that "c" will win.

13. This spinner gives you a lot of data.

14. It is possible that "D" will win. Is it fair IN the game of Is it fair you have to take a lot of samples.

Spinner a

It is 50% chance that A is likely to win. E is 25% chance to win. B is unlikely to win. C and D has the same chance of winning. If C and D combinds togather it will be the same chance of winning as E. B has 0% chance of winning. It is probable that A could loose. It is equally likely

that C and D has the same chance of winning. It is certain that B is going too loose. This spinner is all probability. It is impossible that B could win. It is possible that D could win. There is a possibility that C could win. I need a sample for Pig, Where is the Is It Fair data? It is uncertain that B could win.

Most of Tomo's sentences were about Spinner A. He referred to Pig and *Match or No Match* to write about *sample* and *data*.

Seth drew Spinner B and referred to it in some of his sentences.

1. Probability is likely to be in many board games.

2. On spinner B, D is very unlikely to win.

3. I'm really convinced that with dice, it's all chance.

4. With spinner A C is possible to win, but it's not probable.

5. On spinner B, E and C are pretty much equally likely

6. When you have a sample, it's very foolish to think that's enough data.

7. On spinner A, B has no possibilitys to get spun. In other words B is impossible to spin.

8. Certain is like a 100 d° chance, 100% is the highest percentage.

9. With spinner A and B, it's uncertain which letter will win

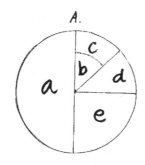

A.

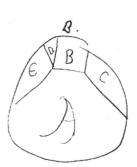

B.

# ASSESSMENT Favorite Activity/ What I Learned

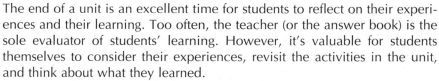

The end of a unit is an excellent time for students to reflect on their experiences and their learning. Too often, the teacher (or the answer book) is the sole evaluator of students' learning. However, it's valuable for students themselves to consider their experiences, revisit the activities in the unit, and think about what they learned.

This assessment gives the teacher information about how individual students responded to the unit, providing useful feedback for reviewing the unit in light of preparing to teach it another time. Use this lesson as a final assessment or as a lead-in to students' preparing portfolios.

In my experience, young children are eager to communicate about what they like. Their own experiences are concrete for them, they typically have preferences, and they usually can provide reasons for their preferences. Reflecting on what they have learned, however, is more abstract and, therefore, more difficult for some children. They have to synthesize their experiences from the unit and think more generally about their learning.

Children can write about their favorite activities and about what they learned at the same time. Writing about their favorite activities helps them think about the specific activities in the unit and prepares them to consider what they learned. To introduce this assessment, remind the children of the whole class lessons and review the activities on the menu. Then present the two-part assignment by writing the following questions on the board:

1. What was your favorite activity in the Probability unit? Why?
2. What did you learn from the Probability unit?

As with all writing assignments, encourage the children to provide you with detailed explanations. Tell them that their writing will help you understand what they think and also give you feedback that will be useful for preparing to teach the unit at a later time. It's always helpful for students to understand the purpose of an assignment.

## FROM THE CLASSROOM

"Who can remember the activities we did when we first started learning about probability?" I asked the class in preparation for the assessment. I waited a bit, as children thought. After about half of the children had raised their hands, I called on Lori.

"I remember we used the 1-2-3 spinners and did two experiments," she said.

"And we cut them apart in all those strips," Lisa added, remembering how we processed the data.

"More 3s came up on the first spinner," Ajani added.

"Then we used the spinners for *Spinner Sums,*" Emelia said.

"Yes," I responded, "we did use the spinners a good deal in the unit." I wrote *Spinner Experiments* on the board.

"Does anyone remember anything else we did at the beginning of the unit, before the menu?" I asked.

"We did that thing with the tiles in the bag," Charlie said.

"Oh, yeah," Abby added, "I remember we had to guess what colors were in there."

"We did that on the menu, too," Lee Ann said.

"Several of the menu activities came from the first lessons," I said, writing *Tiles in the Bag* underneath *Spinner Experiments.*

"There was one game you all liked that I taught at the beginning," I said.

"Pig!" several children called out. I wrote *Pig* on the board as well.

"That was my favorite," Amanda said. "It was the best."

"Me, too," Erin said.

"I liked *High or Low* best," Seth said. "It was fun to argue."

"I'm interested in learning about what each of you liked best in the unit," I said, "and in a moment you'll have a chance to write about your favorite activity. Before you decide, however, think about the lessons we did and about all of the activities on the menu." I referred the children to the list of menu activities and read aloud the names of the activities.

"Also, I'm interested in knowing what you learned from this unit," I said. I wrote on the board:

1. What was your favorite activity in the Probability unit? Why?
2. What did you learn from the Probability unit?

"Please include as much information as you can. Your papers will not only help me know more about what you liked and learned from the unit but will also help me think about what I might change when I teach this unit again to other students."

Emelia thought about the elements of strategy and chance as they related to Pig.

My favorite activity is Pig, because it is so mathematicle. I think that it is two thirds stratagy and one third chance.

I learned that things don't always come out in a way that makes sence. The more you study data the more sence your theory will make. Also if you get into an argument over wether high numbers are better or it's chance it won't get you anywhere.

Seth's favorite was *High or Low*.

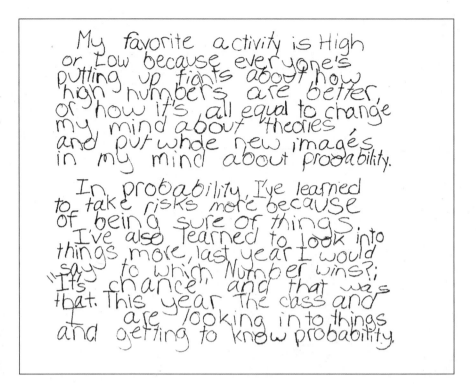

My favorite activity is High or Low because everyone's putting up fights about how high numbers are better, or how it's all equal to change my mind about theories, and put whde new images in my mind about probability.

In probability, I've learned to take risks more because of being sure of things. I've also learned to look into things more, last year I would say "to which Number wins?; It's chance" and that was that. This year the class and I are looking into things and getting to know probability.

The children's papers revealed that *The Game of Pig* was 12 children's favorite activity. Eight chose *High or Low*, four identified *Match or No Match*, and two chose *Spinner Experiments*.

Lisa was one of the children who liked Pig best. She wrote: *My favorite activity in probability was Pig because of how you had to choose a strategy and really learn when to use it. What I mean is, let's just say you like combination. You have to know when to use it. The same thing with all the other strategys too. You also have to learn how high of a number you should go to.*

*One of the things I learned about probability was that it is in life. For example probability is used when the weatherman reports the news of the weather. When he says what he thinks he is predicting. That is one kind of probability.*

*Another kind is equally likely. That is used in life too. Like it is equally likely that the empire state building will come alive as it is a fish will be born without gills.*

Charlie's favorite was *High or Low*. He wrote: *My favorite activity in Probability was High or Low. I like it the most because it has been a fun argument about if high numbers or low numbers are the same. I also like how much fun it was discovering things for this game and it was fun arguing about it. We also discovered a lot of stuff and I think we went pretty far in terms of thinking.*

*In Probability I learned that anything can happen and I also learned more about reasoning. I learned that anything can happen in probability because we would be talking about something and then somebody would say something that would open up a whole new idea or door*

*that we would think about until maybe somebody might come up with another idea.*

Abby had more general thoughts about her favorite activity and what she learned. She wrote: *My favorite activity in probability is when we sit in our seats and argue about somthing. I like it when we do this because you get to say what you think about a game or a spinner in front of the class. Doing this is sort of fun because it is like two different teams thinking different things about a problem and hoever gets the problem right is sort of thought of when you think of that problem. I learned all sorts of things about probability during the year. I mostly learned that we use probability all the time and we never stop useing it until we die.*

Doug compared learning probability to learning the times tables.

① My favorite activity was when Ms.burns would give us big problems they were not problems like twunty devided by seven take away nine and so on and so on. They were problems like which is the best strategy in pig is it unlikley to roll a one and stuff like that. The reason I liked that was because well times tables and stuff you can memorize those but the other kind of math is math were you really have to think. (You dont have to know your timestables to know math).

② Some of the things I learned about probability were well for one I leared you dont need to know your timestables to know math, because I am not that good at my timestables but I am good at other kinds of math. But I am not saying timestables Isint math I am just saying its not everthing I mean I still practice my timestables. I also learned that math can really help you anywere at the stone Or at a toy store or any kind of sture it can even help you when your paying your taxes

# STUDENT PORTFOLIOS

Student portfolios are being used more and more across the country as one way to assess students' learning. In general, a student portfolio is a collection of work that represents a sample of what a child has done. There are different ways to define and structure portfolios and many decisions to make when implementing them in a classroom: What instructional preparation is needed for portfolios? How often should students assemble portfolios? How should students decide what work to include? What should teachers contribute to individual portfolios? What should be done with portfolios once they're completed?

In this section, I describe how I implemented portfolios so that students could communicate about their learning in this probability unit. I begin with a vignette of what happened in my classroom when I introduced student portfolios. I follow the vignette with reflections on my experience.

Trying something new in the classroom always helps me examine my teaching goals and consider new ways to enhance the learning experience for students. My experience with student portfolios has convinced me that having students put together portfolios is valuable. Examining and reflecting on their work helped the students connect more deeply with their own learning processes. Students' reactions to their learning gave me additional insights into individual children's interests and accomplishments. Also, sending portfolios home provided another way to communicate with parents about their child's learning.

## FROM THE CLASSROOM

"Does anyone know what a portfolio is?" I asked the children. They had no previous experience with portfolios in school, and I was interested in what they knew, if anything, about portfolios in other contexts. Lee Ann's and Amanda's hands shot up. I waited a bit, but no one else responded. I called on Lee Ann first.

"My dad is a caterer," she said, "and he makes fancy cakes. He takes pictures of his best ones and puts them in a portfolio, so customers can see what they want."

Amanda then described what she knew. "My sister is a photographer," she said, "and she keeps her favorite photographs in her portfolio."

"Who thinks they could explain what a portfolio is?" I then asked. Only a few students raised their hands.

"Talk about this at your tables," I said. Having children talk among themselves reduces the risk individual children have to take when they're not quite sure of their responses. I let the children talk for a few moments and then called the class to attention.

"What do you think?" I asked. I called on Tom.

"We think it's kind of a scrapbook. My sister has a scrapbook, and she pastes in things she wants to save," he said, reporting for his table and adding something from his own experience.

"It's for some things, not all things," Charlie added.

"Any other ideas?" I asked.

"It's kind of a special book," Kristin said.

"What do you mean?" I asked.

"It's not the kind you read, but to look through," she explained. "It has things to see. It's not a story."

"There are different purposes for portfolios," I said, "and your ideas describe some of them. I want to talk with you about portfolios you'll make to show some of the math work you did during the probability unit." The children were interested.

"In a little while, I'll give each of you the folder of all the writing you've done during the unit. Also, I'll hand out your menu folders," I said. I had filed their daily writing in individual folders. The students kept their work on classroom activities in their menu folders.

"When did we start?" Doug asked.

"It was at the beginning of January," I responded, "just after we returned from vacation." It was now early March.

"That's a long time," Ajani said.

"Two months," Tomo added.

"Oooh, it'll be weird to read all that," Abby said, with a grin on her face that hinted at her eagerness and curiosity. She had been a prolific writer during the unit.

"Before I give you your folders," I said, "I want to talk with you about what you should look for as you read your work. You won't include everything in your portfolio but will make choices based on some categories. I have some ideas for categories, but I'll start with what we learned from Lee Ann and Amanda. Lee Ann said that her father put pictures of his best

cakes into his portfolio; Amanda said her sister chose her favorite photos."
I turned to the board and wrote:

1. Best work
2. Favorite paper

"I have a few other ideas for categories," I said, and then added to the list. I read each category aloud after I wrote it.

3. A paper that describes a mathematical discovery or theory
4. A paper that explains your thinking clearly
5. A paper about an idea you still wonder about or are unsure of

Emelia interrupted. "Could we put in a game we invented?" she asked. Emelia was proud of the game she had invented using Two-Color Counters and dice.

"Yeah," several others chorused who had also invented games.

"What about our favorite game?" Timmy asked. "I like the game that Andrew invented best. Could we put that in?"

"If you wrote about it, you might want to include it," I responded. I wrote on the board:

6. A paper about a game you invented
7. A paper about your favorite game

There were no other suggestions, so I continued my introduction. "What you'll do is read through all of your papers to find examples for your portfolio for at least three of these categories," I said. "Then I'll talk with you about how to organize the papers you chose, and we'll send the work home so your parents can see what you've done in math."

"How many can we pick?" Lisa wanted to know.

"At least three," I said, "and more if you want."

"What if we have two favorites?" Eric asked.

"Then you'll have to choose just one for that category," I responded. "You'll have to choose the favorite of your favorites."

I then gave the children more explicit information. I had a pad of small Post-it Notes for each table and explained to the children how to proceed. "When you read through your folder," I said, "each time you find a paper that you like, put a Post-it on it. Then look up at the board and read over the categories I listed, decide which category it fits best, and write the number of that category on the Post-it. When you've read all of your papers, look again at the ones you marked to make sure that you have at least three papers and only one for a category. When you've made your final selection, exchange your papers with someone else to see if that person agrees that your papers match the categories you chose."

This was a good deal of instruction, so I wrote the directions on the board:

1. Mark possible papers with Post-its.
2. Write the category number on each Post-it.
3. Look over your choices and make changes.
4. Exchange with a partner to see if the categories match the papers.

"What if we don't find three we like?" Ajani said.

"You might look again, get help from your partner, or I can help," I said.

"What if we can't find one for a number on the list?" Amanda asked. "I didn't invent a game."

"You don't have to find papers for all the categories," I said. "You should find papers for at least three of them, and you can choose more, but you don't have to have one for each."

There were no other questions, so I distributed the folders.

### Observing the Children

I was amazed at the intensity with which the children plunged into reading their work. This was the first time I had ever done this with a class, and I had no expectations. The room was completely silent, and children were engrossed in poring over their papers.

After about 15 minutes, Elliot came up to me. "I picked mine," he said. Elliot is usually interested in completing his assignments, but rarely gets involved in depth. He likes to be finished.

"Did you mark your papers with Post-its?" I asked. He nodded.

"Have you looked them over again to be sure your categories match?" I asked. Elliot shook his head no.

"Why don't you do that while you wait for your partner to finish his choices?" I suggested. "Also, you might look in your menu folder and see if you want to include anything in there."

"I already looked," Elliot said. "It's mostly junk." He returned to his desk, gave a cursory look at what he had marked, and whispered to Eric that he was ready. Eric, however, was completely engrossed in reading what he had written. Elliot sat back to wait.

Some children commented to me as I circulated through the room. "This is definitely weird," Abby said as I passed by her desk. "I can't believe how much I wrote."

"Yes, I noticed that you wrote a lot more than you did last year," I responded. Abby was in my second-grade class the year before.

"I made a lot of mistakes," Timmy said. He sat next to Abby.

"What do you mean?" I asked.

"It's hard to read some of it," he responded.

Doug also commented to me about his errors. "I spelled words wrong," he said, "but I used a lot of descriptive words, too."

"This is fun," Amanda said. "I forgot what I did that long ago."

I stopped by Corrine's desk. She had just learned to read earlier in the year, and writing was difficult for her. Also, she had difficulty with school in general, and her understanding of math concepts was weak. I had taught Corrine in second grade, and she struggled then as well.

"How is this for you?" I asked her.

"It's good," she said. "I wrote a lot."

"What did you notice that you wrote about?" I asked.

"I wrote a lot about the games I played," she answered. "Mostly I played with Carrie, but sometimes with Antonio."

"Did you find a favorite paper yet?" I asked.

"I have three," she said. "I have to pick one now." She turned back to her folder.

## A Class Discussion

After about 30 minutes, most of the children had chosen their papers and had read or were in the middle of reading their partner's papers. A few had finished and were quietly playing one of the games from the menu. I called the class to attention.

"How did you feel about reading your work?" I asked. Many hands shot up.

"It was amazing to see how much I wrote," Lori said. Others concurred.

"I felt proud for all I did," Ajani said. Others agreed with this as well.

"I didn't know I thought all that," Charlie said. "I mean, I knew I thought, but I didn't know I wrote it all down."

"I was very interested in my papers," Eric said.

"Yes, I noticed you were very engrossed in your reading," I said.

"He sure was," Elliot said. "I had to wait for him."

"What kept you interested?" I asked Eric. He's a thoughtful boy and, as usual, he responded with care.

"It was interesting to see what I wrote. I noticed that over time I began to write more," he said, "and tell exactly what I wanted. I wrote a lot about probability."

"I thought something like Eric," Lee Ann. "At first I couldn't really write very much about probability, but then my papers got different. I knew so much. But in one of my papers, I found something that I disagree with. It surprised me that I had said it."

"I changed my mind a couple of times," Seth said.

"Me, too," Erin added.

"I made a lot of mistakes," Timmy said, telling the class what he had told me earlier. "It was hard for Alan to read it, and some of the sentences didn't make sense to me either." Some of the children giggled; others commented that they had had the same problem. This was a rare moment that I welcomed, where children could see how writing clearly was essential for communication.

"What pleased you about your work?" I asked Timmy.

"I wrote much more than I thought I could," he answered quickly. Then he thought a bit. "I was surprised that I wrote all this. It's a lot."

"I have something else to say," Seth said. "I was really surprised when I read Doug's papers."

"What surprised you?" I asked.

"He just thinks so different than me," Seth said. "And he writes so different."

"Could you tell more about the differences?" I asked.

"His was more like stories," Seth responded. "Listen to this." He reached for Doug's papers and shuffled through them.

"This was about playing Pig with Elliot," Seth explained, and then began to read: *"Well today I played the game of pig. First my humble chalenger was Elliot the great. In my first roll my luck did not show and I got a zero. Elliot's luck was showing and he got 26. But my next roll was success. I got 41 points. The next roll Elliot got my old luck and got a 1."* Seth stopped reading. "See what I mean?" he asked.

"It sounds like a sportscaster," Alan remarked.

### Another Writing Assignment

As usual, the children who were volunteering their ideas were those who were comfortable with writing and who learned easily. I was curious about the children who were reluctant writers, but I didn't want to call on any to respond. Therefore, I asked the children to write about their reactions to reading their work.

To structure this writing assignment, I wrote on the board:

> Reading My Work
> 1. When I read my work, I felt _____.
> 2. I noticed that _____.
> 3. What surprised me was _____.
> 4. What pleased me was _____.

The children wrote with ease. I've found that whenever children have something to say, something that is real or important to them, they write more easily.

Janos's paper on reading his work showed his typically unique viewpoint.

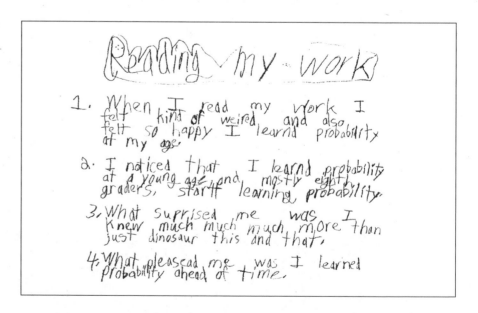

Amanda enjoyed her papers. She wrote: *1. When I read my work I felt good because I thght that was fun. It made me feel good to read from Jan. 3, 1994 to Mar. 3, 1994.*

*2. I noticed that there was a ton of pig riteing. Ther was at lest 8 or more pig riting. I think I relly like pig. lots of my pig ritings said I played whith Lee Ann.*

*3. What surprised me was I was riting so little in the bigening and tords the end there would more more and more riteing.*

*4. What pleased me was that I was riting more. When I started on Jan. 3, 1994 I thoght I was riting alot but now I think that was not so much. now I think I am ritting alot and that is trow. I feel that I am thinking more because I am riting more.*

Elliot evaluated his own progress.

Write

1. When I read my work I felt exsited because I was happy to read my old work.

2. I noticed that I have better ideas now then January. 3.

3. What suprised me was I think more now.

4. What pleased me was that I can understand more that I used to write.

From Ajani: *1. When I read my work it makes me proud for all that I wrote because I thought I couldn't do it.*

*2. I noticed that I got better and better after a few months.*

*3. What suprised me was is all I can think of insted of saying I can't do it.*

*4. What pleased me was that what I can really do instead of siting in front of the T.V.*

Doug was pleased with his use of descriptive words.

> **Reading my work**
>
> 1. When I read my work I felt good I felt good because I did all that work and all those deskriptive words and I also feel good because I made it thrue all of it and I did'nt give up.
>
> 2. I noticed that in the riting every day when I won or lost I discribd the game very good like when I beat Loren in my paper I said I crushed Loren like a peanut.
>
> 3. What supprized me was that in a few of my papers I was making mistakes and miss spelling words.
>
> 4. What pleased me was that I rote about it every day and every day I used deskriptive words.

Eric elaborated on the ideas he had expressed during the class discussion. He wrote: *1. When I read my work I felt good and intrested. I felt good because I was happy to know I had improved.*

*2. I noticed that over time I began to right more. I began to tell exatily what I whanted. I incoriged [encouraged] myself to not give up.*

*3. What surprised me was that so much mathimaticle and sientific stuf came out. Also what surprised me was how much thinking I had to do.*

*4. What pleased me was I was good with thinking about it. Also that I injoide probabiltiy and that I could do such a sufisticated tipe of writing.*

Reading my work

1. When I read my work I felt sort of silly because my first paper had so little writing and at the end I wrote so much and I felt really proud because I thought so much about math.

2. I noticed that I impoved a very very very lot from the beg irning to the end and I thought more.

3. What suprized me was how much I improved is writeing and explaning what I thought in math.

4. What pleased me was how much more I thought about math and how much more I was into probability and how I explaned what I was thinking from beggining to end

Abby's sense of accomplishment was evident in her paper.

Corrine wrote a good deal, but her difficulty with writing was evident. She wrote: *1. Win I was reading my work I was rilly icsidid* [excited] *to see all my riding sins we startid my favrot papers were shake and spill. probabiltiy and life. wich numdir wins.*

*2. I nodist that all of my riting omos* [almost] *is the same liek my games I have alot of shak and spill gams.*

*3. I was sprised with homous* [how much] *I rout for tow mounts* [months].

*4. I was pleased with all my riting over the past tow muns I have rley* [really] *inproved a lout.*

Seth expressed insights into the process of learning.

Reading My Work

1. When I read my work, I felt my class and were up there with the college students.

2. I noticed that I saw the proccess of learning, about writing, and math. I also noticed how fast I changed my mind.

3. What suprised me was when I looked at Doug's work, I saw that Doug thinks so different than I do.

4. What pleased me was when I saw all of my thoughts and ideas.

**The Next Day**

I began class the next day by telling the children how to organize their portfolios. I explained to them that they were to write about why they had chosen each paper and what they thought about it.

I had prepared a form on which they would write their reflections, and I showed it to the class. "Once you've chosen the work you'd like to include," I said, "use a form like this to list your choices." The form had spaces for the category, title, and date for each paper, and lines for a short paragraph. (See Blackline Masters section, page 251.)

"Your paragraph is important," I said. "It explains why you picked the paper. Remember, the goal is to help your family see what you did and to help them understand what you learned. Also, I'm interested in your thoughts about the papers you chose, so I can understand more about what you enjoyed and what was important to you."

"Do we have to write something for every paper we put in?" Tom asked.

"Yes," I responded. "It's important that you think about your choices and explain your reasons for including them. Also, there's room for three papers on this form, but I've made extra copies in case you decide to include more work."

I then gave them directions for assembling their work. "When you've made your choices and written about them," I said, "then you're ready to put together your portfolio. The top sheet will be a letter I've written to your parents. Next you'll put the form you filled in and then the work you chose. We'll staple it all together."

"What did you write?" Seth wanted to know.

"I told your parents a little bit about the portfolio and explained the categories," I said. "Also, I asked them to write back to me what they learned about your work and their reactions to receiving this kind of portfolio."

The children worked on their reflective writing with less enthusiasm than when they wrote the day before, but they plugged away at the assignment. When children finished, they chose activities from the menu. Most of the students assembled their portfolios in 20 to 30 minutes.

Almost all of the children included a piece of work for category 1: best work. Their reasons, however, differed. Doug, for example, wrote: *This paper was my best work because the whole paper I diskribed what I was doing. And at the same time I was using deskriptive words to describe it.*

Abby wrote: *I picked this paper to be in category one because I thought so deeply about this idea and I did a great job.* She had written about the *Roll Two Dice* activity.

Alan also wrote about *Roll Two Dice: I picked this paper because it's long and it is one of my best writings.*

Seth wrote about *Which Number Wins?: I picked this paper because I found out something, I explained my thinking, and I was determined to find that thing out.*

Seth explained that he chose work that gave specific explanations.

**Probability Portfolio**

Category # 1 Title _Which Number Wins?_     Andrew's Version   Date _Mar. 3, 1994_

I picked this paper because I found out something, I explained my thinking, and I was determined to find that thing out.

Category # 3 Title _Pig Strategys_     Date _Jan. 27, 1994_

I picked this paper because I thought it showed a good like saying about why I liked strategy number 2 for Pig.

Category # 4 Title _Probability_     Date _Feb. 9, 1994_

I picked this paper because it showed me exactly what went on that day.

---

Lori included five pieces of work in her portfolio.

**Probability Portfolio**

Category # 4 Title _Probability and Life_     Date _Mar. 1, 1994_

I choose this paper for #4 because I really used all of my thinking on this paper and I gave it a lot of thought to it.

Category # 1 Title _Shake and Spill Is It Fair_     Date _Feb. 2, 1994_

I chose this paper for category #1 because I really discribed what I did that day with probability. I also chose this paper because I really explained everything really good.

Category # 5 Title _Spinner Statements_     Date _Feb. 8, 1994_

I chose this for #5 because I think that's were it really fits in. I also chose this because I discribed how our group was having problems.

**Probability Portfolio**

Category # 1 Title _Pig_     Date _Mar. 3, 1994_

I chose this paper because it really discribed what was happening in the game. I also chose it because it had a little bit of humor.

Category # 3 Title _Shake and spill is it Fair?_     Date _Jan. 14, 1994_

I chose this because I think it really fits the category and I discribed things really well.

Category # ___ Title _____     Date _____

Ajani wrote: *I think this is my best work because I really told what I thought and what were my pig strategeys.*

Eric wrote about *Spinner Puzzles*: *I picked this paper because I was making mathimatical discoverys and connecting my mind with math.*

Erin was one of several children who commented that they thought their papers were funny. She wrote: *Why I chose this paper as my best paper is that I described what I did in a funny way and still explained what happened during the game.*

Amanda was pleased with her selections.

**Probability Portfolio**

Category # 4 Title Equally Likely          Date Jan.11,94
I chose this for category 2 beca-
se I really exsplaned what equally
likely ment. It showed my thinking

Category # 1 Title Pig Strategy          Date Jan.27,94
I piked this writing for category
1 becase I wrote alot and I thght
abowt it and it tells what I
wold do and tells what I did.
And I was really happy with my
work.

Category # 2 Title Math writing          Date Feb.15,94
I liked how I exsplaned how
math can help you And the
techers think I think my thinking
in it was grat.

**Responses from Parents**

I received written responses from the parents of 20 of the 27 students. Of them, 11 were pleased with the portfolios and the unit. Tom's father, for example, wrote: *I am very pleased with this type of material because it is teaching thinking and not just memorization. Tom also seems to regard this as challenging and fun.*

Kristin's mother wrote: *I noticed that Kristin's writing has improved just since January to March. I am very encouraged at what she has to say and I'm very impressed with the thought process. In helping Kristin with her probability words I learned some things also, and it was a good exercise for both of us to do together.*

From Lee Ann's mother: *This kind of assessment gives a parent so much information—about the child—how they are able to write down their thoughts and ideas—and just basic communication skill. I learned that Lee Ann "probably" knows more about probability than I do!!*

Five of the parents were pleased but wanted more information from the teacher. Seth's mother wrote: *The portfolio format seems an excellent one for me to evaluate Seth's work! What he is doing in the classroom is not always clear to me and this provides more information. Reading his samples generated a dialogue about the work, especially his explanation of it. If the teachers would have included a brief description at the top of each category I might have felt less confused. On the other hand, it certainly taught me more about how Seth thinks about problems. I think this assessment portfolio can be highly informative.*

Lori's mother wrote: *My reaction to this portfolio is that Lori was very interested in my attention to it. I would like to have your comments on her learning and her selection of categories. Also, included in her writing, interactions and comments by you. Your written input would help me assess Lori's understanding. I do not consider this an evaluation since it was done by the student. Do you?*

Four parents raised concerns. Tomo's father wrote: *I was interested in the early introduction to probability. It was impressive to see the thought process and the attempt to explain logically the math findings. I believe that this learning system complements but does not replace a learning system based on math mechanics and rote.* (Perhaps Tomo's consistent interest in computing can be traced to his father's valuing of computation skills.)

Two parents were concerned about their children's writing weaknesses. Eric's parents wrote: *It was very informative reading Eric's descriptions of the games. I support the portfolio concept, and especially self-evaluation. The good news is that Eric is engaged and intrigued with the work. He also writes with some enthusiasm and articulation. The bad news is that his spelling is poor and his printing is sloppy. I support the portfolio concept both as a learning tool and a parent-classroom communication conduit.*

Amanda's mother wrote: *I felt uneasy about the lack of discipline for spelling in the writing that comes home.*

Alan's mother wanted more information about the unit in general. She wrote: *I felt that I was reading my son's material in a vacuum. I needed more information at the start of the probability unit to know what was being taught and what goals were expected from the teacher's perspective. More parent INFORMATION needed, either written or with a planned session.*

The parents' comments reminded me that parents' needs and points of view are as varied as those of the students in the class. There's no best way to communicate with all parents, but reaching out to parents is extremely important to support children's learning.

## Reflections on Portfolios

In the following sections, I describe the thinking and planning I did for student portfolios. Also, because hindsight is always valuable after trying something new, I've included the thoughts I had as I looked back on the experience.

## Preparing for Portfolios

The preparation for having students put together portfolios was ongoing throughout the unit. Because the portfolios would reflect children's work over time, I had children write regularly about their experiences so they would have a collection of work from which to choose. At the beginning of the unit, I set up a class math file with a folder for each child. By the end of the unit, I had a chronological record of each student's writing.

I developed a five-step plan for introducing the class to the idea of assembling portfolios:

1. Find out what the students know about portfolios.
   Because I find it's best to start with children's experiences when introducing something new, I planned first to find out what information the children already had about portfolios.

2. Establish categories for choosing work.
   From reading articles about portfolios and adapting the information to what made sense to me, I identified four possible categories for portfolio selections: (1) best work, (2) a paper that describes a mathematical discovery or theory, (3) a paper that clearly explains the student's thinking, and (4) a paper about an idea the student still wonders about or is unsure of. I planned to involve the children by having them contribute additional categories of interest to them.

3. Have the students choose work and exchange with partners for feedback.
   As the children read through their folders, I planned to have them put Post-it Notes on all papers they thought they might like to include and write on each Post-it the number of the category they thought fit the paper. Then, in pairs, they would exchange papers and evaluate whether the categories matched the papers they chose. Finally, they would review their first choices to make their final selections.

4. Have students discuss and then write about their reactions to reading their work.
   After students talked about their reactions to reading their papers, I planned to write prompts on the board to structure their writing:

   > Reading My Work
   > 1. When I read my work, I felt _____.
   > 2. I noticed that _____.
   > 3. What surprised me was _____.
   > 4. What pleased me was _____.

5. Have students write about why they chose each paper and then assemble their portfolios.
   I developed a form on which students could write about each piece of work they chose, including the category, the title and date, and a paragraph explaining why they chose it. (See Blackline Masters section, page 251.) I planned to talk with the children about the importance of their reflections for informing their parents about their work and letting me know what was interesting and important to them.

## Introducing Portfolios to the Class

I spent two class periods implementing my five-step plan. During the first class, I introduced the first four steps: talking with the children about portfolios; presenting my ideas of categories for their work and inviting the children to contribute additional categories; having the children read through their folders, identify papers for various categories, and exchange with partners; and, finally, having the children write about their reactions to reading their work.

During the second class period, I implemented the fifth step. The students reflected on the papers they chose, wrote a short paragraph for each paper, and assembled their portfolios.

## Communicating with Parents

In the letter I wrote to parents, I explained the purpose of portfolios, listed the categories we had established, and asked for their reactions. I used the following letter as a cover sheet for the children's portfolios.

---

Dear Parent,

We've just completed a mathematics unit about probability. The children have reviewed the written work they did between January 3 and March 3. Attached is a sample of your child's work, chosen by your child to fit some or all of the categories listed below. Also, your child has written an explanation about why he or she chose to include each paper.

Categories for Portfolio Work

1. Best work
2. Favorite paper
3. A paper that describes a mathematical discovery or theory
4. A paper that clearly explains the student's thinking
5. A paper about an idea the student still wonders about or is unsure of
6. A paper about a game the student invented
7. A paper about the student's favorite game

This portfolio is an example of the new kind of assessment recommended nationally to evaluate children's learning and communicate with parents. Please comment about what you learned from your child's work, what additional information you would like, and what your general reaction is to this kind of reporting about your child's learning. Also, feel free to include any questions you may have.

---

## Looking Back

I was generally pleased with this first attempt and plan to incorporate much of what I did next time. I definitely plan to have students do regular writing throughout the unit, and I think that my system for keeping their work in individual folders is practical and useful. In the future, I again want to have the students contribute to generating the categories for the portfolio work, look at one another's work, and write about why they chose each piece. I'll continue to send a cover letter to parents asking for their feedback. My goal is to broaden and deepen, as much as possible, the communication between teacher, students, and parents.

However, in the future I plan to make changes. I think that in addition to my letter to parents, each portfolio should have an introduction from the student. I might ask children to write letters to their parents or to use their "Reading My Work" papers as introductions.

Also, I think I should contribute to each portfolio not only a general parent letter but also some information specific to that child. I might choose one or more pieces of his or her work to add to the portfolio and write about how the work I chose helped me assess the child's learning. Or, I might write a narrative about the child's overall experience in the unit—what he or she learned and what I noticed about his or her interest in the unit and approach to thinking about the mathematics.

I realize that writing narratives is time-consuming, but I think the process pushes me to look closely at all the students and, therefore, to think more deeply about each student's mathematical progress.

# CONTENTS

# HOMEWORK

Homework assignments help extend children's classroom learning and also inform parents about the kinds of activities their child is doing in school. The mathematics instruction that most parents had differs greatly from the learning experiences in this unit. Homework assignments can help parents see what their child has been doing and help them better understand the mathematics instruction their child is receiving.

Six homework assignments are suggested. Each homework assignment is presented in three parts:

### Homework directions

The directions explain the assignment and include information, when needed, about what students should do to prepare for the assignment.

### The next day

This section gives suggestions for incorporating the students' homework into classroom instruction. It's important for children to know that work they do at home contributes to their classroom learning.

### To parents

A note to parents explains the purpose of the homework and ways they can participate. These communications help parents understand more fully the math instruction their child is getting in school.

## HOMEWORK

## Spinners

This homework should be assigned with Spinner Face #1 after the first spinner whole class lesson and again with Spinner Face #2 after the second spinner whole class lesson. (See pages 24 and 67.)

**Homework directions**

The children take home the spinners they made for *The 1-2-3 Spinner Experiment*, Part 1 or Part 2, and a blank recording sheet. They do the experiment three times with someone at home and bring the spinners and recording sheets back to class. Not only does this assignment generate more data for your class sample, but it gives parents first-hand experience with one of the activities their child does during the unit. You may choose to give this assignment after one or both of the whole class lessons that use spinners.

**The next day**

The children add the data from the recording sheets they generated at home to the class data.

**To parents**

Dear Parents,
*The 1-2-3 Spinner Experiment* provides experience with thinking about probability and collecting data. In class, your child learned how to make a spinner and use it for a probability experiment. He or she is to do the experiment three times at home and bring the spinner record sheet to class to add to our class sample. The children will analyze the class results and compare the data to the probabilities they predicted.

## HOMEWORK

## The Game of Pig

This homework should be assigned after the whole class lesson *The Game of Pig*. (See page 38.)

**Homework directions**

Ask the students to teach someone at home to play the game of Pig and then play it at least three times. In case children don't have dice at home, show them a substitute. Demonstrate cutting 12 slips of paper, numbering two at a time from 1 to 6, putting them in a bag, and drawing out two, without looking. Use the two numbers drawn as if each had come up on one of the dice. Remind the students to return the two slips of paper to the bag each time before drawing two again. Children may want to draw dots on the slips of paper to make them look more like the faces of a die. It would be helpful to duplicate the rules for Pig (see page 233) for children to take home.

**The next day**

Children report about their experiences playing the game at home, telling with whom they played and the responses they got.

**To parents**

Dear Parents,
Pig is a game of strategy and chance that provides addition practice. The object of the game is to reach a score of 100 or more. Players take turns rolling two dice and mentally keeping a running total of the sums that come up. A player may roll as many times as he or she likes and then record the total score, adding it to the total from previous turns. However, if a 1 comes up before a player decides to "stick" (stop rolling), the player scores zero for that turn. Also, if two 1s come up, the player loses his or her entire score so far and starts again from zero! Your child will explain the rules and show you how to record your scores. Please play at least three games with your child.

# HOMEWORK

## Spinner Puzzles

This homework should be assigned after the menu activity *Spinner Puzzles.* (See page 122.)

**Homework directions**

After children have made spinner puzzles, and you've checked that they've correctly drawn a spinner for each statement, have the children take home their puzzles along with copies of the statements (see page 241). They are to ask someone at home to match each spinner with a statement.

**The next day**

Have children talk in small groups about the reactions family members had to their spinner puzzles. Then ask for volunteers to report their experiences to the class.

**To parents**

Dear Parents,
Your child has completed the task of designing six spinner faces to match six probability statements. The activity gave your child experience connecting the terminology of probability to a problem-solving situation. Please try and match each of your child's spinners to a statement. Also, talk with your child about how he or she decided how to design the spinner faces.

## HOMEWORK

## Spinner Statements

This homework should be assigned after the assessment *Spinner Statements*. (See page 136.)

**Homework directions**

Ask students to take home the *Spinner Statements* sheet (see page 244) and discuss with someone at home which of the 17 statements are true and which are false. Even though children have already discussed the statements with their classmates, discussing them again at home provides additional experience with analyzing the probability statements.

**The next day**

The children report their experiences when they discussed the statements with someone at home.

**To parents**

> Dear Parents,
> This homework assignment gives your child additional experience with the terminology of probability. Please read each statement with your child and discuss whether it is true or false. We have already talked about these statements in class, and discussing them again can help your child cement and extend his or her understanding.

## HOMEWORK

## Pig Strategies

This homework should be assigned after the menu activity *Testing Pig Strategies*. (See page 145.)

**Homework directions**

Have each child copy the class list of strategies for playing Pig, or duplicate them for the class. Tell the children that they are to take their lists home and play Pig with someone at home the same way they did in class: Each player chooses a strategy and then plays 10 games to see which strategy works better.

**The next day**

Have children discuss their results from testing Pig strategies.

**To parents**

> Dear Parents,
> After playing Pig over a period of time, the students brainstormed a list of strategies they used for playing the game. Review the list with your child. Then each of you should choose one strategy and use it while playing 10 games. Talk about your results and which strategies on the list you think are more effective for winning the game.

# HOMEWORK

## Probability Vocabulary

This homework should be assigned near the end of the unit. It is actually an assessment that can be completed in class or at home.

**Homework directions**

Give children the *Probability Vocabulary* sheet (see page 250) and instruct them to use each word in a sentence. Tell them they can refer to the spinner drawn on the sheet, draw another spinner of their own, or refer to any of the activities they've done during the unit. Ask children to underline the words as they use them and to add additional words if they wish.

**The next day**

Collect the assignments and read them to assess how children used the vocabulary.

**To parents**

> Dear Parents,
> This assignment asks your child to write sentences using the vocabulary we've been studying in our probability unit. For each term, your child should write a sentence that describes how the term relates to the spinner shown, to a spinner of his or her own design, or to any of the activities we have done during the unit. Please ask your child to read and explain to you all of his or her sentences.

# CONTENTS

# BLACKLINE MASTERS

The blackline masters fall into several categories:

### Probability Menu

This blackline master lists the titles of all the menu activities suggested in the unit. You may choose to enlarge and post this list for a class reference. Some teachers fill in the boxes in front of each title once they have introduced the activity, then students choose activities to do during menu time. Also, some teachers have children copy the list and make check marks or tallies each day to indicate the tasks they worked on; other teachers duplicate the blackline master for each child or pair of students.

### Menu Activities

Eight menu activities are included. (They also appear in the text following the "Overview" section for each menu activity.) You may enlarge and post the menu tasks or make copies for children to use. (Note: A set of classroom posters of the menu activities is available from Cuisenaire Company of America.)

### Instruction Sheets

Two blackline masters provide instructions. One contains the directions for making a spinner, and the other has the rules for the game of Pig.

### Recording Sheets

Eleven blackline masters provide recording sheets for activities. Duplicate an ample supply of each and make them available to students.

# Probability Menu

☐ Roll Two Dice

☐ Tiles in Three Bags

☐ Shake and Spill

☐ Spinner Puzzles

☐ Testing Pig Strategies

☐ High or Low

☐ Spinner Sums

☐ Match or No Match

# Directions for Making a Spinner

You need: Spinner face
        5-by-8-inch index card
        Paper clip
        ¼-inch length of a plastic straw
        Scissors
        Tape

1. Cut out the spinner face.

2. Cut the index card in half. Mark a dot near the center of one of the halves. Draw a line from the dot to one corner of the card.

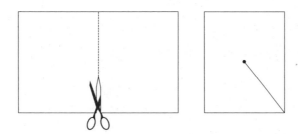

3. Bend up the outside part of a paper clip. This part should point straight up when the paper clip is lying flat on your desk.

From *Math By All Means: Probability, Grades 3–4*  ©1995 Math Solutions Publications

# Directions for Making a Spinner (page 2)

4. Using the paper clip, poke a hole in the center of the spinner face and through the dot near the center of the index card.

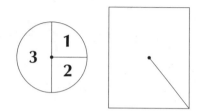

5. Push the bent end of the paper clip through the hole in the card and use tape to secure the rest of the paper clip to the bottom of the card. Make sure the side of the card with the line is facing up.

6. Put the ¼-inch length of plastic straw and then the spinner face on the paper clip.

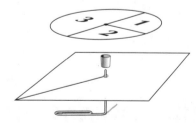

7. Cover the tip of the paper clip with a piece of tape.

From *Math By All Means: Probability, Grades 3–4* ©1995 Math Solutions Publications

# Spinner Recording Sheet

From *Math By All Means: Probability, Grades 3–4*   ©1995 Math Solutions Publications

# Spinner Faces #1

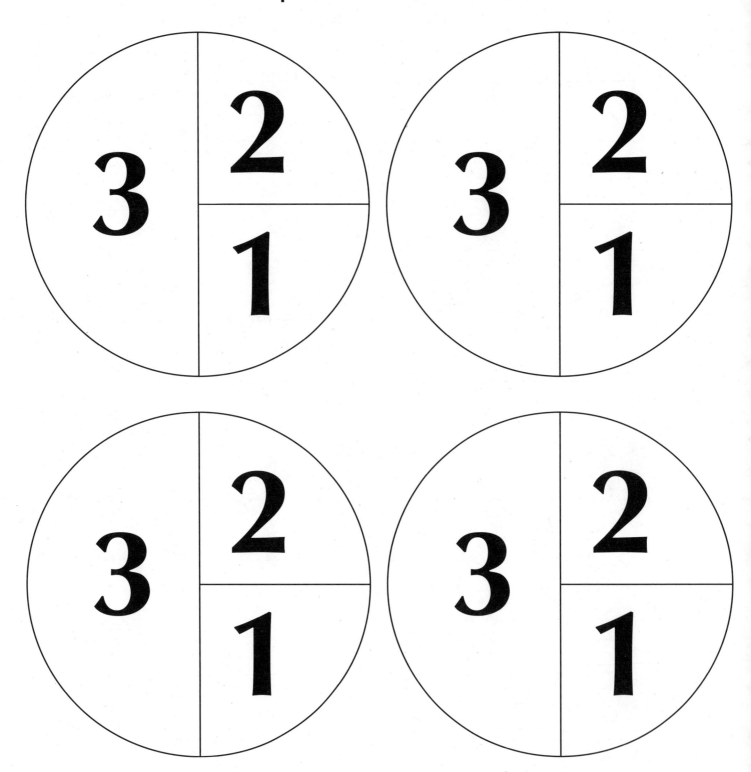

# Rules for Playing Pig

You need: *One pair of dice*

1. The goal of the game is to be the first to get a score of 100 or more.

2. Draw two columns on a sheet of paper. Label one with your name and one with your partner's name.

3. Players take turns. When it is your turn, roll the dice as many times as you like, keeping a running total of what you roll. Don't write down the sums, but add them mentally and say them aloud so your partner can check.

4. When you decide to stop rolling, record the total for that round in your column. Then add it to your total sum from the previous rounds.

5. If a 1 comes up on one of the dice, your turn ends, and you score zero for that turn. If both dice show 1s, your turn ends and your total score so far goes to zero.

# Spinner Faces #2

# Roll Two Dice

$\boxed{\text{I}}$

**You need:** Two dice

Roll Two Dice recording sheet

1. Roll two dice and record the addition sentence under the correct sum. (See the sample below.)

2. Continue rolling until one number gets to the Finish Line.

3. Mark a tally on the class chart to show your winning number.

| 2 | 3 | 4 | 5 | 6 | 7 | 8 | 9 | 10 | 11 | 12 |
|---|---|---|---|---|---|---|---|----|----|----|
|   |   | 1+3 | 3+2 | 3+3 | 1+6 | 5+3 |   |    |    |    |
|   |   |   |   | 4+2 | 5+2 | 2+6 |   |    |    |    |
|   |   |   |   |   | 5+2 |   |   |    |    |    |
|   |   |   |   |   |   |   |   |    |    |    |
|   |   |   |   |   |   |   |   |    |    |    |
|   |   |   |   |   |   |   |   |    |    |    |
|   |   |   |   |   |   |   |   |    |    |    |
|   |   |   |   |   |   |   |   |    |    |    |
|   |   |   |   |   |   |   |   |    |    |    |
|   |   |   |   |   |   |   |   |    |    |    |
|   |   |   |   |   |   |   |   |    |    |    |
|   |   |   |   |   |   |   |   |    |    |    |

Finish Line →

From *Math By All Means: Probability, Grades 3–4* ©1995 Math Solutions Publications

## Roll Two Dice

| 2 | 3 | 4 | 5 | 6 | 7 | 8 | 9 | 10 | 11 | 12 |
|---|---|---|---|---|---|---|---|----|----|----|
|   |   |   |   |   |   |   |   |    |    |    |
|   |   |   |   |   |   |   |   |    |    |    |
|   |   |   |   |   |   |   |   |    |    |    |
|   |   |   |   |   |   |   |   |    |    |    |
|   |   |   |   |   |   |   |   |    |    |    |
|   |   |   |   |   |   |   |   |    |    |    |
|   |   |   |   |   |   |   |   |    |    |    |
|   |   |   |   |   |   |   |   |    |    |    |
|   |   |   |   |   |   |   |   |    |    |    |
|   |   |   |   |   |   |   |   |    |    |    |
|   |   |   |   |   |   |   |   |    |    |    |

Finish Line

# Tiles in Three Bags

You need: One paper bag with tiles—A, B, or C

1. Record which bag you took—A, B, or C.

2. Without looking inside, take out one tile. Record its color. Put it back in the bag, and shake the bag to mix the tiles. Take 12 samples this way.

3. Repeat step 2 two more times.

4. Still without looking inside the bag, look at your data and predict whether the tiles in the bag are:

> 6 red, 3 blue, 3 yellow    OR
> 2 red, 8 blue, 2 yellow    OR
> 1 red, 2 blue, 9 yellow

Write about why you made your prediction.

5. Check your prediction by looking inside the bag. Write about what you learned from looking in the bag.

6. Repeat steps 1 to 5 with the other bags.

# Shake and Spill $\boxed{\text{I}}$

You need: Six Two-Color Counters
  Shake and Spill recording sheet

1. Shake and spill six Two-Color Counters. Record what colors come up by coloring one section of the recording sheet.

2. Shake and spill five more times to fill the recording sheet.

3. Cut out the six sections on your recording sheet. Post them on the class graph in the correct rows.

From *Math By All Means: Probability, Grades 3–4*   ©1995 Math Solutions Publications

# Shake and Spill

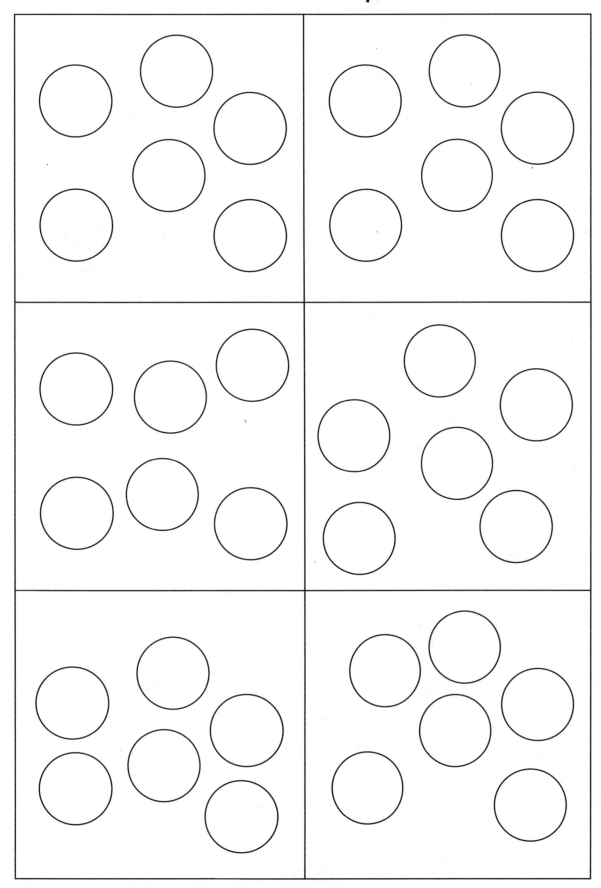

From *Math By All Means: Probability, Grades 3–4*   ©1995 Math Solutions Publications

# Spinner Puzzles

You need: One sheet of 9-by-12-inch paper divided into six sections, with a circle traced in each section.

1. In each circle, draw a spinner face with five sections: <u>a</u>, <u>b</u>, <u>c</u>, <u>d</u>, and <u>e</u>. Design one spinner face to fit each of the following statements:

    1. <u>a</u> is certain to win.
    2. <u>a</u> can't possibly win.
    3. <u>a</u> is likely to win.
    4. <u>a</u>, <u>b</u>, <u>c</u>, <u>d</u>, and <u>e</u> are all equally likely to win.
    5. <u>a</u> or <u>b</u> will probably win.
    6. <u>a</u>, <u>b</u>, and <u>c</u> have the same chance to win, and <u>d</u> and <u>e</u> can't possibly win.

2. To make your spinner faces into puzzles for others to solve, draw them in mixed-up order and do not number them.

3. Fill in an answer sheet for your puzzle. Have someone check your answers and write his or her name at the bottom of the sheet.

4. Solve other students' puzzles.

# Statements for Spinner Puzzles

1. <u>a</u> is certain to win.

2. <u>a</u> can't possibly win.

3. <u>a</u> is likely to win.

4. <u>a</u>, <u>b</u>, <u>c</u>, <u>d</u>, and <u>e</u> are all equally likely to win.

5. <u>a</u> or <u>b</u> will probably win.

6. <u>a</u>, <u>b</u>, and <u>c</u> have the same chance to win, and <u>d</u> and <u>e</u> can't possibly win.

From *Math By All Means: Probability, Grades 3–4*  ©1995 Math Solutions Publications

# Spinner Puzzles Answer Sheet

Name _____

<table>
<tr><td></td><td></td><td></td></tr>
<tr><td></td><td></td><td></td></tr>
</table>

Checked by _____

From *Math By All Means: Probability, Grades 3–4* ©1995 Math Solutions Publications

# Spinner Puzzles Solutions

## Name _____

Name _____

|  |  |  |
|--|--|--|
|  |  |  |
|  |  |  |

Name _____

|  |  |  |
|--|--|--|
|  |  |  |
|  |  |  |

Name _____

|  |  |  |
|--|--|--|
|  |  |  |
|  |  |  |

Name _____

|  |  |  |
|--|--|--|
|  |  |  |
|  |  |  |

Name _____

|  |  |  |
|--|--|--|
|  |  |  |
|  |  |  |

Name _____

|  |  |  |
|--|--|--|
|  |  |  |
|  |  |  |

Name _____

|  |  |  |
|--|--|--|
|  |  |  |
|  |  |  |

Name _____

|  |  |  |
|--|--|--|
|  |  |  |
|  |  |  |

# Spinner Statements

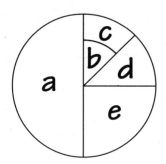

## Circle the statements you think are true.

1. <u>a</u> has a 50% chance of winning.
2. <u>d</u> is twice as likely to win as <u>c</u>.
3. <u>e</u> is twice as likely to win as <u>c</u>.
4. It is probable that <u>d</u> won't win.
5. <u>c</u> can't possibly win.
6. It's just as likely for <u>e</u> to win as <u>c</u> and <u>d</u> together.
7. <u>d</u> has more than a 25% chance of winning.
8. It is certain that <u>a</u> will win.
9. It is possible for <u>c</u> to win.
10. It is possible for <u>e</u> to win.
11. <u>c</u> has the same chance of winning as <u>b</u>.
12. The probability of <u>e</u> winning is 25%.
13. The probability of the spinner landing on <u>d</u> is a little more than 10%.
14. <u>b</u> can't possibly win.
15. <u>b</u> has a 0% chance of coming up.
16. It is uncertain which letter will win.
17. It is unlikely for <u>c</u> to win.

From *Math By All Means: Probability, Grades 3–4*   ©1995 Math Solutions Publications

# Testing Pig Strategies

You need: Two dice
List of Pig strategies

1. Choose a Pig strategy from the list. You and your partner should each pick a different strategy.

2. Play Pig 10 times. Use the strategy you picked for all 10 games.

3. Look at your scores. What did you learn about the different strategies? Would you pick another strategy if you were to play again? Discuss your thoughts with your partner.

# High or Low

You need: Your papers from Roll Two Dice
Two dice
Roll Two Dice recording sheet

1. Count the number of low sums, the number of 7s, and the number of high sums on each Roll Two Dice paper.

2. Write these numbers on the class chart. Circle the number that shows whether a low sum, 7, or high sum won.

3. When you play Roll Two Dice, do you think you are more likely to get a high sum or a low sum? Find a partner who thinks differently from you and play Roll Two Dice again.

4. Post your results.

# Spinner Sums

You need: Two spinners—version #1, #2, or #3
Spinner Sums recording sheet

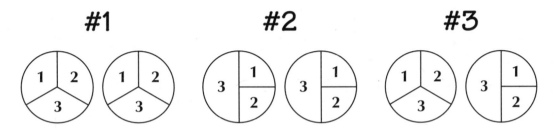

#1          #2          #3

1. At the top of the recording sheet, write your name and the Spinner Sums version number you chose. In the two circles, draw the two spinners.

2. Predict what sum will win.

3. Spin both spinners and add the two numbers that come up. Write the addition sentence in the correct column on the recording sheet.

4. Repeat until one column on the recording sheet is filled in. Make a tally mark on the class chart to indicate which sum won.

5. Write about which sum you predicted would fill the column first and what happened.

# Spinner Sums

## Spinner Sums #___

| | | | | |
|---|---|---|---|---|
| | | | | |
| | | | | |
| | | | | |
| | | | | |
| | | | | |
| | | | | |
| | | | | |
| | | | | |
| | | | | |
| | | | | |
| | | | | |
| | | | | |
| **2** | **3** | **4** | **5** | **6** |

From *Math By All Means: Probability, Grades 3–4*  ©1995 Math Solutions Publications

# Match or No Match

You need: One paper bag
Color Tiles

1. Choose one version below and put the correct number of tiles of each color inside the bag.

> Version 1:  2 blue and 1 red
> Version 2: 2 blue and 2 red
> Version 3: 3 blue and 1 red

2. Draw two tiles and record a tally mark to show whether you got a "match" or "no match."
Do 20 samples this way.

3. Decide whether you think this version is fair. You may want to collect more data first before deciding. Write about your thinking.

4. Repeat steps 1, 2, and 3 for the other versions.

5. Record on the class chart the total number of times your draws came up "match" or "no match" for each version.

From *Math By All Means: Probability, Grades 3–4*  ©1995 Math Solutions Publications

# Probability Vocabulary

Use each of the following probability words in a sentence. You may refer to Spinner A in your sentences, draw your own spinner (Spinner B), or refer to any other probability activity we have done.

Underline the probability words as you use them. You may use the words more than once. Also, you may add additional words if you wish.

1. probability
2. likely
3. unlikely
4. chance
5. equally likely
6. certain
7. uncertain
8. probable
9. possible
10. impossible
11. possibility
12. sample
13. data

Spinner A

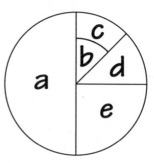

Spinner B

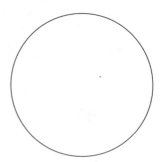

From *Math By All Means: Probability, Grades 3–4* ©1995 Math Solutions Publications

# Probability Portfolio

Name_____

Category # ____ Title _____ Date _____

_____

_____

_____

_____

_____

_____

_____

Category # ____ Title _____ Date _____

_____

_____

_____

_____

_____

_____

_____

Category # ____ Title _____ Date _____

_____

_____

_____

_____

_____

_____

_____

# INDEX